Digital Child Pornography: A Practical Guide for Investigators

CHAD M.S. STEEL

ISBN: 0615947980
ISBN-13: 978-0615947983 (Lily Shiba Press)

DEDICATION

This book is dedicated to all of the victims of child pornography and to the law enforcement officers that bring those who exploit them to justice.

CONTENTS

Part

1

Foundations

1 INTRODUCTION

I desire the company of a man who could sympathize with me, whose eyes would reply to mine.
Mary Shelley, *Frankenstein*

Child pornography is a critical legal and ethical problem that has experienced a resurgence coincident with the growth of the Internet. After international efforts to amend child protection laws in the late 1970's and early 1980's, the prevalence of child pornography cases dropped precipitously and the distribution of child pornography was largely limited to the back rooms of adult bookstores, small cells of individual traders, and a limited, known list of overseas mail order providers. With the growth of the Internet, the ease, cost, and relative anonymity of transactions greatly increased the availability of child pornography and the number of child pornography offenders.

Alongside with the increased availability of child pornography, the field of digital forensics has increased in complexity. A decade ago, the digital forensics on a child pornography cases may have consisted of reviewing a single desktop computer with an 80 gigabyte hard drive and a few CD-Rs. A typical analysis today includes tablets, smartphones, terabyte-sized hard drives, external flash drives, and other digital media devices. It is not atypical to have a single case that involves tens of terabytes of data and over one million images and movies. These quantities have made manual review of content cost-prohibitive and impractical. As such, child pornography investigations are at a critical juncture that calls for new tools and techniques.

This book seeks to address the problems faced in investigating child pornography offenses in the always-on, always-connected age. The book cites the United States federal statutes, but the principles apply to state laws as well as those of other countries. The contents of this book are organized into three sections as follows:

- **Foundations.** The background and modern history of child pornography are covered. The prevalence and types of child pornography are addressed, and a typology of child pornographers is presented, including the psychological reasons for the individuals to be engaged in child pornography. An overview of the current federal laws addressing child pornography is presented, and key cases of recent interest are detailed. How to select investigators to investigate child pornography offenses and how to keep them safe are also reviewed.

- **Digital Forensics**. Digital forensics, as applied to child pornography, is addressed. A methodology for planning for and conducting search warrants in child pornography offenses is provided, and key elements of proof needed that can be gathered digitally are presented. A framework for conducting dead-box analysis for evidence of child pornography offenses is provided.
- **Interviews and Interrogations**. The subjects of child pornography cases take special care and feeding and they require special considerations when interviewing. The process of interviewing and interrogating child pornography subjects, from the planning stages through to obtaining a confession, is documented.

This book is not a basic textbook on investigations – it assumes the reader has a foundational understanding of the investigative process and training in executing search warrants, conducting interviews, and documenting case activity for court. The sections are written to address the unique aspects of child pornography investigations, and to help seasoned investigators hone their skills. It does not address other forms of child exploitation (except as related to child pornography), such as child enticement cases, contact offenses, or sex tourism offenses, however many of the techniques presented can be equally effective in those types of related investigations.

The Importance of Child Pornography Investigations

The main driver behind child pornography investigations is to prevent the sexual abuse of children. While this is understood by those involved in the investigation and prosecution of child pornography, there are still sectors of the public, and even government, that misunderstand the harm, and label the memorialization of exploitation as "just images". As an example, in 2013 Tom Flanagan, the now-former advisor to Canadian Prime Minister Stephen Harper, stated during a public speech "I certainly have no sympathy for child molesters, but I do have some grave doubts about putting people in jail because of their taste in pictures." Flanagan later offered a full statement apology, but his initial comments, unfortunately, reflect the thoughts of a cross section of society, ranging from lawmakers to judges.

Even seasoned investigators can forget the underlying basis for child pornography investigations. One thing that all investigators need to keep in mind is that there is no such thing as a simple "possession" offense in child pornography. Anyone possessing child pornography had to have obtained it from somewhere – meaning there is a distribution offense that occurred. Alternatively, they may have created it themselves, leading to a production offense. Ultimately, the possession offense and the distribution offense will always track back to the production, and the hands-on abuse of a real child.

While defense attorneys claim there is no harm to simple possession, the Joint Hammer case is illustrative of what is wrong with that claim. In 2006, Australian police tracked images of a nine year old Belgian girl being sexually abused that were posted online. The pictures were taken by her father, who was being paid by an Italian filmmaker running a commercial website. In what would become an international effort called Operation Koala in Australia and Operation Joint Hammer in the United States, hundreds of individuals were arrested worldwide for purchasing videos of children as young as three years old being sexually abused.

What is particularly important about Joint Hammer was the method of operation of the website. Individuals from around the world would login to the Italian site and either purchase existing videos or make "requests". The requests would include a laundry list of perversions the purchasers would like to see. Unbeknownst to the purchasers, the filmmaker would contract out their desires as "on-demand" exploitation, and child molesters around the globe were paid to conduct the requested abuse. The video would then be sent to the requestor, and made available online for purchase by any other interested parties.

The global investigation not only resulted in the prosecution of hundreds of purchasers worldwide, but in the arrest of the filmmaker and several of the child molesters. More importantly, 14 child victims were rescued from abuse. This case is one illustration of the direct harm of viewing child pornography – individuals who were not personally abusing children (that we know of), through the act of soliciting and viewing child pornography, unknowingly directed the ongoing sexual abuse of children around the globe.

As a further incentive to investigators, if the Australian team had treated their investigation as a simple possession case, the victims may never have been saved. Shutting down distribution channels and the identification of victims should be the ultimate goal of every child pornography investigation.

Starting in 1994, the United States Congress provided yet another reason to identify victims. They passed the Mandatory Restitution Act (18 U.S.C. § 2259), which provides compensation to those individuals being abused in the images. The act provides a mechanism for monetary damages to be sought from the defendants in all child pornography cases, including those of possession, from victims for their losses, including the costs of:

(A) medical services relating to physical, psychiatric, or psychological care;
(B) physical and occupational therapy or rehabilitation;
(C) necessary transportation, temporary housing, and child care expenses;
(D) lost income;
(E) attorneys' fees, as well as other costs incurred; and
(F) any other losses suffered by the victim as a proximate result of the offense.

Because of this provision, identifying the victims can help them, even as adults, to afford the treatment they may need. After the victim has been removed from the abusive environment, there is a lifelong impact. Images sent across the Internet are there forever – there is no "erase" button - leading to the re-victimization of those abused. Consider the excerpt from the victim impact statement of "Vicky", now in her 20's:

> I wonder if the men I pass in the grocery store have seen them. Because the most intimate parts of me are being viewed by thousands of strangers, and traded around, I feel out of control. They are trading my trauma around like treats at a party, but it is far from innocent. It feels like I am being raped by each and every one of them.

Vicky is the subject of one of the most frequently traded child pornography series. She was repeatedly raped over the course of several years by her father, beginning when she was 10 years old. Her father videotaped the abuse and distributed it electronically, resulting in thousands if not millions of copies being viewed around the world. While the name "Vicky" is a pseudonym, twisted individuals have tried, and continue to try, to track her down. It is for Vicky and the other victims of child pornography that we conduct these investigations.

The Current State of Affairs

The distribution of child pornography on the Internet is widespread. Approximately 1% of all peer-to-peer queries are seeking child pornography, and approximately one in 200 to 500 web-based searches are conducted to find child pornography. The average age of victims in the exploitative images sought is 12 years old, with individuals actively searching for images of victims as young as newborns. This has driven an increase in child pornography arrests over the past decade. As part of the National Juvenile Online Victimization studies funded by the Office of Juvenile Justice and Delinquency Prevention, Office of Justice Programs, United States Department of Justice, Janis Wolak, David Finkelhor, and Kimberly Mitchell documented the growing problem. In 2000, the number of arrests for child exploitation using the Internet was approximately 2,600. By 2006, that number had grown to approximately 7,000. By 2009, it was 8,100. The growth in the number of arrests for these offenses has outpaced increases in the numbers of trained investigators available to handle the cases.

The storage capacity of hard drives has increased approximately sixty-fold over past decade, allowing for the storage of terabytes of data and resulting in a much larger digital forensics effort for each case. It is not unusual to find multiple terabytes of movies and images on the devices seized from a single search warrant. The devices are now more diverse also – evidence of child pornography may be present on computers, flash drives, tablets, smartphones, DVRs, "smart" car systems, and other electronic devices. The tools used to download and distribute the content are varied, and the criminals change their tactics regularly, frequently adopting new technologies before the general public.

The problem of child pornography extends beyond bit-and-bytes. A study by Bourke and Hernandez evaluated individuals incarcerated by the United States Bureau of Prisons for child pornography offenses. In their study, at least 85% of offenders had committed at least one hands-on sexual offense against a child. While their population sample was not necessarily representative of all child pornography offenders, it does show a crossover to contact offenses is present in at least a substantial subset of these cases.

To-date, there has been little research performed on using automated tools to identify child pornography. While there has been extensive work performed on the general identification of pornography, this has not been readily applied to computer forensics and has focused primarily on filtering and monitoring. Much of this may be attributed to the difficulties faced in conducting child pornography research – it is illegal in the United States to possess child pornography, and there are no research exceptions. Additionally, publication in traditional science journals and conferences is difficult given the subject matter, and it is frequently a taboo subject even within the law enforcement community at large.

This book seeks to educate those on the front lines of child pornography investigations – the detectives, special agents, and investigators working the cases. The work is difficult, and if this book can add even a single tool to the collective arsenal and help rescue a single victim, then it was a worthwhile endeavor.

Note on Terminology

The term investigator is used throughout this book and is an intentionally vague title. Child pornography offenses are investigated by teams of individuals, whose titles range from digital forensics specialist to special agent to detective to investigative analyst. Investigator is used as a general purpose title to cover any individual on the investigative team. For the subject, the pronoun "he" is used. While there are female child pornographers, the vast majority are male, and they are the most likely to be encountered in an investigation. That does not mean that female offenders should be discounted, just that they are less prevalent by a ratio of anywhere between 10:1 and 50:1 based on the current research.

The terms male and female are used to denote sex, unless otherwise noted, for the purpose of this text. Sex is the biological state of the individual at birth, based on chromosomes, genitalia, hormonal makeup, etc. Gender is the cultural or personal identity of the individual as a man or a woman. While both sex and gender can play a role in child pornography cases (e.g. when interrogating a subject that self-identifies to a gender different than their biological sex at birth), most of the research and taxonomies use sex as their primary distinguisher.

There has been a recent push to stop using the term "child pornography" and switch to terms such as "child abuse images" to more accurately reflect the contents of the depictions and differentiate them from legal, adult pornography. Additionally, terms such as "kiddie porn" and abbreviations like "CP" are used in common parlance around the squad room. In this book, I have used the term "child pornography" because of its widespread acceptance in the United States, and have avoided abbreviations or attempts to make it less sound less offensive.

2 HISTORY OF CHILD PORNOGRAPHY

The history of man is the history of crimes, and history can repeat. So information is a defense. Through this we can build, we must build, a defense against repetition.
Simon Wiesenthal

Child pornography is not a new problem, though it has received increased recent attention - the Internet has resulted in easier and broader access to both distribute and acquire illicit content. Child pornography has been around since the invention of the camera, and arguably before that in drawings. Child sexual abuse has been documented since ancient times, though the definition of what is a child has changed dramatically. Modern child pornography, at least domestically, can be traced to the commercial enterprises that published literature featuring sexually explicit images of children in the 1970's.

Early child pornography trading, before the Internet and before global commercial distribution methods, was largely a self-limiting crime. Individuals that exploited children might take photographs of that abuse, but their ability to identify other like-minded persons was constrained. Because of this, early collections of child pornography would consist of pictures taken by the abuser or a very small group of individuals that they traded with. Trading was very high risk, as the pictures needed to be developed by a trusted source, frequently the abuser, and identifying individuals to trade with, especially within a small community, was difficult. Transactions took place in private residences, or in "invitation only" back rooms of adult bookstores.

In the United States, there was no federal law against the production, distribution, or possession of child pornography until the Protection of Children Against Sexual Exploitation Act was passed in 1977. While there were obscenity laws on the books and individual states had passed child protection laws prohibiting child pornography, both explicitly and through more general child abuse statutes, this was the first federal law targeting production. The law defined minors as those under the age of 16, and was limited in scope to those producing or distributing material for profit involving interstate commerce. As such, the law largely shut down any domestic production. The major producers of early child pornography magazines – the Europeans – were largely unaffected by this law.

In the 1970's, child pornography was legal in much of Europe. In Denmark, magazines like *Lolita* had a broad distribution, and the Netherland's *Seventeen*, not to be confused with *Seventeen* published in the United States, featured models that were 16 and 17 years of age. Because their production was legal in their respective countries, many studios that now produce adult pornography originally produced a line of underage magazines and videos. Even more mainstream pornography outlets got involved. In a famous case, Eva Ionesco was featured in the Italian version of Playboy (and later Penthouse) at age 11 through erotic photographs taken by her mother. Largely because of the mail distribution of these magazines, the United States Postal Inspection Service and the former United States Customs Service became two of the pioneering organizations in child pornography investigations.

The real crackdown on child pornography in the United States came with the Child Pornography Prevention Act of 1996. Prior to 1996, child pornography possession and not-for-profit distribution was charged under the obscenity statutes – making it politically less attractive to pursue. The Child Pornography Prevention Act criminalized possession of sexual images of anyone under the age of 18, and removed the need for a commercial transaction to have occurred. The legislation came at almost the same time that the Federal Bureau of Investigation formed the Innocent Images National Initiative, geared toward combatting child pornography and backed by the resources of the nation's largest law enforcement organization.

The consolidated efforts of federal and local law enforcement, coupled with stronger laws and prioritization of enforcement, might have ended large scale trading in child pornography. Unfortunately, child pornographers were quick to adopt new networking technologies that would change the landscape dramatically and tip the scales back toward the criminals.

Digital Child Pornography

While many individuals view digital child pornography as purely an Internet problem, the origins of digital child pornography distribution predate the widespread adoption of the Internet technologies that enable it to flourish today.

Before the widespread use of the Internet, Bulletin Board System (BBS) operators (SysOps) ran servers that allowed users to dial in remotely using the phone network. Individual users, connected via their modems to a phone line, would obtain the number to a BBS that hosted content of interest to them and would then dial that number directly. A typical BBS might host forums, have rudimentary "chat" functions, allow local (or early Internet) messaging, and contain downloadable content related to a specific topic. Larger systems had banks of modems, allowing multiple users to connect simultaneously.

Pedophiles with computers were quick to take advantage of the BBS explosion in the late 1980's and early 1990's and used the technology to trade illicit images with likeminded individuals. A typical BBS would have a username and password that the individual needed to know to logon. Once connected, a user would be expected to upload a set number of child pornography pictures to be allowed access to the backroom content. Some boards even required new users to upload "new" images that they had produced themselves or acquired through other channels.

While BBS-based child pornography was theoretically available for download globally, calling into a service that was not local could become very expense, running up huge phone bills. Additionally, the technology of the day was largely based on connections using 14.4Kbs modems, limiting the volume and quality of pictures that could be uploaded and/or downloaded. Images were frequently bitmaps or GIF-based - the first JPEG standard wasn't adopted until 1992 - and were low resolution. Because of the lack of digital cameras, many of the images were scans of magazine spreads from the 1970's. Some of these became common enough that individuals would try to collect all of the pictures from a given magazine series, with certain "rare" images in a series becoming valuable commodities. Movies were generally not available. There were no digital recording mechanisms, audio-to-video convertors to digitize movies from VHS tapes were expensive, storage was largely floppy-disk based and therefore size limited, and computers did not have the processing power to encode and decode them.

Like the backroom of the adult bookstore, BBS distribution became self-limiting. The technological and cost restrictions, in addition to the difficulty in finding an underground BBS, made it hard to scale the distribution. If a BBS did grow to a large enough size, it would attract the attention of law enforcement.

One of the larger BBS's, *Amateur Action*, was run by Robert Alan Thomas out of California. *Amateur Action* was a pay-to-use BBS, with Thomas making approximately $30,000 per month in income from it. Users would pay a user fee, in addition to their own phone charges, to download up to three images per day.

In 1994, United States Postal Inspector David Dirmeyer, operating on a tip from his duty office in Memphis, Tennessee, paid $55 to download samples of the images being served by the BBS out of California. The images included bestiality and BDSM images, in addition to child pornography. Thomas was charged with interstate transportation of obscene materials in a case that would set the stage for the transfer of "bits and bytes" across state lines being legally equivalent to transporting the material via UPS or other common carrier. Thomas also sent VHS tapes containing obscene movies to the same postal inspector. Robert and his wife Carleen Thomas were sentenced on December 2, 1994 to 37 and 30 months of incarceration, respectively, for the violations, which were upheld on appeal.

As with the magazine business, the distribution of child pornography was very limited even with BBS technology. As noted above, BBS providers had technology limitations but they also had privacy limitations – individuals had to call from their home phone and hosting providers had to register a phone number as well, creating a record of their transactions. The perceived privacy of the violators, however, was higher than that of previous traders because they could connect from the comfort of their own homes instead of meeting in person with the proprietor of an adult bookstore. When they connected, they might have to provide credit card information on commercial systems, but they could register with any screen name or "handle" they wanted, hiding their true identity from anyone but the SysOp, their credit card provider, and a law enforcement subpoena.

It would take the convergence of two other technologies to globalize the child pornography problem. The first was the Internet. Developed by the United States Advanced Research Projects Agency (ARPA), the Internet began life as ARPANet, connecting a select few government and academic institutions. By 1983, when ARPANet began using TCP/IP as its underlying protocol, it had barely one thousand hosts connected. Over the next few years, however, bridges between ARPANet, which morphed into NSFNet, and other networks rapidly grew the size of the Internet. Early service providers like America Online, Prodigy, and Compuserve and commercial networks like Telenet and Tymenet connected to NSFNet to greatly increase the user base. By the time the first graphical web browser was introduced in 1993, the Internet already had over 1 million connected hosts.

The two earliest protocols used to transport child pornography were Simple Mail Transport Protocol (SMTP), the standard for sending email since 1982, and Network News Transfer Protocol (NNTP), the backbone for Usenet since 1985. While email and Usenet as technologies both predated the introduction of SMTP and NNTP, respectively, they were largely limited in scope and not "global" applications in their early incarnations.

Early transmission of child pornography via email was limited by two factors - message size and the difficulty in sending binary images. Current mail providers allow us to routinely send multi-megabyte messages and we take for granted the ability to add binary attachments to messages via Multimedia Internet Mail Extensions (introduced in 1992). Early email messages, however, were limited to ASCII text and many mail gateways had limited bandwidth and restricted the size of messages to as small as a few thousand bytes in length. Because of the ASCII limitation, binary attachments had to be "encoded" as ASCII characters then "decoded" back to their original binary values. Unix and DOS-based versions of UUEncode (Unix-to-Unix Encoding) were utilized to do this, but added as much as 40 percent overhead to the size of the original binary, further exacerbating message size restrictions. This, plus the fact that early messaging accounts were generally tied to either a commercial account in true name or an academic account in true name, limited the early transmission of child pornography by email.

The more popular channel for early Internet transmission of child pornography was through Usenet news groups. Usenet took the concept of a forum for exchanging messages on a BBS and made it global in scale. A hierarchy of groups that allowed a user to post a message globally and to read or respond to messages posted by others was created. The hierarchy was topical, with root levels like comp.* (for computer topics), rec.* (for recreational and entertainment topics), and soc.* (for social interest topics) organizing subcategories of interest. A group like rec.arts.sf.starwars.collecting would cater to those who wanted to discuss Star Wars collectibles, while comp.lang.c++ would contain discussions about the C++ programming language. The entirety of the discussion boards that a particular institution was willing to carry would be replicated between servers on a global basis, often at night when interactive usage dropped and bandwidth was available. As with email, binary files could be UUEncoded and added to newsgroups, frequently in multi-part messages for larger files.

The main source of child pornography came from the alt.* Usenet hierarchy. Intended for "alternative" topics, the unmoderated alt.binaries subgroups quickly became a stomping grounds for all kinds of legally questionable activities, ranging from the distribution of early hacking tools to the transmission of copyrighted software to the distribution of pornography, both child and adult. Groups dedicated to sharing child pornography and categorized with names like alt.binaries.pictures.erotica.pre-teens allowed any individual to upload a picture from anywhere on the planet, and for tens of thousands of others around the world to download and view the same picture from their local Usenet server within a matter of hours.

Unlike email, individuals only needed to authenticate themselves to a local server, which may or may not have logged the connection, to send a picture around the world. Individuals who wanted to view images could likewise connect to a local server from their home or office and download illicit content. As long as the local servers did not log the transactions, they could do so with low risk and a high degree of anonymity. The global nature of the newsgroups meant a large amount of content was available at any given time, and most servers kept messages for anywhere between a few weeks and a few months. Child pornography became available any hour of the day, and was cataloged based on individual perversion. The risk of engaging in in-person contact was gone, and producers could share the records of their abuse globally without incurring any personal costs.

In addition to image-centric newsgroups, a whole range of groups under alt.pedophila arose as discussion boards for like-minded individuals to discuss their common interest in sex with children. This provided an avenue for individuals to psychologically validate their deviant behavior. By connecting with others who had the same desires to engage in sexual intercourse with minors, Usenet made it easier for offenders to rationalize their conduct.

While Usenet is still around today, it has mostly been supplanted by large discussion forums such as Google Groups. Many of the larger providers of Usenet access have blocked certain sections of the alt.binaries hierarchy, though determined individuals can still find servers that don't filter them out and Usenet-based trading is still encountered in current cases. Additionally, many of the images traded early-on in Usenet forums are still being distributed using the web, instant messaging, peer-to-peer software and other more recent technologies.

The explosion of child pornography availability occurred commensurate with the explosion of the World Wide Web. In 1993, the Mosaic web browser, the first widespread graphical portal to the web, was released. Almost overnight, the Hypertext Transfer Protocol (HTTP) became the largest volume high level protocol in use on the Internet, driving the exponential growth in Internet usage. The Web allowed anyone to put up a picture gallery, a forum, or a file sharing site, including child pornographers.

The Web, in addition to technologies like instant messaging, peer-to-peer, and onion routing are the primary tools currently in use by Internet child pornographers. Older technologies like Usenet and email still persist to a smaller degree, and new technologies are being adopted on a regular basis. The current state of digital child pornography distribution is covered in the following chapters.

3 MODERN CHILD PORNOGRAPHERS

The dogmas of the quiet past are inadequate to the stormy present. The occasion is piled high with difficulty, and we must rise with the occasion. As our case is new, so we must think anew and act anew.
Abraham Lincoln

How does an individual become a child pornographer? Nowhere is the nature v. nurture debate more applicable. The reasons for engaging with child pornography can range from mere curiosity in the case where the individual has hundreds of thousands of pornographic images, a few of which depict children, to the desire to keep trophies of hands-on molestation perpetrated by the subject. While the extremes at both ends of the spectrum may be the exception, there are multiple ways to evaluate and classify the majority of child pornography offenders that fall between them.

Pedophilia and Mental Illness

Pedophilia, now called pedophilic disorder in the Diagnostic and Statistical Manual of Mental Disorders, Revision 5 (DSM-5) is a paraphilia in which an individual over the age of 16 is attracted to prepubescent children. To be diagnosed with a paraphilia, an intense arousal to atypical objects or individuals, an individual needs to not only have an abnormal sexual attraction, but they also need to feel distress about that attraction beyond the distress imposed by societal norms. Hebephilia, the attraction to pubescent individuals (generally 11 -14 years of age), is not considered a distinct psychological condition by the DSM-5. Though it is not specifically called out, it could be included under the broader category of paraphilia – not otherwise specified (P-NOS).

Sexual desire for children can be diagnosed objectively by using a penile plethysmograph, sometimes called the "peter meter". The penile plethysmograph is a strain gage that is placed over the genitalia and measures the amount of arousal that occurs when erotic images depicting children are displayed. By showing potential pedophiles images that depict mundane objects, adult pornography, and child pornography psychologists can compare and contrast their physiological response and definitely diagnose a sexual interest in children without needing to rely on potentially faulty self-evaluation.

One of the common psychological questions that arise related to child pornographers is whether or not they suffer from pedophilic disorder. There are a few ways to look at the question. First, not all child pornographers meet the clinical definition based on age – an interest in the "developing" child is fairly common in images found as part of child pornography investigations. Any individuals looking at boys or girls between the ages of 11 and 14 is likely to be interested in pubescent youth, a criminal violation but not necessarily a distinct psychological disorder. Similarly, those found with sexually explicit images of children between 15 and 17 are interested in post-pubescent minors which is not directly a diagnosable psychological disorder. In practice, because post-pubescent minors may appear more mature, subjects are not generally charged at a federal level with their possession unless the subject is involved in production or there are other aggravating circumstances.

In addition to the issue of an abnormal attraction, the subject needs to have psychological distress regarding their interest in children to be diagnosed as a pedophile. There is an argument that can be made that individuals involved in groups like the North American Man-Boy Love Association (NAMBLA) may not experience any stress based on their abnormal attraction. While society may place stress on them, some of these individuals genuinely believe that society is wrong and claim to feel no personal apprehension about their interests.

The other side of the question is informative as well – are all pedophiles child pornographers? Again, the intersection of the law with the psychological community has less than perfect overlap. There are many individuals who have an unhealthy attraction to pre-pubescent children that never act on it, either through a contact offense or through the acquisition and trading of child pornography. Similarly, pedophiles may download child erotica images under "non-nude" modeling categories or from nudist websites to masturbate to that do not meet the strict legal definition of child pornography. The interest of pedophiles may extend beyond images as well – they may extensively read or write stories related to incest and child rape, the creation or possession of which may be chargeable under obscenity statutes but are not strictly considered child pornography.

Other aspects of mental illness can drive the collection of child pornography as well. While they do not cause an individual to be attracted to children and do not excuse the subject's actions, they can exacerbate the tendency to view child pornography. These include:

- **Depression.** As with any other stressor in life, depression can reduce the willpower of a pedophile and can cause them to act on their desires. Depression can also cause social isolation, and lead to more time spent alone and without meaningful, healthy adult sexual interactions.
- **Autism Spectrum Disorder (ASD).** ASD, specifically Asperger's Syndrome, has been cited as an excuse for many computer crimes. While having ASD is not a valid justification and does not cause sexual interest in minors, it can amplify the

volume of child pornography downloaded as a repetitive behavior.

- **Obsessive Compulsive Disorder.** Obsessive-compulsive disorder, similar to Asperger's, does not cause an interest in children but may exacerbate a child pornography problem. Obsessions with particular series of child victims or compulsions to go online and download repeatedly can increase the amount of child pornography consumed by these individuals.
- **Sexual Addiction (Hypersexuality).** Not included in the DSM-5, hypersexuality is an addiction to sexual activity. If that activity takes the form of viewing pornography and there is a co-existent paraphilia, consumption of large amounts of child pornography can result.
- **Internet Use Disorder (IUD).** Similar to hypersexuality, IUD is not included in the DSM-5 but is noted as an area for more research. An addiction to Internet use can take the form of excessive viewing of pornographic websites. Coupled with an abnormal interest in children, this can exacerbate both problems.
- **Post-Traumatic Stress Disorder (PTSD).** PTSD, especially that resulting from early childhood sexual abuse, has been shown to have higher than normal comorbidity with pedophilic disorder. This is frequently provided as a rationalization in interviews, though many subjects have admitted post-conviction to fabricating sexual abuse stories in an effort to avoid punishment.
- **Social Anxiety Disorder (SAD).** As with PTSD, SAD and general anxiety disorder have higher comorbidity with pedophilic disorder than in the population as a whole. Individuals who have trouble with in-person interactions may still have active online personas and SAD should not be viewed as lowering the likelihood for a contact offense.

In addition to the above, individuals with pedophilic disorder tend to have higher abnormal personality traits in the areas of narcissism, paranoia, and anti-social characteristics. While not necessarily diagnosable as a disorder, these traits are something for investigators to be aware of when planning on how to approach a subject.

Because paraphilias are not necessarily standalone, individuals diagnosed with pedophilic disorder frequently have more than one comorbid paraphilia. Exhibitionism, voyeurism, and frotteurism, rubbing up against an unsuspecting individual for sexual pleasure, are the most common comorbid paraphilias. Since all of the above involve another individual, it is imperative that the investigators explore instances of the subject "accidentally" rubbing up against minors, exposing themselves to minors, or observing minors without their knowledge or consent.

Even though only a small number of individuals who are investigated for child pornography meet the clinical definition of a pedophile, they do share an abnormal sexual interest in children. As noted elsewhere in the book, possession of child pornography should not be considered in isolation and the possibility of other crimes against children should be explored in all cases.

Conceptual Models

Forensic psychologists and researchers have created several conceptual models to explain the behavior of child pornographers. These models are useful in bringing order to a progression of actions made by subjects, and to assisting in obtaining a confession from subjects by better understanding their internal though processes.

One conceptual model frequently cited to explain child pornographers is the slippery slope. In this model, an individual begins with mainstream adult pornography (e.g. Playboy online), progresses to more extreme adult pornography, and eventually ends up with child pornography. Similarly, the age of the children depicted is likely to start older than the ideal target range desired by the viewer. The model is based on each stage being one step on a downward slope. Once that step is reached, the subject rarely returns to the "higher" steps on the slope. Ultimately, the subject will stop when they hit the age group of strongest interest to them.

The slippery slope model assumes that the subject will need to self-rationalize their behavior. Moving from viewing Playboy magazines to infants in sexual bondage creates a huge degree of cognitive dissonance – it is difficult for a subject to convince themselves that they are normal based on looking at Playboy images, while having the competing fact that they really get excited looking at the infant pictures. Instead, the subjects will move a little bit each viewing. If an individual has already rationalized that looking at 15 years olds is okay, it isn't a significant leap to move to 14 year olds. The speed with which an individual progresses down their personal slope can be anywhere from the length of a single browsing session to several years. Individuals who have difficulty rationalizing their behavior may even need to start each session with more mainstream pornography, or with child erotica, and eventually progress to their target content of choice. In general, the last content an individual viewed during their browsing session is most likely to be the content they were interested in as there is a natural stopping point following masturbation.

The slippery slope model can be applied to the progression from viewer to producer as well. Once an individual is actively involved in trading, it is unlikely that they will stop unless an outside scare causes them to reevaluate their actions. Similarly, an individual who has amassed a large collection may use the content to help rationalize that it is okay to have contact with children, especially if they can imagine the children in the images as consenting. That may lower their resistance to committing a contact offense and put them into a higher risk category.

The slippery slope model is useful in interviewing in that it provides a built-in progression for questioning. It is easier for an individual that admitted to viewing pictures of 17 year olds and perceived no judgment from the investigator to then admit to viewing 16 year olds than it is to immediately admit to the most egregious images present in their collection. By obtaining a series of admissions where each step is only a small change from the prior step, the investigator only needs to obtain minimal incremental rationalizations from the subject to keep getting admissions.

Another model that can be used to explain the actions of individuals is the branching model. The branching model assumes that an individual may not know for certain, or admit to themselves, what their sexual interests are. They may collect a variety of pornographic material, with varying degrees of extremeness, until they hit upon child pornography. Eventually, the initial child pornography will cease to be exciting, and they will branch out vertically by going to a younger age bracket, branch out horizontally to different acts of child pornography, expand to other areas of extreme interest like bestiality, or change their modus operandi and move into trading, distributing, or producing child pornography.

The branching model can help the subject rationalize their interest in children as "one of many" interests they have. They may present curiosity as an excuse to the investigator, which can make for a strong interrogation theme. The branching model also helps to explain individuals that have trouble self-rationalizing the viewing of content that is personally objectionable to the subject but at the same level of egregiousness to the investigator. As an example, some subjects may have an interest in minor boys, but only admit to being interested in young girls. In the extreme cases, the individuals may confess to viewing images of the opposite sex but not of the same sex due to religious or other beliefs that they hold.

Other individuals have previously attempted to create a more stringent typology for child pornographers. The seminal study that largely predates the Internet was based on the work of the FBI's behavioral analysis unit and was published by Carol Hartman, Ann Burgess, and Kenneth V. Lanning as part of the book "Child pornography and sex rings" in 1984. The typology broke individuals into closeted, isolated, cottage, and commercial groups. Closeted collectors did not share their child pornography and did not commit contact offenses. Isolated collectors committed crossover contact offenses in addition to collecting and may have possessed images depicting their offenses. Cottage collectors distributed their collections to others, primarily using the physical means available at the time, for prestige or other psychological gain. Individuals in the commercial category produced and/or distributed child pornography for profit. The typology provided in this book is an updated version of this typology for the Internet age.

Another popular typology in the slippery slope category was created by Tony Krone in his 2004 paper "A Typology of Online Child Pornography Offending". Krone's typology was more detailed (as shown below), and provides an excellent breakdown of the categories in the Internet age. This book's taxonomy makes use of Krone's categories in the development of simplified categories for direct investigative purposes, and eliminates some of the categories due to a blurring of lines and an increase in multi-category offenders. Krone's typology broke subjects into the following groups:

- **Browser.** The browser stumbles upon child pornography and finds it interesting enough to save it. They may be seeking other pornography or illicit content and inadvertently comes across the child pornography, but are excited by it and keep copies of it, frequently co-mingled with adult pornography.
- **Private Fantasy.** These individuals are producers and create text-based descriptions of or visual representations of children engaged in sexual activities. The information is created for personal enjoyment alone.
- **Trawler.** The trawler is a web-based viewer of child pornography who searches using open websites for others sharing child pornography.
- **Non-Secure Collector.** The non-secure collector uses peer-to-peer technologies to download child pornography for their collections. They connect without using technologies like TOR and are likely to take minimal precautions to hide their actions.
- **Secure Collector.** The secure collector uses private forums and exchanges that require the establishment of bona fides a priori to obtain child pornography. They employ security and utilize methods to obtain content that they believe will protect them from prosecution.
- **Groomer.** The groomer uses child pornography as a means to an end. Their collection is used to groom a minor for the purposes of establishing an online

relationship.

- **Physical Abuser.** The physical abuser may use child pornography to facilitate a hands-on offense. Custom child pornography, including detailed "tutorials" involving animated children, may be present on their systems to assist them with this.
- **Producer.** The producer records their own activities for personal use or distribution. They may also record the activities of others, such as a spouse, without personally committing the abuse.
- **Distributor.** The distributor may fit into any of the above categories and provides child pornography to others.

Whatever model is used to understand their behavior, the more content a subject views the more "normalized" that content becomes to the subject. This makes it easier for the subject to feel less isolated, as greater quantities being available are indicative of more individuals out there with interests similar to the subject. Subjects needing further reassurance may reach out to others on forums or over chats to feel a greater connection to people with similar interests and to assuage personal doubts. The mere existence of groups such as NAMBLA can further assist the subject in convincing themselves that they really have mainstream interests.

The Collection

The above models focus on categorizing the subject based on their actions, but another optic to use is to view their collection. An understanding of the collection itself is of equal interest to the investigator and especially helpful when conducting a forensic examination, though the "viewer" class of child pornographer has recently redefined the state of the game. Ken Lanning, in his work Child Molesters: A Behavioral Analysis, details six characteristics of the collection, noted below with commentary:

- **Important.** The subject's child pornography collection is a vital part of their life. They may keep it with them in its entirety or keep key portions of it with them at all times. The use of child pornography may take up a substantial portion of the subject's time, and they may devote significant financial resources to storing their collection. The subject may also make multiple backups of their collection, in the event of a catastrophic computer failure.
- **Constant.** An offender's collection is something that has permanence to them, and they will always attempt maintain a collection unless acted upon by outside forces. The collection will generally grow over time, and not shrink.
- **Organized.** The degree of organization present in some collections is such that it would impress Melvil Dewey. Subjects may extensively collate their images and movies, and arrange them to meet other psychological needs. They may also distribute their collection across digital media in a way that may appear haphazard, but may have meaning to the subject.
- **Permanent.** On offender's collection is something that they will preserve similar to how another person may preserve their wedding photos or a family heirloom. When the subject experiences a scare through a close call with law enforcement,

through discovery of their collection by a family member or friend, or experiences extreme guilt, they may temporarily destroy part of their collection, but they will rebuild it quickly thereafter, often re-obtaining the same images.

- **Concealed.** The subject will take all reasonable steps to conceal their collection from others, to the extent that it does not impede their access to it. Because rapid access to their collection is weighed against the risk of disclosure, subjects with technical skills may avoid using encryption because of the delay in accessing their collection due to the additional actions required to decrypt. Subjects will similarly avoid using cloud-based file storage in many cases, not just to avoid monitoring by the provider but to avoid bandwidth-imposed delays in viewing their movies and images.
- **Shared.** Every subject would like their collection to be in the open and would share it with others if they believed they would find acceptance and avoid legal repercussions in doing so. This competes with the need to conceal their collection from those that the subject believes would not understand it or would turn them in to authorities.

Child pornography images are rarely the only abnormal pictures found on a subject's storage devices. Studies have shown, and experienced examiners can attest, that there are higher incidence rates of finding images and movies of sadism and masochism, bestiality, and extreme sex acts on the computers of child pornographers. Forensic examiners most frequently find co-existent cartoon depictions of children engaged in sexual activity imported from Japan. These depictions fall into one of two categories - anime (animated movies) or manga (static comics).

Because of censorship laws in Japan dating back to the Meiji Restoration, animation and pornographic material have a different focus than they do in the United States. Obscenity laws in Japan banned depictions of male-female sexual intercourse and pubic hair. As a result, intercourse appears "blurred out" through pixelation in many Japanese movies and images, though unpixelated versions are available for export. Additionally, younger individuals without pubic hair are featured engaging in sexual activities, hence the attraction of this content to those interested in child pornography.

There are many variants of anime and manga, and a whole subculture exists dedicated to the imagery depicted. Hentai, or sexually explicit anime, frequently features graphic depictions of rape, often involving younger protagonists. The various genres are further subdivided based on the content, and a common theme is the inclusion of fetish and paraphilia oriented material and extreme sex acts that would not be possible with live actors. Understanding the terms and their history provides insight into the individual subject and provides additional search terms for analysis. A few of the areas that investigators may encounter are as follows:

- **Lolicon.** An abbreviation for "lolita complex", lolicon refers to an obsession with sex involving minors. Lolicon manga and hentai depict minors engaged in sexual activity, frequently including extreme and abusive sexual acts. These can include BDSM depictions and rape. The term is regularly used in the United States by child pornographers as a search term and as a file tag for animated content involving minors.

- **Ecchi**. Ecchi is the Japanese animated equivalent of child erotica. It includes erotic depictions, frequently of minors, that are sexualized but contain no explicit sexual content. Ecchi frequently focuses on pantsu images, or images of schoolgirls flashing their panties.
- **Yaoi**. Yaoi is a subgenre of boy-love fiction, depicting homosexual acts primarily focused on pubescent youth. Yaoi content is very different than most other hentai and manga in that its primary consumers are female – over 85% by some estimates.
- **Shotacon**. Shotacon, or shota, is similar to yaoi pornography only it depicts pre-pubescent boys, generally engaged in sexual activity with older men. Unlike yaoi images, shota images are primarily viewed by homosexual men.
- **Yuri**. In the United States, yuri refers to Japanese animation depicting sexually explicit girl-love. The movies and comics feature pubescent (or younger) females engaged in lesbian sexual activity. This is roughly equivalent to yaoi, though the audience is primarily male for yuri content.
- **Futanari**. Futanari, or futa, is pornography that depicts hermaphrodites. Generally, the depictions consist of females, frequently schoolgirls, who also have a penis. The closest American equivalent would be "shemale" pornography, but the futanari images generally depict younger females with anatomically exaggerated features.
- **Shokushu Gouka.** Shokushu gouka, or tentacle rape, depicts a female being raped, generally in multiple orifices, by the penis-like tentacles of various creatures. Because creatures do not fit into the definition of "male", these unusual movies were permitted in Japanese art and animation whereas ordinary sexual activity was not. The genre dates back to a famous 19th century woodcutting "The Dream of the Fisherman's Wife", which depicted a woman being raped by two octopi. The form of erotic woodcutting has a long history in Japan under the umbrella term of shunga.

Japanese animation and comics are not generally chargeable as child pornography at a federal level in the United States, though they can be charged as obscenity. Because they do not depict the abuse of an actual child, they are more permissible around the world, however their strong correlation with child pornography consumers and their catering to individuals who are interested in visual depictions of sexual abuse involving minors make them of concern in child pornography investigations.

Viewers, Collectors, Traders, Distributors, and Producers

The several taxonomies noted above are used to evaluate the threat of a child pornographer or to determine the likelihood of recidivism. In terms of investigations, a simple taxonomy that represents a general progression in threat and impact can be used. Categorizing offenders from those who view child pornography through those who produce child pornography is an effective way of evaluating the level of offender that the investigator is dealing with and prioritizing investigative resources based on the overall severity of the offense. While the taxonomy below represents a progression, it is not a strict progression. An individual may produce a video as a trophy from a contact offense, but may never share that video. Similarly, an individual may be distributing child pornography for commercial purposes but have no personal interest in the content from a viewing or collection standpoint. These cases are the exception, however, and individuals generally start as viewers and rarely begin by distributing or producing, at least since the ready availability of content the Internet.

Viewers

Viewers are a relatively new class of child pornographer. Prior to the Internet, individuals had to physically possess images of child pornography for a non-transient period of time, unless they visited a companion who possessed the child pornography. With the advent of the World Wide Web, subjects can go to sites dedicated to child pornography and view movies or images while online without directly saving a copy of them. Technically, possession also occurs when a copy of the movie or image is stored in a cache directory on the computer, but storing the content for posterity is not the intent of the viewer. Additionally, if the subject uses In-Private browsing or clears their cache, there may be no evidence of the temporary possession on the local hard drive, and the subject would just be charged with the accessing and/or viewing provisions of the relevant federal statutes.

Subjects that progress to other categories with child pornography generally start out as viewers. Frequently, they will put search terms into Google or another search engine looking for content based on their initial interest. Although the number of individuals in this category was on the rise, recent attempts by Microsoft's Bing and Google to block search terms associated with child pornography may change the dynamics of the category. The sophistication of the user can be gauged by their search terms - viewers may initially search for terms like "young teen sex pictures" and eventually begin searching for more discriminating terms such as "PTHC" or "R@ygold", which return fewer false positives for them. Their terms may become more specific over time as well, with specific age ranges or acts described in the search terminology, e.g. "8yo blonde girl incest sex". Their searches will likely end up eventually pointing them to Thumbnail Gallery Porn (TGP) sites, to self-hosting sites, or to web forums.

Commercial TGP sites frequently advertise child pornography, and are easier to find through Google searches consisting of more commonly used terms. The TGP sites provide thumbnails of pornographic material to the viewer, who then clicks on pictures that interest them to be transferred to an appropriate gallery containing images or movies based on the clicked-upon picture. In reality, many of the TGP sites have implied child pornography mixed in with adult pornographic images. The implied child pornography contains a young looking individual, or nudist photos of a minor that are difficult or impossible to charge. When the subject clicks on the image, they may be transferred to a foreign site that hosts child pornography, often commercially, or more frequently to a commercial pornography site within the United States that hosts unrelated adult pornography.

Some of the TGP sites will also link to commercial nudist or "youth modeling" sites that contain child erotica available for a fee. These sites cater to individuals that search for and view what they believe to be unprosecutable images and movies. Users may even use tools like Google Images as a pseudo-TGP mechanism by entering terms related to nudism or young models. Viewing this content shows a sexual interest in children, and much of the borderline content is chargeable if the subject admits to viewing it for sexual satisfaction.

TGP sites are notorious for being rampant with malware and for having links that lead to other TGP sites, sometimes circularly linking back to the original site. TGP sites generally have a low probability of linking to actual child pornography. Because of this, they are more frequently visited by individuals who have not already found more reliable avenues to view child pornography.

Self-hosting sites are those that allow an individual to post content without pre-screening by the provider. Early web-based child pornographers would setup temporary sites on free hosting providers like GeoCitites, knowing that they would be taken down a week or two later. As the monitoring on specific self-hosting services becomes more sophisticated, child pornographers move on to other, similar services. Online forums post links to the sites for users to browse or download from while they are available.

Today, Flickr-knockoff sites are frequently used to host child pornography. Sites like imgsrc.ru and imgsrc.su, while ostensibly monitoring for child pornography, allow users to password protect personal image galleries with little policing of their content. Because password distribution via forums became onerous, the child pornography community came up with a decoding system. Image forums would have postfixes to their names like "EZEZE". "EZ" became a consensus code for the community for "12345", and combinations of this password were then encoded in the forum name, so that "EZEZE" would always be accessible to those who knew the scheme as "12345123454321". Similarly, these sites will use CAPTCHA-type questions in the forum name that prevent automated scanning systems from accessing and reviewing the content. Frequently, these will take the form of easily searchable questions like "How many players are on the field on a baseball team <the number spelled out>?" While mechanisms exist for member reporting of contraband and automated provider reviews on many of these sites, the offending posters are rarely reported to law enforcement and will pop back up under a different name shortly after being blocked.

One of the earliest and still highly prevalent methods of web viewing of child pornography is through forums, both public and private. Message boards are setup, frequently on servers in countries with lax enforcement of anti-child pornography laws, for posting images and discussing sexual acts with children. Message boards are differentiated from chat rooms in that the content is static and non-transient on web forums – once uploaded (and sometimes approved by a moderator), the content is viewable to any members of the forum until it is taken down or the message expires. The message board concept is a direct descendant of the BBS model that allowed for dial-up access to child pornography systems in the 1980s and 1990s as detailed in Chapter 2.

Message boards are generally grouped into subforums based on more specific content. A child pornography board may be grouped into "hard core" and "soft core" images, or it may be grouped into subforums based on age, gender, or the sexual activity depicted. The subforums are further broken up into threads – groups of messages in response to a specific topic started by a forum member. Individuals post both text and pictures in a message as part of a thread. The message can be posted anonymously, if permitted by the forum moderator, or by using a login handle chosen by the member. Many boards allow for anonymous reading of messages, but require registration and logging in by the member to post a message.

The child pornography forums not only provide a source of images, but a like-minded community of individuals that a subject can interact with semi-anonymously. The community reinforces that subject's personal proclivities toward sex with children by providing text-based reassurances and by showing the subject that others have similar interests. Further, because there are extremes in all forms of content including child pornography, the subject is likely to encounter others that the subject can rationalize as being "worse" than they are.

Message boards can be publicly accessible (from a foreign hosting provider), can be invitation-only, or can require the uploading of images for access. Open access boards may operate under the guise of "amateur" pornography boards, and make minimal efforts to police their content. They may even include a legal disclaimer that all models are over 18, and that any offending content will be taken down and reported. For more overt boards, the user must generally be invited by a current member of the board. These invitations can come through postings to the open message boards, or through the open section of a private board. The open sections may discuss and include image of adult pornography, with a members-only set of forums not accessible unless the moderator invites the subject to join. Some boards require the subject to upload child pornography as a condition of joining, sometimes requiring large quantities of "new" child pornography to be provided. The moderators generally believe that this will prevent law enforcement from accessing their boards. If one of these boards is encountered during an investigation into viewing or possession, the investigator should seek to obtain consent to take over the persona of the individual being investigated for possession in order to investigate the distribution offenses occurring on the board.

Within the message boards, individuals may be grouped into hierarchies based on the quantity or quality of content they have posted. In some cases, producers can obtain greater status by providing new content or by taking requests for molestation-on-demand. Higher level categories may grant additional benefits, such as the ability to moderate threads or approve and revoke user memberships. Some individuals will thrive on obtaining better "status" within the community by posting frequently, and the status goal can become equally important as the sexual goal for certain subjects.

In addition to having viewable images, message boards can provide links to file providers or to .torrent files that allow for child pornography to be downloaded. These links may be password protected files hosted on legitimate providers, or files hosted on transient file sharing services. Thus, message boards can serve as a viewing platform, a gateway toward possession of child pornography, and a distribution mechanism for producers.

The line between the types of sites is a blurry one. Sites like imgsrc.ru contain forums in addition to housing shared images. Other sites, like motherless.com, have become a haven for child pornographers by integrating all of the features into one site. Individuals can upload images and talk about them, and then make their images searchable in a TGP-like fashion.

One final hybrid category consists of sites that automatically decode and display the images found on Usenet newsgroups. While the groups are mostly thought of as a historical footnote as noted in Chapter 2, the inclusion of web-based front ends has allowed them to continue as a niche location for child pornography distribution. Encoded binary files and anonymous posting services give subjects the ability to post semi-anonymously, and for other subjects to download the posted content semi-anonymously from a completely different server after the content is replicated.

Viewing investigations are extremely time sensitive. Contraband files may not reside on the electronic device seized, and investigators must find the links that have been accessed and obtain copies of all of the content viewed as quickly as possible. Because many of these sites are transient in nature, a few days delay may mean not being able to obtain the content viewed for charging purposes. Techniques for downloading viewed content are discussed in the section on digital forensics, and investigators should consider obtaining a trap and trace order to get timely access to links in viewing cases.

Cases of individuals viewing and accessing child pornography are becoming more frequent with changes in technology. Higher bandwidth in the home means that real-time viewing of movies and images over the Internet is more convenient than ever. Additionally, if the subject is using a shared computer the ability to view the content and not leave easily found traces on the shared machine is desirable. Finally, individuals may require additional rationalizations to store images permanently (or semi permanently) by possessing them. In fact, environmental factors and encounters with law enforcement can actually cause an individual to go from a possessor to a viewer.

Collectors and Distributors

Possession and distribution are inextricably linked as offenses. The mechanisms that some individuals use to download child pornography are the same mechanisms that others use to distribute the same material. Possession can be inadvertent (e.g. through cache files) or intentional (e.g. a fully cataloged collection). Distribution is always intentional, though individuals using peer-to-peer file sharing programs may claim they did not realize they were sharing, and can be anything from a one-to-one transaction via email to running a commercial enterprise that produces and distributes child pornography.

The mechanisms for distribution and consumption of child pornography are primarily Internet-based. There are still hardcopy images, magazines, videos, and similar content available, but they represent a small minority of the evidence encountered by investigations. On the Internet, possession can be broken up into four categories based on the technology used – web-based mechanisms, peer-to-peer mechanisms, chat rooms, and one-to-one connections.

Web Distribution

Web-based mechanisms for viewing child pornography are also distribution platforms. The same individuals that view content can right-click to save the same content locally, or, in the case of movies, use third party download software. In general, individuals saving content directly from websites have already viewed the child pornography, know what it contains, and have made a conscious decision that they need a copy for later viewing. In that sense, web-based acquisition is highly targeted. As noted above, web-based mechanisms include TGP sites, self-hosting sites, and web forums. The mechanisms for possession are the same across all of the options, but the types of distributors tend to be different for each of the avenues.

Those distributing child pornography over TGP sites tend to be commercial producers. Because TGP sites are created to generate revenue, the distributors are either sexualized "child model" photography sites or traditional adult pornography sites with younger appearing models. Both may use generally available payment mechanisms, and both are likely to generate profit directly from user subscription fees.

The "child model" sites may actually be producers of child pornography or obscenity – the exploitation of prepubescent children by having them pose in underwear, swimsuits, or lingerie in a sexualized manner is potentially chargeable. A variant on these are alleged "nudist" picture sites that require subscriptions to join. While there are nudists who have sites dedicated to their interests and are not involved in child pornography, their sites tend to discourage photography, especially of minors. In contrast, the TGP-linked sites focus their content almost exclusively on visual depictions of minors, frequently in suggestive poses. Both categories of sites are likely to be hosted in more lenient jurisdictions, either domestically or overseas.

The adult sites linked to by TGP sites may be hosted anywhere and are generally protected by the First Amendment. These can range from Hustler's "Barely Legal" sites to foreign hosted sites, primarily in Eastern Europe, containing amateur models. The foreign sites may have birth certificates of dubious origin on file for the models, and in many cases the depicted models may only be in their mid-teens. These youth are frequently exploited by the producers, and they might be victims of human trafficking, or may be coerced through drugs or alcohol. In most cases, because the models are purporting to be of legal age where the content was produced, there is little likelihood of prosecuting the commercial enterprises behind the sites or even receiving cooperation in definitively identifying the ages of the models for a domestic prosecution of possession.

Subjects that post images to self-hosting sites like imgsrc.ru, in contrast, are primarily non-commercial distributors, though the platform itself generates revenue through ads. The sites tend to be of a single child or a small group of children, either victimized by the distributor or part of a private collection. These sites tend to be self-limiting in the number of images that can be posted – if too many are uploaded by a single user, it draws too much attention to that particular user and their content is more likely to be taken down. This creates two dynamics of interest to investigators. First, individuals will post the content most meaningful to themselves. These will either be their favorite "trophy" images, or the images that they have collected and are most proud of. Second, individuals may have multiple accounts on the same provider under different usernames. If the provider is being subpoenaed, or more commonly asked to provide information through a mutual legal assistance treaty (MLAT) request, the investigator should ensure that all accounts linked to the IP address of the distributor are provided and not just the initial account under investigation.

Web forums have yet another dynamic at play for collectors and distributors – that of written feedback. Individuals can upload images and receive immediate comments on what they have posted. In general, and in contrast to other types of feedback forums, the comments are more likely to be supportive of the material uploaded and may even request the trader provide additional content. Those looking to obtain child pornography from web forums can make requests based on content they like, and can go to another channel such as email or chat to further trade with individuals if they want to do so. The interactivity between distributor and consumer is moderately high, but can be throttled back by the distributor on demand. Distributors get the added benefit of immediate support for their activities from a large number of individuals.

Web forums tend to be less transient than self-hosting sites. In some cases, the sites are up long enough for their users to build a sense of community and for individual members to attain some degree of recognition within the group. When a site does get taken down, the membership will likely seek another forum, and may use the same handles on the new forum. Activities such as requiring a user upload content before being allowed to participate not only make it more difficult for law enforcement to infiltrate the forums, but also start the indoctrination process and create a sense of in-group mentality by having the joiner's first act be a proof of trust, using the illegal act as a bonding mechanism.

Peer-to-Peer Distribution

Peer-to-Peer distribution of child pornography can take the form of a mesh-based network like eDonkey that allows individuals to search distributed computers for content of interest, and defaults each member of the network as both a sharing hub and a content search/download tool. It can also take the form of a tracker-based tool that requires an aggregator that can be searched for pointers to content of interest, a model popularized by BitTorrent. Peer-to-peer tools generally allow content to be acquired faster than using web-based mechanisms, though there will be less discrimination in the content acquired. Some of the content may be mislabeled, either intentionally or through poor categorization, and subjects need to know the proper terminology to be able to acquire the content they want. Because of how these networks work, there is a brief delay between the user deciding to view content and the content becoming available, with a higher false positive rate in obtaining the exact content they desired. Since an individual can search for terms of interest and flag a large number of files at a time, or even automate the downloading of similar files as they come online, some subjects will use peer-to-peer connections as a batch download tool. They may start a peer-to-peer session before going to work or before going to sleep at night, and then view all of the content that has been downloaded the next morning, discarding the files they are not interested in.

Unlike web forums, there is no contact between distributors and consumers and there is no built-in feedback mechanism in peer-to-peer distribution. Some subjects will use web forums to post links to .torrent files to share files using BitTorrent to indirectly receive feedback. Alternatively, subjects may discuss peer-to-peer software on forums. These are more likely to be the exception rather than the rule, however. In general, peer-to-peer acquisition of child pornography attracts individuals who do not want direct interaction. Distributors can upload content semi-anonymously, and once they have uploaded the content they can disengage from the network. This does not provide the same level of psychological bolstering that posting to a forum does in terms of receiving immediate written feedback or even ratings, but it does reduce the risk associated with posting content. Similarly, for consumers, their interaction with the network is also perceived as transient. They can stay connected only long enough to download content, there is no logging inherent in the networks, they do not have to upload any content to be able to download material except in rare quota-based peer-to-peer systems, and they do not have to interact with others, even indirectly.

Peer-to-peer communication using the BitTorrent client is currently the highest bandwidth file-trading protocol on the Internet. Files are shared by creating a .torrent descriptor file by the individual wanting to distribute the content. The file points to a tracker, though most clients now support non-tracker based peer-to-peer sharing also, which contains information on where pieces of the file can be downloaded. The .torrent descriptor file can be sent via one-to-one communication using email, instant messaging, or chat software or one-to-many communications by posting to a tracker search engine or a web forum. As a user downloads a file using a client like Vuze or µTorrent, they share pieces of the file automatically. Because of this, anyone downloading child pornography with BitTorrent generally distributes the same content simultaneously. Evidence of an individual creating a .torrent file shows further intent to share a file.

The Gnutella network was one of the earliest peer-to-peer networks. Using clients like BearShare, Limewire, and Phex, individuals connect to an ultranode, which provides them a list of other ultranodes and connected peer machines. The subject can then search the network through the connected systems, which sends a distributed query request for names of tagged files. Any machines connected to the network that have a filename containing the query string respond, and the user can download files directly from that client, or piecewise from multiple clients if the file exists in multiple locations.

The Gnutella network became rife with child pornography – at one point the single most frequent query on the network was "PTHC". Files that are downloaded are immediately placed in a shared folder, where they are made available automatically for searching and distribution to anyone else connected to the network. Child pornographers will frequently batch download large numbers of files, then view them at once, deleting the content they are not interested in and moving the content they are interested in from the default download directory into another directory of their choosing.

Filenames on the Gnutella network tend to have long descriptors that include extensive detail on their contents. In some cases, individuals will intentionally mislabel files to encourage their downloading – for reasons ranging from the desire to propagate malware to delivery of religious messages to simply trying to subvert child pornographers. This subversion of filenames results in a high false-positive rate of files that do not contain what they advertise. Because of this, the child pornography community has evolved their terminology, including terms like "NoBull" and the permutation of it, "Nabult", to indicate that the file is "not bullshit" and really contains what its filename is advertising.

The Gnutella network led to several spin-off networks based on the same architecture. Ares, a gnutella-like client that is currently popular, runs on a separate but similar network. Another protocol, Gnutella 2.0, has been adopted and implemented by several of the more popular clients as well.

Currently, the most popular peer-to-peer software in use by child pornographers is eMule. A SourceForge project, eMule connected to the eDonkey network. EDonkey used centralized tracking servers to coordinate searching on the network. The servers were originally run by a now-defunct corporate entity, but have been supplanted by community-maintained servers. EMule is similar to Gnutella for investigative purposes except that it does not allow the browsing of all of the files shared by an individual host. Only files that have triggered hash hits associated with child pornography and have been enumerated by trackers can be browsed.

Other peer-to-peer networks that were popular in sharing child pornography were those using the FastTrack protocol, namely Kazaa, Kazaa Lite, and Kazaa Lite Resurrection (the latter two were unauthorized clients). While Kazaa itself used centralized servers and after numerous lawsuits has shut down, Kazaa Lite and Kazaa Lite Resurrection still exist. As with the Gnutella-based networks, the FastTrack-based networks generally shared files automatically once they were downloaded, and allowed for searching of centralized indices of files from all attached clients. Even though the main Kazaa client is no longer extant, investigators may come across the knock-offs or still-installed versions of the original software that were previously used by the subject.

One of the final peer-to-peer variants that is currently in active use by child pornographers is GigaTribe. Hosted in France and difficult to get law enforcement cooperation from, GigaTribe uses central servers that allow users to share files directly from their hard drives. Unlike the other peer-to-peer networks, the paid version of GigaTribe allows users to encrypt and password protect their content, preventing global browsing. Instead, they can allow others access to their content, which they may utilize forums, chat rooms, or email to enable. Although GigaTribe is a peer-to-peer network, in practice the investigations and the mindset of the distributors are closer to those using shared hosting sites. From a prosecutorial standpoint, however, there are fewer links in the chain – the offending content is actually hosted on the computer of the individual doing the sharing, making it easier to link to the original source. Distributors looking to share amongst a small group of trusted friends are likely to use GigaTribe.

Because individuals on the Gnutella network and other peer-to-peer networks share files that may depict known victims and can be confirmed by hash value to be child pornography, efforts have been made to log any individual sharing previously identified or suspected content. Gridcop, an effort funded by TLO, and RoundUp, a tool used by most of the ICAC taskforces, both track this sharing. RoundUp focuses on the Gnutella network, while Gridcop's CPS tracks Gnutella, FastTrack, Ares, BitTorrent, eDonkey, Gigatribe, Motherless, IRC, and several other sharing mechanisms. As a result, investigators can get an historical picture of the activities associated with a particular IP address or GUID (a number that uniquely identifies a particular installation of peer-to-peer software). Investigators can also use law-enforcement specific peer-to-peer clients like ShareazaLE to download offending content from subject's machines for evidentiary purposes and to obtain probable cause to apply for a warrant.

Chat Rooms

Chat rooms are one-to-many conversation centers that allow an individual to monitor conversations between others, join in a conversation, or take a conversation offline into a one-to-one discussion. Many of the chat rooms dedicated to child pornography have the ability to transfer files using web-based or installable clients, allowing them to be used as a sharing mechanism. Chat rooms are differentiated from web forums in that chat rooms do not generally store their conversations – an individual can only see chat content from the moment they join into the future. There are two primary chat mechanisms used by child pornographers – Internet Relay Chat and video chat rooms. Specific web forums may also have a chat function, which is generally over a web-based client, with behavior similar to that seen in IRC.

Internet Relay Chat (IRC) began in the late 1980's as an IP-based, client-server mechanism for holding live conversations. With IRC, a server, or server network, is setup and hosts various channels, defined by a #name. Individuals connecting to the server select a handle, join a channel, and can then listen in on communications that are occurring. Server networks like DALnet and Undernet have historically been used by child pornographers who setup channels dedicated to trading illicit content.

Subjects that use IRC tend to monitor multiple channels and may have multiple personas. The "magnanimous" desire to share content and to make a name for oneself tend to be less prevalent in IRC channels – because the content is transient, so is any recognition. Subjects using IRC as their primary acquisition mechanism are generally looking to directly trade content with others who have private collections. By targeting particular channels, they can ensure they only communicate with individuals that have similar interests. Requests can be made of the channel as a whole, and then private conversations broken off to perform the actual trading. Collectors that are looking to complete a series of a particular victim or looking for very particular paraphilia-based content can make directed requests to a large number of individuals and obtain immediate responses. Additionally, as with web forums, individuals can discuss child pornography collecting and can obtain some self-assurance from other like-minded individuals using these channels.

File sharing is done by engaging in a private conversation with another individual, using their handle, in a particular channel. Once the private conversation begins, the subjects generally engage in a mutual escalation protocol to establish trust. The parties may start with basic questions like "Are you law enforcement?" under the erroneous belief that investigators must answer that question in the affirmative. The parties may then trade erotica-based images to further establish trust. Eventually, one party must make a leap of faith and send images or movies to the other party, hoping the individual on the other end reciprocates the gesture. Individuals participating in IRC generally do not establish long-term contact with other offenders using that mechanism – they may go to another mechanism such as email or break off contact after a single trade. Additionally, because handles are throw-away identifiers, one subject may have multiple identities in an IRC channel.

One aggravating problem with IRC-based offenders is the direct exploitation of children by joining chats dedicated to the interests of younger individuals. These chats can involve the subject sending adult pornography to children as a grooming mechanism, distributing child pornography to children, or requesting self-pictures of children. Often, though not always, the offenders will pose as peers of the children that they are chatting with. These offenders will also monitor chat rooms extensively, looking for troubled youth to prey upon and learning the lingo of that particular age group and demographic. This allows them to better pretend to be of the appropriate age. In the worst case, subjects may extort children into producing images of themselves, sometimes called "sextortion", by threatening to disclose the contents of private conversations. The highest risk offenders will use IRC as a tool to setup in-person meetings with children to engage directly in sexual activity. The investigation of sex travelers using IRC and performing undercover operations as child targets is beyond the scope of this book, but these individuals are also likely to be possessors, distributors, and producers of child pornography.

IP address tracking gives investigators the ability to identify individuals that trade with them in child pornography forums. Individuals may have multiple handles, sometimes using them at the same time in multiple forums. Fortunately for investigators, there is frequently commonality in either the handle name, using an uncommon numerical postfix, for example, or in the other identifying information they present to the community. The Gridcop CPS system provides limited after-the-fact tracking of IRC activity as well.

The second type of chat forums utilizes video for anonymous or semi-anonymous interactions. Services including Omegle, Zumbl and Chatroulette have been previously co-opted by child pornographers as a way of obtaining live camera feeds of minors. All three services noted have implemented monitoring and moderators to address the issue, but as one site increases its security the offenders move to a different platform. These systems differ from single user programs like Skype in two ways – the subjects are generally anonymous and they connect at random with others globally instead of selecting a directed connection.

Because of the random nature of these services, offenders have a low probability of encountering minors, and an even lower probability of encountering a minor that they can entice to remove their clothing. This would generally discourage subjects, but the concept of a live feed can reduce the likelihood that law enforcement is present on the other end. Subjects that encounter minors can entice them using grooming techniques, or take their interactions into another channel by trading email addresses or instant messaging IDs.

One-to-One Connections

The most intimate form of child pornography distribution is through one-to-one connections. These involve a level of direct interaction not present in other methods and require that both the distributor and the consumer share a piece of information such as an email address or instant messaging identifier that can be used to trace their communications. There is a low risk, however, of detection unless one of the parties involved is law enforcement or one of the parties is caught by law enforcement. Additionally, the parties involved can very precisely specify content they are interested in, can trade techniques, can offer support for each other's activities, and can have ongoing contact to acquire new material. One-to-one connections include email, instant messaging, ICQ, directed chat clients, and MMS.

In most situations, one-to-one connections are formed after an individual identifies someone like-minded using another method like a chat room or a web forum. When one-to-one interactions are encountered during an investigation, the investigator should seek to find out how the interaction began. The sharing of identifiers is generally done after some level of trust has been built up, frequently based on the escalation protocol noted above. Subjects may continue to have interactions with like-minded offenders as long as there is content still being traded or other support provided.

Child pornographers are likely to have many identifiers setup for these interactions, and may have a unique backstory for each persona they have created. For subjects with more than a few identifiers, they are likely to keep a spreadsheet or document detailing the biography, username, and password associated with each account. Each persona may be targeted at a different demographic and a different forum – subjects may pretend to be a homosexual, middle aged male with one persona and a grade school-aged bisexual female with another. In some cases, the personas are used to send child pornography to minors as part of a grooming ritual.

The easiest method of trading child pornography one-to-one is through email. Although email can be a one-to-many interaction, it is generally not used that way by child pornographers. Subjects who meet using other technologies will frequently trade email addresses following a successful transaction. Subjects that adhere to stricter protocols are likely to have a single, throwaway email address for each trading relationship. These accounts may still be linked by an emergency password recovery account, cell phone number, or registered user identity and any subpoenas issued should request other accounts with these features in common. Similarly, these accounts are likely to be accessed using the same IP addresses, unless the subject is extremely diligent about using anonymizers.

Emails are most likely to contain a simple request->response format at first. Over time, they may expand to include details about personal fantasies or other child pornography related discussions. They rarely bleed over into general personal conversations due to a fear of law enforcement and a need to maintain the persona that was created for that account, with the exception being groomers communicating with children. Email transactions are slow and have a limited capacity, so they are more likely to be used for images than movies. Additionally, email transactions require a more patient offender – responses to requests are not instant, and may require several days of waiting. Because of this detachment, email correspondence can be less personal than other real-time one-to-one transactions and require less of a backstory for each persona.

Instant messaging, whether using services like Yahoo! Messenger, MSN Messenger, AOL Instant Messenger, and Google Talk!, or using older services like ICQ ("I-seek-you"), allows for real-time, one-to-one interaction between child pornographers. In the early 2000's, it was estimated by some researchers that instant messaging (IM), specifically ICQ, was the primary distribution platform for Internet child pornography.

IM is similar to email in that it requires a client to register with a username or handle that can be used to contact them. In most cases, an email address is required behind the client, so offenders must either use their real email address or create a throwaway address to register for IM services. In some cases, such as Google Talk!, the user signs up for an email account and can begin using the IM functionality immediately as part of the service.

With IM software, a consumer contacts a distributor to begin a conversation, though in practice, both parties are likely to be both consumers and distributors on IM. After the escalation protocol, the two parties can begin trading child pornography directly from their collections on their computer. Most IM clients allow for content to be shared in two ways – by direct incorporation into the message stream or by download from the distributor's hard drive. Direct incorporation is frequently used for images – the distributor can drag-and-drop an image straight into their messaging client to have it appear on the consumer's IM stream within the client. This may be used as part of a preview process, either to establish bona fides or to allow for the consumer to decide what particular content interests them. For larger content, including movies or archived images, the users are more likely to use the download functionality of the clients. This permits the sharing of individual files, or folders in some cases, and direct download of content while both users have their software clients running.

IM is one of the most interactive options for child pornography trading. It requires the individual to have content already available that they can provide, and to interact in real-time with their trading partner. The volume that can be traded using IM is generally low – the requirement that both parties remain active and that high upload bandwidth is available can limit activity either technologically or by requiring longer periods of interactivity than both parties may be comfortable with.

Most child pornographers will adopt one of the more fully-featured clients. Clients like Trillian, Adium, and Pidgin can interface with multiple IM services from within the same client and support multiple identifier usage. For investigative purposes, these clients may log the chats that occur, including any associated downloads. By tying a download to a request, it can further substantiate the "knowingly" condition of a receipt charge. For the server-based chat functions, legal service on a provider can return a list of chat contacts and potentially a chat history, including logs.

One final feature of interest in modern IM clients is the ability to use a webcam as part of a chat. Webcams permit additional interaction that some child pornographers seek, especially those looking to groom minors and to encourage them to perform on camera. When the persona that a subject uses does not match their actual appearance, they may claim that their webcam is broken, misconfigured, or that their computer is too old to have one installed to avoid a two-way video chat. On the other hand, they can validate that the individual they are chatting with is a minor and not law enforcement through the integrated webcam feature.

The riskiest form of one-to-one trading of child pornography is using Multimedia Messaging Service, or MMS, using smartphones. MMS allows individuals to trade multimedia content, including images and movies, as part of text messages. In general, MMS messages containing child pornography are images that were taken with a cell phone's camera by one of the parties as part of a sexting interaction. Sexting images are usually taken by consenting minors as part of same-age relationships, but can also be coerced or extorted from minors by adult subjects. Because it requires providing an easily traceable phone number and is more intimate than other methods, MMS messages are rarely used to exchange child pornography by two adults except in cases where the parties already know each other's true identities and at least one of the parties is committing hands-on offenses, though images that minors have sexted to each other have occasionally been forwarded by adults and distributed onward.

Although it is not a distribution technology itself, the use of TOR to interact with other child pornography services is growing in popularity. TOR (The Onion Router) routes connections through multiple anonymous proxies, hiding the address of both the sender and the receiver. Users can connect to websites, chat forums, and other services openly sharing child pornography over the "darknet" of services provided through TOR. The greatest barrier to widespread adoption of TOR is the speed – TOR connections are an order of magnitude slower than non-anonymized connections. TOR connections make determining the location and identity of the party on the other end difficult, which is an advantage for those trafficking in child pornography but a disadvantage to investigators. The addition of untraceable payment mechanisms like Bitcoin have encouraged a resurgence in commercial child pornography services, though recent arrests like those of the operators of the Silk Road website may discourage further growth in this area.

Contact Offenders and Producers

The core reason for strict penalties on child pornography possession and distribution is that the images all depict the physical abuse of minors. The most controversial area of research is the quantification of what percentage of individuals that possess child pornography have committed or will commit a contact offense against a child. There is one school of thought that believes viewing child pornography may satisfy a psychological need that would otherwise be fulfilled by molesting a child directly. The other school of thought says that repeated viewing of child pornography lowers inhibitions and results in a higher likelihood of an individual becoming a contact offender. Perhaps the most accurate statement about those who view child pornography is that the images don't necessarily depict what the possessors have done, but they do depict what they want to do.

The arrow is generally thought to proceed in one direction – individuals that possess child pornography eventually go on to commit contact offenses and become producers. This conceptual model neglects several categories of individuals that don't fit as neatly into the progression as one might predict. Those that do not fit into the standard progression include the following:

- **Story-centric Child Pornographers.** Subjects may only have a few images, but write stories about the children that they abused. They may also have stories about abuse that others have written. The stories may be altered to include names of children that the subject knows, or the subject may fantasize that they are part of the stories by including their own name. With these individuals, there is a potentially higher risk of production without a large quantity of child pornography being present or being traded.

- **Commercial Producers.** There are individuals involved in human trafficking and the prostitution of minors that may have no interest in collecting content or even possessing it beyond what they produce for distribution. These subjects will view their activities as a for-profit criminal enterprise and their victims as chattel, without the need to rationalize the victims being willing participants.
- **Non-contact Producers.** Though it may seem contradictory, there are individuals that may assist in the production of child pornography and not touch a child or be interested in doing so themselves. Spousal abusers, where one spouse is greatly subservient to the other, may include one party that digitally memorializes abuse without laying a hand on the victim. While these individuals bear equal ethical and legal culpability, their motivations may not involve excitement at the images of children and they may not actually possess any images.
- **Trophy Producers.** Some individuals who produce child pornography may do so as trophies of their actions or as extortion material against their victims. These subjects may not have extensive collections of images or distribute the images to anyone else. In fact, subjects in this category may enjoy having exclusive access to the images or use the threat of distributing them to control a victim.
- **Older Producers.** Individuals who began molesting before access to Internet-based distribution mechanisms was readily available may have started with production and moved on to possession and distribution once the technologies became available. Although the majority of offenders will have adopted the newer technologies, there are still technophobes that may shun the Internet but maintain a home production capability.

When does a collector/distributor become a contact offender and then a producer? The research is mixed on this topic. In their seminal paper "The 'Butner Study' Redux: A Report of the Incidence of Hands-on Child Victimization by Child Pornography Offenders", Michael Bourke and Andres Hernandez looked at this specific area by examining individuals convicted of child pornography offenses at Butner Federal Prison. At the time of their conviction, 26% of the inmates had admitted to a prior contact offense. Following treatment, including polygraph examinations, 85% of the inmates admitted to at least one sexual contact with a minor. Michael Seto, R. Karl Hanson, and Kelly Babchisin in "Contact Sexual Offending by Men with Online Sexual Offenses" found in their meta-analysis that the number of self-reported child pornographers who engaged in contact offenses was approximately 55%, though they also identified a subgroup that was deemed not likely to offend.

Although the numbers above show a large, if not guaranteed, crossover risk, most of the individuals involved did not become producers of child pornography. Their contact offenses were not visually documented, and their child pornography collections did not include images of their own actions. There may have been multiple reasons for this – memorializing their actions increased their legal risk, they may not have had the technical capabilities on hand to do so, creating a video or images of the abuse may have interrupted the act itself, or they may not have thought of doing so until after the physical act was completed. Because of this, it should not be assumed that a lack of production of child pornography means that a contact offense has not occurred – only that the investigators have not found any memorialization of an offense.

4 CHILD PORNOGRAPHY AND THE LAW

I shall not today attempt further to define the kinds of material I understand to be embraced within that shorthand description ["hard-core pornography"]; and perhaps I could never succeed in intelligibly doing so. But I know it when I see it. . .
Justice Potter Stewart

The legal system is highly location dependent. The definition of what constitutes child pornography differs on a state-to-state basis, and the penalties vary dramatically based on venue. When international law is taken into account, the offenses range from non-existent - in Japan, possession without intent to distribute is legal - to severe - Saudi Arabian law allows for up to 1,000 lashes for using a camera phone to take illicit images. Even within the United States the laws vary greatly – some states have decriminalized possession by teenagers of pictures consensually shared, while others have stricter standards than the federal system. Covering all applicable laws would be an impossible task, and many times there are options available for choosing your venue. For the purposes of this book, United States federal law related to child pornography and online child exploitation is provided as an exemplar of the legal complexities surrounding child pornography offenses.

This chapter covers the current federal statutes as well as summaries of relevant case law. Key decisions are cited, and represent the more recent opinions relevant to child pornography investigations. Because statutes and case law change as new technologies are adopted, investigators are encouraged to contact the Child Exploitation and Obscenity Section of the Department of Justice for the latest legal interpretations and the relevant judicial decisions in their circuit. This chapter assumes a basic understanding of federal laws related to search and seizure, specifically of computers, and general constitutional rights as they relate to investigations.

What is Child Pornography?

Child pornography is defined by federal statute 18 USC § 2256, which states:

(8) "child pornography" means any visual depiction, including any photograph, film, video, picture, or computer or computer-generated image or picture, whether made or produced by electronic, mechanical, or other means, of sexually explicit conduct, where—

(A) the production of such visual depiction involves the use of a minor engaging in sexually explicit conduct;

(B) such visual depiction is a digital image, computer image, or computer-generated image that is, or is indistinguishable from, that of a minor engaging in sexually explicit conduct; or

(C) such visual depiction has been created, adapted, or modified to appear that an identifiable minor is engaging in sexually explicit conduct.

Included in the definition are several other definitions. First, a minor is defined in the same chapter as a person under the age of 18. Sexually explicit conduct is further defined narrowly:

(A) Except as provided in subparagraph (B), "sexually explicit conduct" means actual or simulated—

(i) sexual intercourse, including genital-genital, oral-genital, anal-genital, or oral-anal, whether between persons of the same or opposite sex;

(ii) bestiality;

(iii) masturbation;

(iv) sadistic or masochistic abuse; or

(v) lascivious exhibition of the genitals or pubic area of any person;

In the United States, child pornography is distinguished from child erotica, which may contain nude or seminude depictions of minors. Further, even if nudity is present, whether lascivious display of the genitalia has occurred is not always obvious. In US v. Dost (*United States v. Dost*, 636 F. Supp. 828 (S.D. Cal. 1986)), the defendant was found to have photos of girls aged 10 and 14 years of age which were alleged to be child pornography. To determine whether they met the threshold of child pornography, the court developed what is now known as the six factor Dost test:

1. Whether the focal point of the visual depiction is on the child's genitalia or pubic area;
2. Whether the setting of the visual depiction is sexually suggestive, i.e., in a place or pose generally associated with sexual activity;
3. Whether the child is depicted in an unnatural pose, or in inappropriate attire, considering the age of the child;
4. Whether the child is fully or partially clothed, or nude;
5. Whether the visual depiction suggests sexual coyness or a willingness to engage in sexual activity;
6. Whether the visual depiction is intended or designed to elicit a sexual response in the viewer.

Not all of the elements of the test need to be present for a finding that an image is child pornography, but the test is widely accepted in the federal system. The difference between the child erotica and child pornography is not always readily apparent. Consider the following two cases:

- In US v. Knox (*United States v. Knox*, 32 F.3d 733 (3d. Cir. 1994)), Stephen A. Knox was arrested by United States Customs officials and the Pennsylvania State Police when he received two videotapes depicting minors in "bikini bathing suits, leotards, underwear, or other abbreviated attire". He was found to have additional videotapes in his residence, and was convicted of possession of child pornography. Though no nudity was present, the courts held that the video met the standard for child pornography, which was upheld on appeal.
- In City of Cincinnati v. Contemporary Arts Center (*City of Cincinnati v. Contemporary Arts Center*, 57 Ohio Misc. 2d 15, 566 N.E.2d 214 (Ct. Mun. Ct. 1990), a case made famous for testing the definitions of obscenity, the Cincinnati Contemporary Arts Center and its director, Dennis Barrie, were charged with displaying the images of a nude, minor male and female created by artist Robert Mapplethorpe. The court applied the obscenity test, determining that the images were not obscene and therefore could not be considered child pornography.

The cases above highlight the fact-specific issues surrounding the definition of child pornography that may be present. Specifically, the Mapplethorpe case applied the Miller test (*Miller v. California*, 413 U.S. 15, 93 S. Ct. 2607, 37 L. Ed. 2d 419 (1973)) for obscenity as a baseline for determining if an image is pornographic:

1. Whether "the average person, applying contemporary community standards", would find that the work, taken as a whole, appeals to the prurient interest;
2. Whether the work depicts or describes, in a patently offensive way, sexual conduct specifically defined by applicable state law;
3. Whether the work, taken as a whole, lacks serious literary, artistic, political, or scientific value.

Unlike the Dost test, the Miller test requires all three elements to be present.

The definition becomes even more blurry when images that did not involve actual children are considered. Originally, the 1996 Child Pornography Protection Act contained broad provisions banning virtual child pornography, specifically, the definition included any visual depiction that "is, or appears to be, of a minor engaging in sexually explicit conduct". In the landmark case of Ashcroft v. The Free Speech Coalition (*Ashcroft v. Free Speech Coalition*, 535 U.S. 234 (2002)), a trade association for the adult entertainment industry challenged the law, citing the inability to film works such as Romeo and Juliet under the included definitions. The Supreme Court agreed, striking down the provisions related to virtual child pornography as a violation of the First Amendment and reasoning that the primary concern of the child pornography laws was to protect children, and no children were harmed in virtual child pornography.

Congress, worried about the implications of the Ashcroft v. The Free Speech Coalition decision, revised the law with the PROTECT Act of 2003. Congressional concerns were raised about the increase in computing power available to child pornographers. They postulated that a child pornographer could alter a photograph of a real child enough to have it reclassified as virtual, and were concerned about the possible court defense that the images were not "real" children and just very good computer generated imagery, which would result in the government having to prove the identities of victims to successfully prosecute a case. 18 USC § 2256 was amended to include the definition of "indistinguishable from", which removes the requirement for the government to specifically identify the individuals in the images and show that they are minors:

> ...the term "indistinguishable" used with respect to a depiction, means virtually indistinguishable, in that the depiction is such that an ordinary person viewing the depiction would conclude that the depiction is of an actual minor engaged in sexually explicit conduct.

Further, 18 USC § 2252a was amended to include an affirmative defense:

> (c) It shall be an affirmative defense to a charge of violating paragraph (1), (2), (3)(A), (4), or (5) of subsection (a) that—
>
> (1)
>
> (A) the alleged child pornography was produced using an actual person or persons engaging in sexually explicit conduct; and
>
> (B) each such person was an adult at the time the material was produced; or
>
> (2) the alleged child pornography was not produced using any actual minor or minors.

The defense that "the alleged child pornography was not produced using any actual minor or minors" was successfully used in the case of US v. Carlos Simon-Timmerman (*United States v. Simon-Timmerman*, 673 F. Supp. 2d 76 (D.P.R. 2009)). Simon-Timmerman was arrested for possession of child pornography by an Immigration and Customs Enforcement Special Agent while travelling to Puerto Rico when he was found with a DVD of Little Lupe in his possession. Both the Special Agent and a pediatrician testified that the actress in the films was a minor. The defense was able to successfully refute that when they found the actress, Lupe Fuentes, who appeared in court and provided evidence that she was 19 years old when she made the movie, and the defendant was released.

For images that are "indistinguishable from" those of real children, the courts have upheld that expert testimony from digital forensic examiners is sufficient, even without a rigorous methodology and a known error rate. In US v. Bynum (*United States v. Bynum*, 604 F.3d 161 (4th Cir. 2010)), the appellate court upheld testimony by a seasoned FBI digital forensics examiner that the images present were not virtual, citing the experiential nature of the expertise and likening it to testimony on drug language.

While the child pornography statutes were amended to remove penalties for possessing generated images of children engaged in sexual activity, the obscenity statutes were amended to include them. Specifically, 18 USC § 1466A, created under the above-mentioned PROTECT ACT of 2003, states:

> (a) In General.— Any person who, in a circumstance described in subsection (d), knowingly produces, distributes, receives, or possesses with intent to distribute, a visual depiction of any kind, including a drawing, cartoon, sculpture, or painting, that—
>
> (1)
>
> (A) depicts a minor engaging in sexually explicit conduct; and

(B) is obscene; or

(2)

(A) depicts an image that is, or appears to be, of a minor engaging in graphic bestiality, sadistic or masochistic abuse, or sexual intercourse, including genital-genital, oral-genital, anal-genital, or oral-anal, whether between persons of the same or opposite sex; and

(B) lacks serious literary, artistic, political, or scientific value;

(c) Nonrequired Element of Offense.— It is not a required element of any offense under this section that the minor depicted actually exist.

Based on 18 USC § 1466A, various forms of Hentai, Manga, and comic erotica depicting children may be considered obscene, though the statute does require possession of at least three images. While the Miller Test requires looking at the whole of a work to determine if it is obscene, the subjects may remove and only retain specific pieces of a work (e.g. a screen capture of animated child sex), changing what constitutes the "body of work" that is analyzed under the test. The obscenity statutes are not frequently charged, but there is case law under the above statute:

- In US v. Whorley (*United States v. Whorley*, 550 F.3d 326 (4th Cir. 2008)), Dwight Whorley was found to be in possession of both child pornography and Japanese anime depicting sexually explicit activity involving children, as well as emails containing obscene text. Whorley was convicted and appealed, claiming that 18 USC § 1466A was an unconstitutional limit to First Amendment freedom of speech since no actual children were involved, and that the emails containing textual content could not be considered obscene. The court rejected both of Whorley's arguments and upheld his conviction.
- In US v. Handley (*United States v. Handley* No. 1:07-cr-030, (D.Io 2010)), Christopher Handley purchased a "loli manga" magazine from Japan, which was delivered via mail to his home. A search of his residence found thousands of "loli manga" magazines, videos, and digital images, though Handley had no child pornography. Handley pleaded guilty to possession of obscene materials and causing the mailing of those materials (18 USC § 1641) and was sentenced to six months in prison.
- In US v. Kutzner (*United States v. Kutzner* No. CR-10-0252-S-EJL, (D.Id 2010)), Stephen Kutzner was found to have obscene images of characters from The Simpsons engaged in sexual activity that he downloaded from an adult website. While Kutzner was also in possession of child erotica depicting real children and admitted to downloading child pornography, he was convicted of obscenity for the possession of the cartoon depictions of child sexual activity.

The Supreme Court declined to hear an appeal on the Whorley case, but the definition of what is child pornography, both virtual and actual, has been successfully interpreted in a fairly broad manner in multiple district and circuit courts.

Proving Age

While proving obscenity is challenging, proving the age of victims depicted can be even more difficult. Ideally, all individuals identified in movies or images can be provided to NCMEC and matched against known victims. If the victim is unknown, the prosecution must show probabilistically that the individual depicted is a minor. If the victim is known from a previous case, NCMEC can provide the name of the original investigating body and the assigned investigator. The courts have generally held that the original investigator can positively identify the depicted victim and that investigator is required to testify as to the age of the child to avoid heresy. This requires coordination, preparation, and potentially funding if the original investigator resides in a different jurisdiction.

Originally, the Tanner scale was used as a method of determining the age of victims present in child pornography images. The Tanner scale, developed by Dr. Tanner to measure maturation, looks at factors including breast development, pubic hair presence, and the development of male genitalia. The scale ranges from I (pre-pubescent) to V (fully mature). Because of factors like early onset puberty exist at one end of the spectrum, and individuals who never go through puberty at the other end, it is difficult to correlate the Tanner stages to individual ages. Additionally, legitimate adult entertainment providers will seek out young-looking stars and shave their pubic hair for movies like those in the Hustler Barely Legal series. Add in false environmental cues to age such as a high school setting and cheerleader outfits and determining the age of the individuals portrayed becomes even more difficult.

Because of the difficulty in determining age accurately, many United States Attorney's Offices have a policy of only charging pre-pubescent images, unless a known victim is portrayed. While this targets the most egregious offenders, children who have reached puberty early may fall through the cracks of the system. As such, alternatives to determining the age of victims are needed.

Despite the limitations of the Tanner scale, medical testimony has been admissible as to age:

- In US v. Anderton (*United States v. Anderton*, 136 F.3d 747 (11th Cir. 1998)), Thomas and Reba Anderton were charged with receipt and possession of videos containing child pornography. At trial, the prosecution presented expert testimony from a doctor who specialized in adolescent growth and development. The doctor testified that the victim depicted was between eleven and fifteen and a half years of age. The defense presented a clinical psychologist and sex therapist who testified that the age was indeterminate. The Andertons were convicted and appealed the decision. The appellate court ruled that the expert testimony was sufficient to present to the jury and allow them to determine the reliability and credibility of the government's witness.
- In US v. Clark (*United States v. Clark*, 762 F. Supp. 2d 203 (D. Me. 2011)), Matthew Clark's shared residence was searched as part of an unrelated animal welfare complaint. During the search, evidence of child pornography was found and ultimately Clark was found to be in possession of VHS tapes and computer images of what appeared to be child engaged in sexual activity. Several images were identified by NCMEC as known victims. The remaining images were evaluated by an endocrinologist using the Tanner scale and found to be minors, based on both the testimony of the doctor and the opinion of the judge.

Ultimately, prosecutors can make their jobs easier by ensuring all of the images identified are first sent to NCMEC for possible identification, and that the unknown images are actively pursued for identification. If identification is not possible, the best recourse is to judiciously choose which images to charge, with pre-pubescent being the best option, and to obtain a formal opinion from a pediatrician or pediatric endocrinologist as to their age before going forward with an indictment. The Tanner scale can be used as one factor in the age determination, but the doctor should base their testimony on their training and experience as well.

Intent and Possession

Convicting an individual of possession requires a definition of "knowingly possesses", which is absent from the definitions in 18 USC § 2256. The question is not a simple one when it comes to electronic evidence - does a deleted file constitute "possession"? Does an individual have to have intentionally sought out child pornography to meet the definition of "knowingly"? These questions have been addressed in various circuits with different views on what constitutes both elements of the statute.

The limits of possession have been addressed in multiple circuit court decisions. The decisions have addressed the differences between viewing and possessing images, and what constitutes doing so knowingly (proving intent):

- In US v. Romm (*United States v. Romm*, 455 F.3d 990 (9th Cir. 2006)), the government charged Stuart Romm with possession of child pornography based on files deleted from his hard drive folders, including 40 images from his deleted Internet cache. Citing Black's Law Dictionary (1999), the court held the definition of possession to be "[t]he fact of having or holding property in one's power; the exercise of dominion over property". The court found that, because Romm admitted to downloading and masturbating to the images, and not simply having them appear in his cache as a result of an unwanted pop-up, he "knowingly possessed" the images and upheld the lower court's conviction.
- In US v. Stulock (*United States v. Stulock*, 308 F.3d 922 (8th Cir. 2002)), Edward Stulock purchased a VHS tape containing child pornography from a distributor that was later raided by federal and state agents. After finding Stulock's purchase record, agents executed a warrant on his home and found the VHS tape as well as a computer that, when examined, was found to have child pornography on it. Stulock's computer had over 1,000 images deleted from a "Temp" directory that he used to extract images from .zip archives, and three images from his browser cache that were extant. The possession charge only addressed the files in the browser cache, which the district court acquitted Stulock on as being insufficient evidence of possession, given Stulock's defense of "aggressive pop-up" advertisements that inadvertently put child porn on an individual's computer. The possession count was not brought to the circuit court, but the court did comment on the fact that the thousands of images found on his machine and the evidence as a whole substantiated receipt for the purposes of the other counts.
- In US v. Flyer (*United States v. Flyer*, 633 F.3d 911 (9th Cir. 2011)), Andrew Flyer was identified by an undercover FBI agent as sharing files with names associated

with child pornography over Limewire, a peer-to-peer software package. The agent downloaded two files from Flyer, whose computer was subsequently seized and who was charged with both possession and transportation across state lines of child pornography. The transportation count was vacated by the testimony of a defense expert who showed that the transfer was intrastate because the FBI agent and Wright were both in Arizona. While interstate transportation is generally a rebuttable presumption in child pornography cases, the court cited the opinion in US v. Wright (*United States v. Wright*, 625 F.3d 583 (9th Cir.2010)) that "a defendant's mere connection to the Internet does not satisfy the jurisdictional requirement where there is undisputed evidence that the files in question never crossed state lines". On the possession count, the court cited US v. Navrestad (*United States v. Navrestad*, 66 M.J. 262 (C.A.A.F.2008)) and overturned the possession conviction based on the fact that the images were in unallocated space and not under the control of Flyer, who had no forensic software to recover them. The government cited US v. Shiver (*United States v. Shiver*, 305 Fed.Appx. 640 (11th Cir.2008)) as supporting the theory that deletion shows an act of control. The appellate court agreed with the argument but found that there was no evidence provided that the control occurred within the dates chargeable for the offense.

The above cases provide insight into what constitutes possession and how difficult proving intent can be from forensic evidence alone. Based on the differing opinions across the circuits, prosecutors should not rely on the simple presence of child pornography files, deleted or otherwise, to prove possession. Possession should be a constructive charge based on both digital forensics and the subject's statements. Prosecutors should look to the following to assist in charging possession:

- **Interview statements.** If the defendant admits to downloading or viewing child pornography, the time period of the activity should be established. Additionally, establishing how the defendant obtained the child pornography, that the subject's actions were performed with the intent to find images of minors engaged in sexual activity, and that the defendant obtained sexual satisfaction for doing so will corroborate possession.
- **Digital Forensics Timelines.** Showing the time of the possession and what actions were taken immediately prior to and following the subject's obtaining the images can assist in showing it was a knowing act, and dispute claims of unwanted "pop-up" ads placing the content on the device. Additionally, performing a timeline analysis can assist in showing that a particular individual was at the keyboard at the time of the download on shared computers. Contemporaneous logins to email or social networking sites can assist with this.
- **Digital Search History.** One of the most effective techniques in showing intent in possession cases is by analyzing the subject's search history in the application used to acquire the child pornography. Showing that the individual searched for "3YO RAPE" or "PTHC" can greatly reduce the likelihood of a pop-up defense or an "accidental download" defense succeeding.
- **Digital Metadata.** Showing a user moved a file, especially to a directory they created and named for the purpose, viewed a file using a program external to the browser or

download software, or selectively deleted files to avoid being caught can show control over the content. The dates and times associated with the above actions should be recovered to the greatest extent possible.

- **Non-Digital Evidence.** Magazines, DVD's, print-outs of websites, and other evidence found around the computer that is contemporaneous with the possession can assist in showing, based on a totality of the evidence, that possession occurred on the date in question.

In addition, the prosecution should be prepared to argue that routing can take place interstate in cases where distribution is based on a local download, and obtain digital evidence of advertising the content interstate. In US v. Flyer, the prosecution could have shown that routing is not always direct even within a state as most ISPs go to their backbone before handing off traffic, or that the subject connected to a Limewire hub in another state as part of the initial connection to provide a list of shared files.

The above guidance only addresses possession of the child pornography. The prosecution should not overlook possession of the computer or other device containing the contraband. Establishing that no other individuals had access to the computer, or at least did not have access at the time of the offense, and that the computer belonged to the subject can be done up-front in an investigation, before addressing the child pornography offenses, to bolster later possession charges.

A final defense related to intent is the "virus did it" defense. This is the electronic equivalent of the infamous SODDI ("Some Other Dude Did It") defense, and is generally used by invoking a mysterious virus or malicious hacker who, for reasons unknown, downloads child pornography to the subject's machine. The defense has been successfully employed in other countries, and has been attempted in several court cases domestically. Within the federal system, the representative case is US v. Brown:

- In US v. Brown (*United States v. Brown*, 2012 WL 5948085 (E.D. Mi. 2012)), Brown was charged with possession and receipt of child pornography. After being convicted, Brown filed a Rule 29 motion claiming the government failed to provide evidence that he knowingly possessed and received the material. Brown claimed that he did not download the two videos of child pornography on his computer, first citing that his wife and their babysitter had access to the computer, then pointing to the presence of a virus found in a Limewire music file downloaded around the time the child pornography was downloaded. Based on a complete forensic exam showing that Brown played the videos, and a log file analysis showing his actions leading up to the download, the defense failed and Brown's motion for acquittal was denied.

Though not in the United States, two high profile cases in the United Kingdom did successfully use the SODDI defense in relation to viruses. The best strategy against a SODDI defense is a corroborated statement from the subject and a thorough forensics examination. In addition to the forensic elements noted above, a thorough virus scan should be conducted on any device analyzed. Any viruses or malware found should be thoroughly researched and noted in the forensic report. The presence of up-to-date anti-virus software at the time of the download of any contraband should also be confirmed and noted in the report.

While the above strategies go toward proving "knowingly" for the possession of the files, the prosecution must also show that the subject believed the individuals that were being depicted were minors. The word "knowingly" became an element in all of the offenses due to the X-Citement Video case:

- In US v. X-Citement Video (*United States v. X-Citement Video*, Inc., 513 U.S. 64, 115 S. Ct. 464, 130 L. Ed. 2d 372 (1994)), Rubin Gottesman was charged with production of child pornography for making and distributing videos that included sexual acts by a then-underage Traci Lords. In a case that ultimately went to the Supreme Court, the defense argued that the existing law at the time was unconstitutional in that, grammatically, the term "knowingly" did not apply to the production clause, making that clause unconstitutional. The Supreme Court disagreed, finding that, if a particular reading of the law is constitutional, then that reading trumps the unconstitutional reading. With respect to the child pornography law, they concluded that "knowingly" applied to all of the sub-clauses in their entirety.

Possession, Receipt, and Distribution

Possession of child pornography is the lowest level offense that is generally charged at the federal level under 18 USC §§ 2252 and 2252A. In practice, both statutes are analogous though 18 USC § 2252A is slightly broader in scope and is therefore more frequently charged. The relevant text of the statute is as follows:

(a) Any person who—

(1) knowingly mails, or transports or ships using any means or facility of interstate or foreign commerce or in or affecting interstate or foreign commerce by any means, including by computer, any child pornography;

(2) knowingly receives or distributes—

(A) any child pornography that has been mailed, or using any means or facility of interstate or foreign commerce shipped or transported in or affecting interstate or foreign commerce by any means, including by computer; or

(B) any material that contains child pornography that has been mailed, or using any means or facility of interstate or foreign commerce shipped or transported in or affecting interstate or foreign commerce by any means, including by computer;

(3) knowingly—

(A) reproduces any child pornography for distribution through the mails, or using any means or facility of interstate or foreign commerce or in or affecting interstate or foreign commerce by any means, including by computer; or

(B) advertises, promotes, presents, distributes, or solicits through the mails, or using any means or facility of interstate or foreign commerce or in or affecting interstate or foreign commerce by any means, including by computer, any material or purported material in a manner that reflects the belief, or that is intended to cause another to believe, that the material or purported material is, or contains—

(i) an obscene visual depiction of a minor engaging in sexually explicit conduct;

or

(ii) a visual depiction of an actual minor engaging in sexually explicit conduct;

(4) either—

(A) in the special maritime and territorial jurisdiction of the United States, or on any land or building owned by, leased to, or otherwise used by or under the control of the United States Government, or in the Indian country (as defined in section 1151), knowingly sells or possesses with the intent to sell any child pornography; or

(B) knowingly sells or possesses with the intent to sell any child pornography that has been mailed, or shipped or transported using any means or facility of interstate or foreign commerce or in or affecting interstate or foreign commerce by any means, including by computer, or that was produced using materials that have been mailed, or shipped or transported in or affecting interstate or foreign commerce by any means, including by computer;

(5) either—

(A) in the special maritime and territorial jurisdiction of the United States, or on any land or building owned by, leased to, or otherwise used by or under the control of the United States Government, or in the Indian country (as defined in section 1151), knowingly possesses, or knowingly accesses with intent to view, any book, magazine, periodical, film, videotape, computer disk, or any other material that contains an image of child pornography; or

(B) knowingly possesses, or knowingly accesses with intent to view, any book, magazine, periodical, film, videotape, computer disk, or any other material that contains an image of child pornography that has been mailed, or shipped or transported using any means or facility of interstate or foreign commerce or in or affecting interstate or foreign commerce by any means, including by computer, or that was produced using materials that have been mailed, or shipped or transported in or affecting interstate or foreign commerce by any means, including by computer;

(6) knowingly distributes, offers, sends, or provides to a minor any visual depiction, including any photograph, film, video, picture, or computer generated image or picture, whether made or produced by electronic, mechanical, or other means, where such visual depiction is, or appears to be, of a minor engaging in sexually explicit conduct—

(A) that has been mailed, shipped, or transported using any means or facility of interstate or foreign commerce or in or affecting interstate or foreign commerce by any means, including by computer;

(B) that was produced using materials that have been mailed, shipped, or transported in or affecting interstate or foreign commerce by any means, including by computer; or

(C) which distribution, offer, sending, or provision is accomplished using the mails or any means or facility of interstate or foreign commerce,for purposes of inducing or persuading a minor to participate in any activity that is illegal; or

(7) knowingly produces with intent to distribute, or distributes, by any means, including a computer, in or affecting interstate or foreign commerce, child pornography that is an adapted or modified depiction of an identifiable minor shall be punished as provided in subsection (b).

In practice, the possession of smaller quantities of child pornography is more frequently charged at a state level, though this is a matter of policy and not law. Receipt, which has a higher sentencing guideline range, is generally the lowest level charged federally. Because they are separate offenses, it was originally common to charge both receipt and possession at a federal level. This matter is still being litigated, with the circuits split on whether or not this is allowable. The 7th Circuit found in US v. Halliday (*US v. Halliday*, 672 F.3d 462 (7th Cir. 2012)) that a defendant could be charged twice, for receipt and possession, if the offenses applied to different circumstances - in this case images with different timestamps. Additionally, while the court originally found that "a receipt provision, includes a scienter requirement, such that a person who seeks out only adult pornography, but is sent a mix of adult and child pornography, would not have violated that statutory provision", it quoted the 9th and 3rd Circuit cases of United States v. Davenport (*US v. Davenport*, 519 F.3d 940, 943-44 (9th Cir. 2008)) and United States v. Miller (*US v. Miller*, 527 F.3d 54, 71-72 (3d Cir. 2008)), which found that possession was a lesser included offense. In general, receipt should be charged if the facts support it, with possession counts added where there is separate conduct that would make charging receipt more difficult.

Distribution charges carry the highest point increases at sentencing of any of the offenses outside of production scenarios, depending on who the material was distributed to and the reason for the distribution:

- Distribution without profit has a two point minimum increase.
- Distribution for financial gain has a minimum five point increase with a maximum 30 point increase based on the gain, though in practice the amounts are generally smaller and correspond to fewer points.
- Distribution for non-financial gain has a five point increase.
- Distribution to a minor has a five point increase, six points if the material was intended to entice the minor into illicit activity, and seven points if the activity involves the minor crossing state lines for sex.

Distribution is frequently charged under the stricter 18 USC § 2252 because of higher mandatory minimum penalties. There are multiple methods of distribution using electronic media. While physically providing or selling media containing child pornography does occur, most cases will involve digital distribution, frequently to an undercover investigator. The primary methods for digital distribution that are routinely charged are by posting to web forums, sending images over email, and sharing files with peer-to-peer software:

- In US v. Budziak (*United States v. Budziak*, 2012 WL 4748704 (9th Cir. Oct. 5, 2012)), FBI agents downloaded child pornography that Budziak had present in a shared folder over Limewire. The court concluded, concurrent with other circuits that "Following the First, Eighth, and Tenth Circuits, we hold that the evidence is sufficient to support a conviction for distribution under 18 U.S.C. § 2252(a)(2) when it shows that the defendant maintained child pornography in a shared folder, knew that doing so would allow others to download it, and another person actually downloaded it."
- In US v. Richardson (*United States v. Richardson*, 713 F.3d 232 (5th Cir. 2013)), Bennie E. Richardson, IV was found guilty of distributing child pornography when a Houston Police lieutenant downloaded images Richardson had been sharing through Limewire. During his interview, Richardson admitted to knowing that files in

his shared folder could be accessed by others, but claimed that the downloading by others was an affirmative act on their part and did not require his active participation. The court disagreed, holding that Richardson possessed child pornography, left them in a folder he knew to be shared, and that they were actively downloaded by the police lieutenant.

- In US v. Battaglia (*United States v. Battaglia*, 624 F.3d 348 (6th Cir. 2010)), Ross Battaglia was convicted of 18 USC § 2252A(a)(2) for distributing child pornography via email and 18 USC § 2252(a)(2) for receipt and possession of child pornography. Battaglia received the base level 22 sentence for the violation of 2252A(a)(2), in addition to a five point enhancement for trading child pornography for non-pecuniary gain under the receipt charge and contended that it amounted to double counting. The court found that the charge and enhancement related to separate conduct, and both the distribution charge and the enhancement were affirmed.
- In US v. Williams (*United States v. Williams*, 128 S. Ct. 1830, 553 U.S. 285, 170 L. Ed. 2d 650 (2008)), Michael Williams posted seven sexually explicit images of children to a message board in response to chats with an undercover United States Secret Service agent. Williams was convicted of pandering, and appealed the decision. The 11th Circuit found that the statute was overbroad and infringed upon First Amendment rights. Upon appeal to the US Supreme Court, the high court overturned the ruling of the 11th Circuit, and found that "offers to provide or requests to obtain child pornography are categorically excluded from the First Amendment".

The most egregious charge, production, also has the highest penalties associated with it. Production is frequently charged as a contact offense at a state level when interstate transportation of the child involved cannot be proven and the resultant images are not distributed. If the images are distributed over the Internet, however, 18 USC § 2251 can be applied, in addition to provisions of 18 USC §§ 2252 and 2252A. 18 USC § 2251 starts out at a base offense level of 32 and sentencing is modified based on the following enhancements:

- The age of the individual involved modifies the base offense by four points if the child is below 12, and by two points if the child is between 12 and 16.
- If a computer is used to entice the child to commit the act or travel across state lines occurs, an additional two points are added.
- If the child is in the legal custody of the offender as a parent or other guardian another two points are added.
- An additional two points are added for general sexual acts, or four points if the acts involve force.
- Distribution adds two points.

As expected, the penalties for production can add up quickly. Production cases are frequently pleaded down to lesser charges of distribution, but the federal system still successfully prosecutes multiple production offenses each year:

- In US v. Evers (*United States v. Evers*, 669 F.3d 645 (6th Cir. 2012)), Ovell Evers, Sr.

had his 13 year old niece perform oral sex on him and filmed the event with his camera. Evers was charged with production of child pornography and was convicted. Evers appealed the search of his computers, contending that the warrant to search them was overly broad. Upholding decisions from previous computer search cases, the circuit court found that the search of the computer was properly outlined in the statement of probable cause and that subsequent analysis offsite was a standard practice and within the scope. The conviction was upheld, but the forfeiture of an unrelated computer that did not contain child pornography was overturned and the device was returned to Evers.

- In US v. Malloy (*United States v. Malloy,* 568 F. 3d 166 (4th Cir. 2009)), Michael Malloy, a 33 year old United State Capitol Police officer, was convicted of using a camcorder to videotape himself and a friend having sex with a 14 year old girl. Malloy appealed, stating that he was unaware of the age of the victim and was not allowed to put forth an affirmative defense to that effect. Similarly, Malloy argued that the videotape remained in his home and that he was charged in violation of the Commerce Clause of the United States Constitution. Both arguments were rejected. The court held that there was no "knowingly" requirement applicable to the age of the victim and that the conduct fell under the auspices of an interstate enterprise, child pornography, citing "[b]ecause Congress possessed a rational basis for concluding that the local production and possession of child pornography substantially affect interstate commerce, `the de minimis character of individual instances arising under the statute is of no consequence.'" [*United States v. Forrest*, 429 F.3d 73 (4th Cir. 2005)] (citing *Gonzales v. Raich*, 545 U.S. 1, 125 S. Ct. 2195, 162 L. Ed. 2d 1 (2005)) and that Malloy's lack of knowledge that such a market existed was not a requirement for conviction.

For any of the above offenses, it is important to categorize the content of the images. The current sentencing guidelines provide for an additional four point enhancement for images that include "sadistic or masochistic conduct or other depictions of violence". Many investigations will stop at identifying the number of images and confirming whether they included previously identified or unknown victims. Requesting details, either visual or written, on the image contents can provide the basis for this enhancement, and a written description of the acts depicted may be admissible, even if the images themselves are considered prejudicial.

Statute of Limitations

By default, the statute of limitation on charging an individual who has committed an offense at a federal level is five years unless otherwise cited. There have been multiple modifications to that timeframe on child pornography offenses, and determining what is within statute is based on when the event occurred, the age of the victims at the time of charging, and the continuance of the act.

The statute of limitations was eliminated for federal crimes against children in 2006 by the Adam Walsh Child Protection and Safety Act. Any child pornography offenses, with the exception of the obscenity statute, that are charged for an offense that occurred after 2006 have no statute of limitations. Because, in general, possession is a continuous offense and distribution is generally found in a timely manner, production offenses that occurred prior to 2006 are the crimes that are the most likely to be charged for acquisitions that occurred prior to 2006.

The five year statute of limitations applied to possession and distribution when the offense occurred before the passage of the Adam Walsh Act as there was no grandfathering clause enacted. There is an exception, however, for production that occurred between 2003 and 2006. The PROTECT Act of 2003 removed the five year statute of limitations on the production of child pornography and made chargeable it for the life of the child. This provides a small window that may be useful to prosecutors in older production offenses that are uncovered as part of current investigations.

Restitution

Victims in child pornography cases are able to seek restitution from any individuals that are found guilty in federal court. The restitution order in these cases is mandatory under 18 USC § 2259, requiring that the court "shall direct the defendant to pay the victim, through the appropriate court mechanism, the full amount of the victim's losses as determined by the court". The amount of restitution can include:

(A) medical services relating to physical, psychiatric, or psychological care;
(B) physical and occupational therapy or rehabilitation;
(C) necessary transportation, temporary housing, and child care expenses;
(D) lost income;
(E) attorneys' fees, as well as other costs incurred; and
(F) any other losses suffered by the victim as a proximate result of the offense.

Unlike other restitution orders, the victims exploited through child pornography can receive full restitution from multiple sources for their expenses. In many cases, where the abuse was charged in state court, victims can receive significantly higher restitution judgments from those who possess an image depicting their abuse than they received from the abuser. The issue of whether the losses due to possession need to be a proximate result of the offense has been raised:

- In US v. Aumais (*United Sates v. Aumais*, 656 F.3d 147 (2d Cir. 2011)), Gerald Aumais was convicted of transporting child pornography across the United States border from Canada. One of the victims depicted in his images, "Amy", sought restitution in the amount of $48,483. The Appellate Court found that Amy's losses were based on assessment performed before Aumais was arrested and therefore could not be a proximate result of his offense, and as such restitution was not required.

In US v. Aumais, the court also speculated that the law required double compensation (full compensation from all parties), which would seem to go against precedent in other restitution cases. Amy's restitution was further denied in the case of US v. Paroline (*United States v. Paroline*, 672 F. Supp. 2d 781 (E.D. Tex. 2009)) under similar circumstances. US v. Paroline has been accepted by the Supreme Court for review and their decision will likely impact future restitution orders.

Other Issues

There are multiple legal issues that are not directly related to the statutes, but heavily impact child pornography cases. Most of these issues deal with computer technology and the adaptation of the law to computer-related issues. The Computer Crime and Intellectual Property Section (CCIPS) of the United States Department of Justice acts as a clearinghouse for computer concerns, and works closely with CEOS on issues that arise in computer-facilitated child pornography offenses.

One of the earliest legal concerns in many child pornography investigations comes during the request for a warrant. Frequently, the information in the warrant may be included months after the act, causing staleness challenges. While most warrants with issues are resolved at the magistrate judge level and written opinions are not available, there are several cases that have reached an appellate level that deal with these concerns:

- In US v. Seiver (*United States v. Seiver,* 692 F.3d 774 (7th Cir. 2012)), the defendant, Ronald Seiver, downloaded an explicit image of a thirteen year old girl. A warrant was sought and was granted seven months after the fact, and Seiver claimed that A) the warrant was stale, and B) the argument that "collectors" of child pornography keep their materials for extended periods did not apply because the investigators only had evidence of a single image being downloaded and not a collection. The opinion found that the information was not stale, holding that, even if a file has been deleted, "it is possible that the deleted file will no longer be recoverable ... [or] the computer will have been sold or physically destroyed", but "rarely will they be so probable as to destroy probable cause ... for probable cause is far short of certainty". The court additionally stated that computers and computer equipment are "not the type of evidence that rapidly dissipates or degrades".
- In terms of staleness in child pornography cases, Brachlow v. State (*Brachlow v. State*, 907 So. 2d 626 (Fla. Dist. Ct. App. 2005)) provides an even longer allowable period. Although a State of Florida case, the court cites several federal cases in their decision. Gary Brachlow was accused by a former minor co-habitant of molestation that occurred four years earlier. According to the complainant, Brachlow made videotapes of the molestation and kept them in a safe. A search warrant was issued, and drugs were found in plain view in Brachlow's residence, for which he was charged and convicted. The court held that, based on the expert testimony of a special agent from the Florida Department of Law Enforcement, that it was "highly likely that a sexual offender, such as appellant, would keep child pornography hidden but readily accessible and that such material was not destroyed". The court found that the warrant was not stale, and that the items found should not be suppressed.

In many cases, all the investigating agency has available is an IP address that has been found to be downloading or distributing images or movies. The courts have held that an IP address that has been linked to a residence is sufficient for probable cause to search that residence:

- In US v. Perez (*United States v. Perez*, 484 F.3d 735 (5th Cir. 2007)), Javier Perez shared images of child pornography with a woman via instant messaging. The woman complained to police, and the IP address associated with the instant messaging account was traced back to Perez's residence. A search warrant was executed and thousands of images of child pornography were found. The court cited US v. Grant (*United States v. Grant,* 218 F.3d 72 (1st Cir. 2000)) in stating "even discounting for the possibility that an individual other than [defendant] may have been using his account, there was a fair probability that [defendant] was the user and that evidence of the user's illegal activities would be found in [defendant's] home" and upheld the inclusion of the evidence.
- In US v. Gillman (*United States v. Gillman*, No. 09-6109 (6th Cir. Aug. 2, 2011)), Joseph Gillman was found to be using peer-to-peer software to share a video depicting child pornography. Gillman's IP address was identified when law enforcement downloaded the video, and a search warrant was executed on his residence. Gillman sought to suppress the evidence, citing the possibility of an open wireless access point. The court denied the motion, and the appellate court affirmed that decision, citing probable cause as existing for there to be evidence in the residence even if the *possibility* that another individual used the wireless network existed. US v. Gillman further highlighted the government's ability to download images from an IP address that is sharing those images openly via a peer-to-peer network without a warrant.

Frequently, the government makes use of the Child Protection System (CPS) to identify individuals sharing child pornography over peer-to-peer networks. A product of TLO, Inc., CPS was proposed by the defendant as being a government actor in US v. Crowe (*United States v. Crowe*, No. 11 CR 1690 MV (D.N.M. Apr. 3, 2013)), and the systems used by TLO were requested to be provided to the defense. The court denied the motion, but upheld the defense's access to the ShareazaLE software for their expert to analyze at an appropriate law enforcement facility.

One area of increasing legal interest is password protected computers. While compelling the production of a password may constitute a Fifth Amendment issue, at least one case was able to circumvent that by requiring the production of the contents of a password protected drive. As part of In Re Boucher (*In Re Jury Subpoena to Sebastien Boucher*, No. 2: 06-mj-91 (D. Vt. Feb. 19, 2009)), customs agents found evidence of child pornography on the hard drive of Sebastien Boucher when he entered the United States from Canada. The computer was then shut down, activating the PGP encryption on the drive with the child pornography. The court required Boucher to produce the unencrypted contents of the drive, which the agents knew contained child pornography from observation, but not the password. While this represents a single case, the issue of compelling passwords for encrypted drives is still being debated.

While the case law regarding child pornography is in constant flux, the precedents established by several of the cases above can be used to bolster arguments in child pornography prosecutions. Because this book represents a point-in-time primer and the laws will likely have progressed by the time it goes to print, the reader is encouraged to contact CEOS for the latest case law and for guidance when challenges arise in prosecuting child pornography cases.

5 INVESTIGATIVE RESOURCES

The race of mankind would perish did they cease to aid each other. We cannot exist without mutual help. All therefore that need aid have a right to ask it from their fellow-men; and no one who has the power of granting can refuse it without guilt.
Walter Scott

Investigating child pornography is different than investigating most other types of criminal activity. There are certainly other crimes that are equally heinous, with assaults, rapes, and homicides being contenders. There are equally despicable offenders as well, including those who prey on the elderly, abuse those who cannot defend themselves, and commit atrocities that leave innocent victims scarred for life. There are even hands-on crimes against children - investigating neglect, physical abuse, and sexual abuse cases takes a special type of investigator. What sets child pornography offenses apart from other crimes is the need for the investigator to view the criminal act itself. With the advent of high definition video and ubiquitous smartphone cameras, those investigating child pornography cases may need to see, hear, and document thousands or more acts of children being sexually abused, then sit calmly across from the abuser and show compassion. This takes a specific skillset for members of the investigative team and requires special handling of the investigative process. Fortunately, there are some unique resources available to support these investigations.

Hiring Crimes Against Children Investigators

Unlike other criminal conduct, not everyone with core investigative skills is cut out to investigate crimes against children. While all investigations require some specialized training such as understanding vehicular dynamics, examining blood spatter evidence, or recreating ballistic trajectories, crimes against children, especially the investigation of child pornography, requires both specialized skills and the right psychological profile. The child pornography investigator must be willing and capable of handling the material encountered, and possess the temperament to deal with both subjects and victims. An investigator should NEVER be assigned a crimes against children case against their will or without adequate vetting. Doing so may harm both the investigation and the investigator.

Selecting individuals for crimes against children squads can and should be a fairly stringent process. First, investigators need to have developed core investigative skills. The basic training provided by the police academy or federal training center should be considered a starting point. Unless the department is small, investigators should get some seasoning by investigating other offenses to both raise their confidence and hone their general investigative skills. Doing so ahead of time will keep the general stress of starting a new job from compounding any stressors resulting from the investigations themselves. A minimum of one to three years as a detective or special agent is recommended before assignment to these cases.

Following a break-in period performing other criminal investigations, investigators should be asked if they would be willing to work child exploitation cases. The investigator should be provided the details of what it entails, should be encouraged to talk with individuals currently working child pornography cases, and should not be disadvantaged in their career if they decline. If the position is made available in an open competition, the qualified applicants should similarly be provided details on the position and allowed to speak to current child pornography investigators. Once it has been established that the investigator still wants to continue being considered for the position, the department/agency should engage their psychologist, if one is available, to do a psychological pre-screening. If psychological testing is not available to the individual doing the hiring, they should look at the following factors:

- **Compartmentalization.** Investigators must, for their own sanity, be able to compartmentalize their work and to separate their job from their other responsibilities. Ultimately, this means not bringing their work home with them and being able to “turn off” the investigation when not on duty.
- **Detachment.** Similar to compartmentalization, detachment can be measured, in psychological terms, as a small positive on the psychopathy axis in standardized testing. Why do we look for detachment? It allows the investigator to not become too emotionally involved in the case at hand. To avoid cases turning into crusades , especially because they don’t always turn out positively, a detached investigator views the facts dispassionately and treats each case on its own merits.
- **Compassion.** A small amount of compassion is a good thing – too much can be a problem in child pornography investigators. The investigator should be able to empathize with the subject in order to be able to confront them calmly. Similarly, they should be able to empathize with both caregivers and victims to be able to obtain information under difficult conditions. The investigator should not be overly empathetic with victims, however, to the point where they lose objectivity or blur the lines between investigator and victim advocate. Individuals who have difficulty with over-empathizing may be better suited as victim/witness coordinators or social service workers. Both are equally important roles in protecting children from victimization.
- **Objectivity.** Experiences that may affect an investigator’s objectivity should be examined. Encumbrances to objectivity can include a past history of being molested

themselves or having someone close to them molested, or having children. Although many fantastic child exploitation investigators have children, the investigator needs to have the appropriate detachment and compartmentalization with respect that aspect of their life. Finally, having strong religious beliefs that introduce taboos when talking about sexual activities or cause judgment of the actions under investigation can be an encumbrance. As with other potential encumbrances, investigators may personally hold strong religious beliefs or none at all, as long as they are compartmentalized.

- **Resiliency**. Because investigators will be dealing with difficult situations and regularly viewing objectionable content, resiliency is extremely important. Over time, some images or movies viewed in child pornography cases may become part of the permanent wetware between their ears. A resilient investigator can keep the images from directly affecting their personal life and can recover faster when handling particularly difficult cases.
- **Emotional Extroversion.** While introverts are frequently attracted to digital forensic analyst positions, though not necessarily detective/special agent positions, having the ability to talk to others is important in child exploitation cases. The introverts need to be able to express concerns and talk about troubling content early and not internalize their emotions. Similarly, extroverts need to avoid any "tough guy/gal" acts and speak openly about things that bother them in child exploitation cases.
- **Normophilic Interests**. The term normophilic is used to define an individual with normal sexual interests that are not clinically classified as deviant. There have been instances of pedophiles accepting jobs in law enforcement, and any individual showing an excessive interest in pictures or movies should be excluded from investigative positions on child pornography squads. Some agencies have done specific-issue polygraphs on child exploitation squad applicants to ensure they do not have hidden interests in children or issues in their background that would be problematic.

While it may seem excessive to do psychological screenings of each candidate, there is a duty to protect the investigators as well as the integrity of the cases. Unfortunately, there have been instances where individuals on the investigative and prosecutorial side of the criminal justice system have gone astray:

- Assistant U.S. Attorney John D.R. Atchison from the Northern District of Florida was charged with crossing state lines to have sexual relations with what he believed to be a five year old that he met over the Internet. He committed suicide while in prison awaiting trial.
- Philip Woolery, a 17 year veteran of the Grapevine Texas Police Department, was convicted of the production and receipt of child pornography. Woolery was caught purchasing child pornography online, and was found to have videotaped sexually explicit acts with a young boy in a swimming pool.
- Jonathan N. Gamson, a 25 year veteran of the Tampa Police Department was convicted of the possession of child pornography, including sexually explicit images of an infant, after being caught trading online as part of Operation Gondola.
- Donald Sachtleben, a former Special Agent with the Federal Bureau of Investigation

who retired after 25 years of service, pleaded guilty to possession and distribution of child pornography after being caught in a Gigatribe sting operation.

The above examples all have a few things in common – all of the individuals appeared to be upstanding members of society and had families. They all had distinguished themselves over long careers protecting and serving the public. Unfortunately, the also all had a hidden interest in child pornography.

Once an investigator has been brought on to the child exploitation squad, they should be put on a probation period, both for their personal safety and for performance. During a three-to-six month period, the investigator should be mentored by a senior investigator and evaluated on their casework. At the end of the probation period, the investigator should be evaluated a second time by the psychologist for any negative life impact from their work. The investigator, the squad chief, and the psychologist should all sign off on continued work in the squad, with the option to return to another position without penalty.

Managing Crimes Against Children Investigators

While hiring good investigators to handle crimes against children is difficult, retaining them and keeping their performance high is even more challenging. The effects of viewing contraband images and working with offenders can be cumulative, and if proper attention is not given to caseloads, downtime, and the mental health of the team both the investigations and the investigators may suffer. Local rules may dictate what polices and procedures may be implemented when managing crimes against children squads, but the following are some suggested polices that can be put in place specific to crimes against children investigative units.

- **Mandatory Vacation.** This is a good general policy for investigators, but especially so when crimes against children are involved. Passionate investigators can get so wrapped up in closing cases that they voluntarily skip their vacation time. Forcing them to take their vacations will ensure they "get away" from the offensive content for at least a couple weeks out of the year.
- **Open Investigative Spaces**. While the crimes against children area should be closed off from other investigative spaces because of the nature of the content that will be viewed, the internal spaces should be open. Having other like-minded investigators within eyesight and earshot will reduce the sense of isolation that can occur when analyzing media related to these cases.
- **Maximum Analysis Time Limits**. Putting a one or two hour maximum time limit on cataloging images and movies can ensure investigators take a needed break. Requiring half an hour of downtime between viewing sessions to grab a cup of coffee, take a walk, or hit the gym can break the cumulative mental impact of viewing objectionable material. Similarly, investigators should be limited to a maximum of three sessions of cataloging and analysis per day.
- **Mandatory Case Debriefings.** Most investigators won't seek debriefings after a case if they are optional. In addition to allowing colleagues to learn from successes or missteps, a debriefing builds a sense of camaraderie between team members and they can share impactful experiences so that they will know that they are not

"alone".

- **Multi-investigator Assignments.** If possible, cases should have both a primary and a secondary investigator assigned. In addition to providing coverage during vacations and when other cases take the primary investigator offline, the secondary investigator provides at least one other individual who can talk about their shared experience on cases.
- **External Rotations.** It can take years to develop top notch child exploitation investigators, and losing top talent is always an issue. If investigators are showing signs of burning out, the team lead should offer a rotation to a different assignment, with the ability to return after taking a breather. Any rotations into child exploitation squads should go through the same vetting as permanent placements, but can be an effective way of seeing how an investigator handles the job in the short term. Finally, having former investigators on other squads can reduce the isolation felt by those on the child exploitation squad and foster a greater understanding of and respect for the squad's activities in the department.

The final and most important recommended policy is the implementation of mandatory, periodic counseling sessions with a staff psychologist. By making them mandatory, the stigma attached with seeing a staff psychologist is diminished. Ensuring they happen periodically allows the psychologist to detect behavioral changes in staff members from their baselines session. The check-ups should happen at least twice a year, and they can occur more frequently if an investigator starts showing signs of job stress. Stress signals in child exploitation investigators are the same as those for other investigators and include things like difficulty sleeping, relationship troubles, and changes in demeanor. There are a few unique expressions of stress based on the material encountered in child pornography cases that can manifest themselves as well:

- **Hyperrestriction.** This affects investigators with children more frequently, but those without kids may start offering unnecessary and unwanted advice to others who are parents. If an investigator starts acting irrationally cautious with their children out of fear of child predators, that is a sign of psychological stress. While there are real threats, irrational behaviors can indicate the investigator needs a break. Overly cautious actions can include not letting their children go over to the houses of friends, keeping them from participating in extracurricular activities, or placing age-inappropriate restrictions on them. Investigators not allowing their five year old to cross the street alone is age-appropriate, while the same restriction on their 15 year old is hyperrestrictive.
- **Hypervigilance.** Because investigators see child predators from all walks of life on a daily basis, they can start to believe that they are a higher proportion of the population than they are in reality. If an investigator believes that they are seeing a child predator every time they encounter an adult alone with a child, they are likely experiencing hypervigilance. This can lead to depression based on an overly negative view of society.
- **DVR Syndrome.** Eventually, every child exploitation investigator will view an image or a movie that "stays with them". This is normal based on the nature of the work, unless the image becomes intrusive into the investigator's daily thoughts. If an

investigator keeps "replaying" a certain image in their head and it comes back unbidden to the point of distraction, that is not normal. In general, the image should be most prominent shortly after viewing it, but should slowly become less prominent over time. If an image is still regularly coming to mind without prompting a week or two after it has been viewed, this is a cause for concern.

- **Child Avoidance.** There is a tendency after identifying a child predator to "connect the dots" backwards and look for behaviors that are, in hindsight, suspicious. Some of these behaviors may be normal for those who do not have an unhealthy interest in children – for example, sitting on a bench in the park, going to a movie alone, or coaching a Little League team. Because these behaviors occur at locations that are likely to result in encounters with children, investigators may start to avoid those activities for fear of being associated with sexual predators. They may also avoid ever being alone with a child, including their own child or a close relative, for the same reasons.
- **Sexual Dysfunction.** Viewing graphic images of child sexual abuse can and will have an impact on the sexual health of anyone. It is normal to not feel "in the mood" after spending a day going through tens of thousands of pictures during a forensic review. Danger signs can include any long-term impact to the libido – a lack of desire even during vacations and weekends, for example – or an inappropriate mental juxtaposition of healthy, adult sexual relations with what they see at work, resulting in avoidance or even revulsion.

Investigators should all be provided with training on the warning signs of job fatigue noted above so that they can watch for them in their own actions and those of their colleagues. In general, it is much easier to address these problems early on before they develop into bigger issues, and a staff that looks out for their colleagues is never a bad thing.

Managing child exploitation cases can be challenging. The investigators may require a little more latitude with stress-reducing gallows humor, they may not get the same recognition as higher-profile squads that "make the stats" for a department, and the risk of burnout is higher. On the other hand, helping protect children from sexual abuse and getting dangerous predators off the street is some of the most rewarding law enforcement work available.

Resources

Working as part of a small department, it may seem like there are few resources available to assist in child exploitation cases. In reality, there are numerous resources that exist explicitly to help in child pornography investigations. These resources can provide guidance, training, and tools to assist investigators, often at no charge. While there are different resources available in different jurisdictions, a few of the nationally available resources that can provide assistance are noted below.

National Center for Missing and Exploited Children

The National Center for Missing and Exploited Children (NCMEC) is a unique program, specially authorized by Congress to be the United States clearing house for resources related to finding missing children and stopping the sexual exploitation of children. Founded in 1984, they provide several unique resources that are helpful to law enforcement, and they provide many other resources for the general public and related to missing children as well:

- **Victim Identification.** NCMEC is the US Government-authorized repository for known child pornography movies and images. They have identified and saved thousands of children, and any images or movies found by an investigator can be submitted for analysis by a NCMEC professional against their database. If a hit is found, the investigator is provided a law enforcement contact and information about the image series it is identified with. The investigator can then follow up with the case agent on that series. In addition, for previously unknown victims, NCMEC works with law enforcement globally to locate and identify the sexually abused children depicted in the images.
- **Training.** NCMEC provides regular training on a variety of topics related to child exploitation, all free of charge to law enforcement. The training ranges from forensic reconstruction and drawing to procedures for dealing with at-risk children. They offer on-site training in Alexandria, Virginia in addition to regional training around the country.
- **Team Adam.** Comprised of retired law enforcement officers, Team Adam can supply a virtual SWAT team of skills in child sexual exploitation cases. Team members can provide detailed technical support on computer forensics issues, and provide assistance in dealing with the victims and their families after an incident. Their assistance can be provided to law enforcement around the country on-site or on a remote, consultative basis as needed.
- **Sex Offender Tracking.** Given the high sex crime recidivism rate in child sex offenders, the national sex -offender registry was established. NCMEC can provide additional resources related to previously convicted sex offenders, including information on residence and employment history and links to the United States Marshal Service, for finding sex offenders who have violated the terms of their release.
- **Victim and Family Support**. NCMEC provides direct support to the victims of sexual exploitation and to their families. This support can include assistance ranging from immediate crisis intervention through to the linking of in-need individuals with state and local resources. Their services are available on a 24x7 basis via their hotline (1-800-THE-LOST).
- **Law Enforcement Services Portal**. The Law Enforcement Services Portal (LESP) is a website that allows for the digital submission of images and for a manual search of the NCMEC victim identification program database. Investigators can upload lists of hash values to check against the known images list at any time, and can use a taxonomy-based guide to identify potential known victims based on their physical descriptions.

Innocent Images National Initiative

Started in 1995, Innocent Images is an international program to combat online child pornography and child sexual exploitation around the world. A part of the Federal Bureau Investigation's Cyber Division, Innocent Images is staffed by law enforcement officers and analysts from the FBI, and has ties through legal attaché to law enforcement agencies across the globe.

Because of the resources available to the FBI, Innocent Images focuses on large producers and distributors of child pornography online, in addition to coordinating proactive efforts on peer-to-peer and chat room investigations. They can provide assistance to investigators attempting to identify subjects or victims in other countries through their global taskforce contacts, and can assist in finding local investigators domestically on cases outside the primary investigator's jurisdiction.

Like NCMEC, Innocent Images performs both victim and subject identification tasks. Both NCMEC and Innocent Images maintain databases of known identifiers such as email addresses and screen names, and can search them for links to other cases or to other linked identifiers. Finally, Innocent Images can provide the full resources of the FBI on larger cases that may be too complex for smaller departments.

Through their Regional Computer Forensics Labs (RCFLs), the FBI also makes available a knock-and-talk tool known as ImageScan. Free to law enforcement following a one-day training session that is also free, ImageScan consists of a CD and a USB drive that can be used to do a live preview of a suspect's computer for images and filenames potentially related to child pornography. ImageScan is user friendly, and is designed to perform a quick assessment of a computer to determine if seizure and further analyses are warranted.

Department of Justice – Child Exploitation and Obscenity Section

The United States Department of Justice has an entire section dedicated to crimes against children – the Child Exploitation and Obscenity Section (CEOS). CEOS provides a global clearinghouse for legal issues related to child pornography cases, and supports other United States Attorney's Offices with both expertise and trial attorneys. CEOS manages large, multi-jurisdictional child pornography cases and has administrative subpoena authority to obtain information that can be used in multiple jurisdictions.

CEOS owns Project Safe Childhood, the United States Department of Justice strategy to protect children online. The strategy integrates many of the other resources listed here, and provides coordination and deconfliction of efforts between local, state, and federal agencies.

The CEOS High Tech Investigative Unit (HTIU) specializes in forensics related to child pornography cases. They maintain information on the latest techniques used by online child pornographers, and can provide technical assistance in complex cases.

Internet Crimes Against Children Taskforces

The Internet Crimes Against Children (ICAC) Taskforces are a regional collaboration of investigators organized by the Department of Justice to investigate crimes against children that are facilitated by technology. The ICAC taskforces provide training to their member organizations, and bring together federal, state, and local resources.

The ICAC taskforces represent a huge step forward in the coordination of efforts to protect children online. Internet predators can be identified by one agency, and through taskforce contacts a second agency that may have better resources, a more solid jurisdiction, or a concurrent case can leverage that identification and prosecute the offender. Individuals investigated can be taken to court at a federal level or a state or local level, depending on the severity of the crime, the most applicable statutes, and the most appropriate venue. Many of the taskforces are co-located with larger federal entities, including the FBI and the United States Department of Homeland Security – Homeland Security Investigations.

United States Marshal Service/Dru Sjodin National Sex Offender Public Website

Originally called the National Sex Offender Registry, the National Sex Offender Public Website (NSOPW) was renamed as part of the Adam Walsh Child Protection and Safety Act in honor of Dru Sjodin. Sjodin's life was taken at the age of 22 by a convicted sex offender, Alfonso Rodriguez, Jr., who had recently been released from prison after serving time on a 23 year sentence. The NSOPW maintains information on convicted sex offenders nationally, and can provide links to local sex offenders and information on how to obtain additional details on them.

In conjunction with the NSOPW, the Adam Walsh Child Protection and Safety Act established a new law, 18 USC § 2250, which made failure to register a federal felony or to register false information on the NSOPW. The United States Marshal Service (USMS) was tasked with enforcing the law, and made it part of their fugitive recovery efforts to track down violating sex offenders. The USMS resources can be brought to bear on recidivist subjects of child pornography investigations that "skip town", and can help track down subjects who violate the terms of their parole through engaging in banned online activities.

Gridcop

Gridcop is a multifunctional portal for investigating online child exploitation cases. Built out of Operation Fairplay, a tool developed by the Wyoming ICAC to track peer-to-peer child pornography distributors, it was brought into the TLO family by the late Hank Asher. Asher was dubbed the "father of data fusion" for his work in developing many of the current subject tracking systems including as Choicepoint/CLEAR. It is available free to law enforcement, and has expanded to include several items of interest to child pornography investigators. A few of the items include:

- **CPS.** CPS is the online web interface that tracks individuals sharing child pornography over peer-to-peer and IRC networks. Both historical and current data on six different peer-to-peer networks and multiple IRC source are collected, allowing for searches by IP address, GUID, username, and filename. Any IP addresses or other identifiers identified as part of a child pornography case should be checked against the CPS system.
- **ForensicScan, IRC-LE, and ShareazaLE.** Gridcop provides a home for numerous software packages tailored toward child pornography investigations. In addition to custom LE-focused clients for the major peer-to-peer and IRC networks, they have developed ForensicScan, a tool that quickly navigates a file system and extracts information relevant to child exploitation cases, including likely offending images and movies. All of their tools are made available free to law enforcement with

community support available online.

- **Forums.** Gridcop hosts forums dedicated to their tools and to general discussions related to crimes against children cases. Because of the wealth of knowledge of registered investigators and the law enforcement-only environment, questions can be safely posed regarding assistance with online exploitation cases. Additionally, free and knowledgeable community support is available for child pornography forensics efforts, using both the Gridcop supported tools and commercial or open source tools.

There are numerous other resources available – the COPINE project (Combating Paedophile Information Networks in Europe) provides expertise across the pond, Interpol works to combat human trafficking and coordinate global investigative efforts, and the Child Advocacy Centers work with investigators where hand-on offenses are suspected. While the resources listed above are in no way exhaustive, they provide a starting point for engaging with others involved in child exploitation investigations.

Part

2

Digital Forensics

6 FORENSIC CONCEPTS

Before turning to those moral and mental aspects of the matter which present the greatest difficulties, let the inquirer begin by mastering more elementary problems.
Sir Arthur Conan Doyle, *A Study in Scarlet*

Because modern child pornography is a problem of bits-and-bytes, a thorough digital forensic analysis is critical to obtaining the evidence needed to secure a conviction. Child pornographers tend to be early adopters of technology, and each search warrant executed presents a potential new challenge in the form of new computer equipment, cell phones, or storage devices. Additionally, child pornographers tend to adopt newer software technologies quickly and to be early users of new online services. For the digital forensics analyst, this may mean that go-to tools like Guidance Software's EnCase and AccessData's Forensic Toolkit may not have a way of parsing the evidence, and the analysis may require the analyst to find point solutions or even develop their own tools to parse a new logfile, analyze a new memory chip, or understand a new piece of software.

To write a book, let alone a few chapters, that covers every possible technology associated with child pornography is impossible, and the book would be outdated by the time it went to print. Because of this, digital forensics is covered in three parts in this volume – forensic concepts, live forensics, and static (dead-box) forensics. Each chapter focuses on the evidence that the analyst should look for, and not on specific tools or technologies used to obtain that evidence. The foundation provided should serve the analyst well in augmenting their existing knowledge with domain-specific knowledge of particular use in child pornography investigations.

The Challenge

Originally, digital forensics consisted of manually reviewing a few floppy disks found in the possession of a child pornographer after they were caught connecting to a BBS trading child pornography or buying a magazine from a previously known overseas provider. Finding the physical devices was relatively easy (5.25" disks aren't that small), and the number and quality of images that could be placed on an individual disk was limited. Additionally, there was likely only a single computer with few relevant peripherals to be found when executing a typical search warrant and no network connectivity beyond a modem.

Today, digital forensics requires a whole new approach. An effective forensic approach to child pornography cases involves online research, live forensics on-scene to assist in executing a search warrant and conducting an interrogation, and high volume forensics on device images seized from the offender. The digital forensics challenges an investigator will face today that were not as prevalent in past decades include the following:

- **Ubiquitous Connectivity.** IPads, Smartphones, portable storage devices, and laptops may all be enabled with Internet connections. They may have 4G capabilities built in, or have high speed 802.11 connections that allow the device to connect to any local network. An individual device may have multiple methods of connecting to the Internet as well. A laptop may have a wired Gigabit Ethernet connection, an integrated LTE card, connectivity to a DSL modem over USB, and a Bluetooth connection to a smartphone acting as an access point. Most current digital forensics is also likely to involve network forensics.
- **Large Storage Volumes.** It is not atypical to find 10 terabytes of storage devices in the possession of a child pornographer. They no longer have to "prune" their collection to fit within their storage budget. To conduct an effective forensic examination, the digital forensics lab must have enough storage space to accommodate drive images from every device seized. Because of the time it takes to review large quantities of information, even using automated tools like FTK and EnCase may not be possible. The investigator may need to rely on more rapid tools like bulk_extractor to perform a triage and selectively review higher priority devices first.
- **Internet Storage.** Storage used to be local, allowing the investigators to seize all relevant items immediately and at a single location with a properly scoped search warrant. Today, much of the evidence may be stored on the Internet, explicitly using cloud storage drives like Dropbox or iCloud, as part of email services, or in the log files residing on servers around the globe. Each of these locations requires additional legal authority to search, and in some cases they may be located overseas in places with less-than-friendly legal reciprocity
- **Encryption.** Strong whole disk encryption and container-based encryption is available for free with tools like TrueCrypt, is easy to deploy, and is almost completely transparent to the user. It is not unusual for investigators to encounter encryption that, if the machine is not seized properly, can make forensics impossible. Once a device is encrypted and locked, the investigator may have to rely on brute-force or dictionary-based password attacks, which are not likely to succeed if strong passphrases are used.
- **Device Diversity.** An individual may have an Android phone, an iOS-based iPad, a PlayStation 4 running a FreeBSD variant, a laptop with Windows 8 installed, a digital camera running a proprietary OS, and an Ubuntu partition on their desktop. No individual examiner can be an expert in all of the possible devices from both a hardware and software standpoint. Additionally, each device may be running numerous applications, each of which have their own forensic footprints and may

need specific expertise to fully exploit. Since child pornographers tend to hoard their collections, investigators may also encounter older technologies that require purchasing second-hand equipment to review and image. Because of this, the forensic examiner needs to take an approach that uses specific forensic tasks that focus on outcomes and not on the underlying technology.

- **Small Form Factor Storage.** With microSD cards, close to a terabyte of storage in items smaller than a dime is inexpensively available. This is both a blessing and a curse to investigators executing a warrant for digital media. It is a blessing because, given the small size, investigators can justify opening any containers and having a reasonable expectation of finding relevant items. It is a curse as well – subjects can hide large quantities of storage, their whole child pornography collection in some case, in locations where it is difficult to find, forcing investigators to take a more reasoned approach to searches.
- **Device Interconnectivity.** Many of the devices found, especially storage devices, may have been connected to multiple other devices. The microSD card found may have been placed in the subject's smartphone, their digital camera, and two different computers. Tracking the transfer of material between devices requires the investigator to invest additional forensics effort beyond simply finding the contraband.

Gone are the days when an investigator could image a hard drive, hash the files, check the hashes against a list of known-bad content, and call that an analysis. Even carving and manually reviewing all of the images and movies on all of the seized media is insufficient, if not impossible. Doing so does not address questions of ownership of the material, transmission of the content, potential production, or intent to distribute it. A single image that matches a known hash value from NCMEC on an old floppy disk is likely to have a much different forensic story behind it than a movie taken with the subject's cell phone camera and found in an "Uploads" directory in their Instant Messenger. The following chapters are meant to be a primer, providing a methodology for meeting the forensic challenges above in child pornography cases and giving investigators a few focus areas for further learning. Investigators are encouraged to seek general digital forensics training – organizations like the Defense Cyber Investigations Training Academy and the Federal Law Enforcement Training Center provide excellent instruction in digital forensics, ranging from cell phone analysis to field triage. Commercially, providers like SANS and Guidance Software provide similar training.

Forensic Concepts

The next few chapters detail the methodology for approaching live and dead-box digital forensics, but several basic concepts need to be explained before they can be put into a framework. This book assumes that investigators know how to handle evidence, deal with chain of custody issues, and document their actions. With that understanding, there are a few areas of digital forensics that can build upon that knowledge to better facilitate and guide digital forensic examinations. Experienced digital forensics examiners can skip the remainder of this chapter and move on to the areas of focus for their analyses in the remaining chapters.

Digital Evidence Integrity

Preserving evidence in as close a state as possible to how it was found is the goal of any forensic review. In a traditional evidence gathering procedure, for example preserving fingerprints, there is a protocol that is used based on whether or not the prints are on a porous surface, if the material is wet or dry, and if the prints can be stabilized for transport. Options range from simply putting the item into a paper envelope to creating an on-scene fume chamber to solidify the prints using cyanoacrylate. Similar procedures are available for preserving digital forensic evidence. A seized smartphone that is still active will have a different set of procedures than a standalone hard drive found powered off. The procedures vary, but there are guiding principles related to maintaining integrity that apply to any device:

- **Document Actions in Detail.** The old court adage is "If it isn't documented, it wasn't done". This is never truer than in digital forensic examinations. If you shut off a device, move the mouse, or simply bag-and-tag the evidence, it must be documented. There can never be too much documentation – including digital photographs, videos, sketches, and write-ups of the location where the digital evidence was acquired.
- **Stop Any Current Destruction.** If the device is in a state where not acting will result in the loss of evidence, either by a remote kill switch, by the shutdown of an encrypted machine, or by a disk-wipe program running in the background, this needs to be addressed as a priority. The action taken may range from keeping a device active to magnetically shielding connections to a device. For provider-based evidence, it may be as simple as faxing a preservation notice.
- **Obtain Any Information Needed Immediately With Minimal Interaction.** There may be transient information, like current network connections or the contents of RAM, that need to be obtained before taking further preservation actions. By obtaining these, there may be slight alterations to the system state but they should be minimal and explainable. The chapter on live forensics is dedicated to acquiring transient digital information.
- **Create an Image as Soon as Possible.** Images are electronic, bit-for-bit copies of the contents of digital media. Images can be uniquely identified by hash functions (see below), and an image is considered a best-evidence copy of information for court purposes. If imaging is not possible, a logical copy of the relevant files should be obtained and preserved on indelible media or as part of a logical image as soon as possible.

Once an image is created of the digital device, the original device and the image itself can be entered into evidence. A working copy of the image can then be loaded onto the forensic machines for analysis. If there is a challenge to evidence as part of a suppression hearing, the documentation, the hash value obtained, and the lab's procedures go a long way toward showing that the evidence gathering and analysis procedures did not result in any substantial destruction of meaningful information.

Hashes

Not to be confused with hash tags, a hash is a mathematical signature of the contents of a file or a device. The hash itself is a small set of characters, generally between 128 and 4096 bits, which is created based on a mathematical function that iteratively uses all of the contents of the device to generate it. The hash algorithm is generated in a way that changing even a single bit will completely change the resultant output signature. This allows a file or a disk image to be hashed using the same algorithm at any point, and if it has been altered even slightly, there will be a completely different output signature. It is generally mathematically impractical to knowingly generate the same hash value, called a collision, when using more recent hash functions. Investigators may encounter hash algorithms like MD5 or SHA-1, two of the most popular, or more recent hash functions like the NIST-approved SHA-3.

In addition to assisting in assuring evidence integrity, hashes are used in three other ways in most forensic examinations – for positive and negative file matching and for password guessing.

Positive and negative file matching usually involves the use of a hash database – a set of known hashes based on previously encountered content. For positive file matching in child pornography cases, there are hash databases maintained by NCMEC, the FBI, and Homeland Security Investigations that contain hash signatures of previously encountered child pornography images depicting known victims. Additionally, applications like CPS from TLO maintain larger hash databases of suspected child pornography, images under active investigation, and confirmed non-child pornography - generally commercial pornography with young looking actors confirmed to be over 18. One of the initial steps in any child pornography examination is hashing every file seized and comparing it to known hash databases to see if there is any low-hanging fruit – exact copies of existing, known-bad content.

Negative hash databases are used to exclude known-good files – generally operating system files and application-related files – so that they do not need to be manually reviewed. NIST maintains a software reference library, the National Software Reference Library (NSRL), and the major forensics vendors supply their own databases of known files to reduce the review workload in cases.

While hashing can be useful, there are limitations. Altering a single bit in an image (e.g. a single pixel), which can occur when file formats change, a logo is added, or cropping occurs, completely changes the hash output. Because of this, positive hash databases have become less useful over time. To address this issue, newer types of hash algorithms have been created. Two of the most popular types of approaches are fuzzy hashing and PhotoDNA.

Fuzzy hashing creates hashes for pieces of a file for the purposes of "closeness" matching. Two files can be compared by evaluating how different their hashes are from each other. Instead of producing a yes/no match, the output is a percentage of how close the file contents are to each other. The major forensic tools include the capability of doing fuzzy hashing, and Jesse Kornblum, the developer of the technique, makes his ssdeep software available as open source.

PhotoDNA is similar to fuzzy hashing in that it creates a unique signature for pieces of a rendered image. These pieces are stored in a table, so that any alteration to part of an image (e.g. by inserting a logo), changing the size of an image, or changing the file format of an image results in largely the same hash value. Similar to fuzzy hashing a distance function can be used to determine how close two images are to each other. PhotoDNA has been proposed as a new database format for collections of known child pornography, and several forensic packages now include the technology.

The final problem with hashes comes with the transition to movies as the illicit content of choice for child pornographers. Most of the databases store hashes of static images – movies are altered more frequently format-wise and time-wise and are less suitable for hashing. While thumbnail programs combined with the newer hash techniques hold some promise, as do facial recognition databases, there is no silver bullet solution, though this is very active area of current research.

File Carving and Unallocated Space

Data that is deleted by a subject is rarely unrecoverable, though newer solid state drives are better at "wiping" data than traditional hard drives. When a user attempts to delete data, they do it through one of three mechanisms – deleting individual files from the file system, formatting their drive, or wiping their drive.

When a subject deletes the child pornography they downloaded using the "delete" key or by dragging the files into their recycling bin and then emptying it, they don't actually remove the file contents from the disk. On most file systems, files are stored using a "directory" that maps filenames and other metadata to locations on the disk where the contents of the file are located. When a file is deleted using traditional methods, the directory entry is either deleted or marked as deleted and made available for overwriting. The actual file contents remain in place until the operating system overwrites those areas on the disk with new information. Those areas are labeled as "unallocated space" by the operating system. Unallocated space is sometimes called "slack space", though that can also refer to unusable portions of a drive sector at the end of a file or other data structure that may contain small amounts of residual information. Subjects can inadvertently destroy data permanently by deleting files then filling their hard drive with new movies, images, or other content. Most forensic suites automatically recover any files deleted this way as part of their core functionality.

If the directory entry is completely overwritten, the contents of files may still be recoverable by file carving. Carving looks at every sector on a disk for "signatures", unique values that identify the type of file content present in that sector. Specialized software then attempts to re-create the file, usually without the filename or information on what directory the file originally resided in. Specialized tools are now available to do intelligent image carving by comparing sector contents and reassembling them using complex processing algorithms. Even if a file cannot be carved, text that is present in unallocated space can be indexed by the major forensic packages for keyword searching by the investigator.

The second method of deleting data is by formatting a hard drive. Formatting the drive does not actually delete any data – instead it removes the pointer to the directory noted above. The directory and underlying files can still be recovered using commonly available forensic tools and a reasonably talented examiner. Many subjects believe that doing a "full" format instead of a "quick" format erases the drive's contents. In reality, a full format only checks each sector to determine if there are any read issues and flags it as a bad sector if any are encountered.

The third method involves wiping the drive, using specialized software or hardware. Wiping software works by overwriting all of the sectors on a device with a pattern of ones and zeroes. Some wiping software will perform multiple "passes", overwriting zeroes then ones then a random value, though even a single pass will make the data unrecoverable through forensics. Wiping software, however, may have flaws in its implementation and may not wipe as advertised or may fail to complete due to operator error or hardware issues. Because of this, it is always valuable to at least triage wiped drives.

Hardware wiping consists of running a device through a degausser. Degaussers generate extremely large magnetic fields that are passed over the media, causing the physical equivalent of digitally wiping the drive at once. Degaussers capable of wiping hard drives tend to be expensive to purchase and power hungry, making them uncommon in home environments.

Although not really a method of wiping files, physical destruction of a drive can be encountered as well. Data from the undamaged portion of a physically mangled drive may be recoverable through advanced techniques available at commercial providers like Kroll Ontrack or through federal forensics labs, but employing these techniques is not likely to be cost effective or feasible in all but the most egregious cases.

Cache, Swap, Hibernation, Shadow and Temporary Files

Cache, swap, hibernation, shadow, and temporary files are generated by the operating system or by applications and not directly by the subject, though they may contain evidence of the subject's activities. Because these files are automatically generated, they will be present on a typical system unless the subject has taken steps to remove them.

Cache files are created by an application to speed up its operation by storing content locally that can be accessed more rapidly than remote content. Web browsers are the most common location for cache files – the browser will store copies of images or other content that it has previously downloaded so that the next time that content is accessed, it can be loaded from local storage on the smartphone, tablet, or computer without requiring transmission over the network. Unless a subject takes steps to clear their cache or uses private browsing modes on their web browser, a record of the sites they previously visited, including images, is going to be present. Some browsers, Safari being the most prominent, even store thumbnail screenshots of websites visited.

Swap files or paging files are copies of RAM that are offloaded to the drive to increase the amount of memory available to running programs. These files tend to be very large, and can contain fragments of data that has been deleted from other locations on the drive as well as semi-permanent copies of ordinarily transient information from memory. Swap files are regularly overwritten, and may be wiped by the operating system during machine startup or shutdown. Analyzing the swap file is difficult but possible, and can be done in cases where the subject was believed to have been engaged in acquiring or transferring child pornography shortly before their device was seized.

Hibernation files are similar to swap files in terms of their potential contents except that they contain an entire copy of the contents of RAM and are intentionally stored when a machine is shut down. The hibernation file is used to quickly boot a device and to restore the system into the state that it was in prior to shutdown. Because hibernation files contain the same information as paging files (only as a complete copy and not fragments), they can similarly be analyzed for recent operating information. Additionally, a hibernation file can be created for the current contents of RAM by putting a laptop or similar device into hibernation mode in lieu of shutting it down or powering it off, with the trade-off that the creation of the hibernation file may overwrite a small portion of the hard drive.

Shadow copies are replicas of the file system that are created by the operating system prior to performing updates to allow the user to "roll back" their device to a known-good state. A given system may have multiple shadow copies available that permit the examiner to reload a prior version of the system (with the appropriate virtualization software). If a child pornographer has recently removed relevant information from their system, reverting to a shadow copy may restore some of that information. Alternatively, shadow copy files can be directly reviewed using specialized forensic software.

Temporary files consist of data that is created by an individual application or the operating system for temporary use. They are not user generated, and may contain relevant data that the user is not aware they have stored on their system. Using peer-to-peer software creates temporary files that contain partial versions of images and movies as they are downloaded. Web browsers create temporary files when downloading content. Any application may create a temporary file storing details about the current session, including everything from user identities to chat logs. Understanding what relevant temporary files an application creates and how to exploit them can uncover hidden evidence even if the subject deleted the primary evidence of their child pornography activities.

Write Blocking and Imaging

Imaging, mentioned earlier in this chapter, is the creation of a file (or files) that contains an almost exact duplicate of the contents of a drive, partition, folder, or other piece of electronic information. Although images for devices ranging from DVDs to printer memory chips can be obtained, in general it is disk or flash-based media that is imaged. To understand how imaging works, an investigator needs to understand at a rudimentary level how information is organized on these media devices.

In general, a drive consists of areas that can store blocks of information, either as part of flash memory or on a magnetic platter. The smallest addressable amount of space on a drive is referred to as a sector. Each sector consists of anywhere from 512 bytes to 4096 bytes, and is the smallest amount of information that can be written to that media. A hard drive is organized into large numbers of sectors called partitions, each of which contains a file system. Different file systems, such as FAT32, NTFS, or ext3 can be present on different partitions, depending on the operating system. If the disk has multiple operating systems installed, there may be partitions present that are not viewable to the other operating systems if they do not have the appropriate file system support.

When a device is booted normally, it reads the partition table to determine what partition is active, generally one that contains the operating system or a boot manager. The system then attempts to load the operating system on the active partition, and in the process is likely to update file times, overwrite unallocated space, and generate new log entries.

To avoid generating new data after a device is seized, it is connected to an analysis machine using a write blocker. The write blocker allows the analysis machine to view the contents of a storage device without writing anything to the device. Write blockers can be hardware or software-based, and support USB, IDE, SATA, FireWire, and other types of connections to the target drive.

After connecting to the write blocker, an "image" of the storage device is created as a file (or group of files) on the drives in the analysis machine. The image is a copy of every sector present on the storage device at the time of imaging, and the image files can then be analyzed instead of the device itself, which can be put into evidence. Image files can be raw images, sometimes called "dd" images after the program originally used to create them, where each sector in the image is the same size as the original sector. Other formats, including the EnCase Expert Witness Format, sometimes referred to as .e01, store metadata about the image with the raw data, and allow the raw data to be compressed to save space. More advanced image formats like the open source Advanced File Format are fully extensible and support both compression and encryption of images.

When performing a consent search of a child pornographer's devices, the examiners should create images of each device as soon as possible. Depending on the terms of the consent, the images are derivatives that become the property of the investigating agency, and may be able to be subsequently searched even if consent is revoked. Investigators should work with their prosecutor's office to ensure their consent forms contain this provision.

Registry, Configuration, and Log Files

Windows uses a registry, most Linux machines use .conf files stored under the /etc directory, and Apple uses property list (.plist) files to store system settings. Individual applications may use XML files, .ini text files, or proprietary format files to store individual application settings. All of these files can contain information of interest in child pornography cases, including:

- System and software installation times
- Users present on a system
- Devices that have been connected to a system
- Personally identifiable information on system users
- Internet account names and passwords
- Current network settings
- Most recently used files, websites visited, and networks connected

Each of the configuration files above have different ways to store the same type of information, and expertise in analyzing a particular operating system is usually necessary to fully exploit its configuration files. Application-specific configuration files can contain even more information of forensic value. A simple configuration file for an IRC client can show all of the usernames a subject has utilized, the chat rooms that they have added as favorites, the location of chat transcripts, the upload and download directories for files transferred, and the individuals that they have in their contact list.

In contrast to configuration files are log files, which are used by the system to record specific events. Log files generally contain an event identifier, a description of the event, and the date and time the event occurred. This gives the examiner the ability to show the actions of the subject and when they took those actions. System-level logs may show when the operating system was installed, when a user logged in, what applications or files they accessed at a particular time, when patches were applied to the system, and when a particular software package was installed.

Application-level logs store forensically useful information about the operation of a particular application. This can include the time the application was installed, files the application opened, network connections the application made, websites the application viewed, and other relevant details. A peer-to-peer log file might contain the sessions established by the user, what machines they connected to, the searches they conducted, the files they uploaded/downloaded, and their viewing of those files from within the peer-to-peer application.

Encryption and Compression

Both encrypted and compressed files can look the same to a novice examiner when viewed through a forensic tool – they will appear to be a random series of characters. Both are encountered frequently in child pornography cases, but the technologies are used for very different purposes.

Compression, using programs like gzip, WinZip or WinRAR, or the built-in compression in many operating systems, reduces the size of a file on the device by removing redundant portions of data and replacing them with a smaller placeholder. Compression can be lossless, where the file is exactly the same when decompressed (Zip and GIF files), or it can be lossy (JPEG, MPEG-2, and MPEG-3 files), where the file is similar but not an exact replica. Text and executable files are always compressed using lossless compression, and multiple files can be stored together in an archive. Image, audio and movie files can be stored using lossy compression, making changes in the file that are imperceptible to the human eye or ear and result in minor loss of visual or audio information. Most forensic tools automatically decompress archived files and extract the files contained in them, though older or more obscure formats may not be recognized by all programs and may require manual review. Additionally, archived files can be stored within other archived files, and many forensic programs do not automatically extract embedded archives.

Encryption, on the other hand, seeks to protect information from unwanted disclosure to unauthorized parties. In many cases, the examiner is the "unauthorized" party from the subject's perspective. The subject can use tools like PGP, TrueCrypt, or Bitlocker to encrypt an entire drive or individual files and folders on a drive. Additionally, the subject can create an encrypted "container" that is loaded through the operating system and acts as a virtual drive to store information. Encrypted files or drives cannot be viewed without the password or passphrase that the user utilized to encrypt the device, or the key that the system uses to decrypt the contents. Child pornographers may selectively encrypt movies or images on their system to hinder prosecution if their device is seized.

Most encryption is symmetric – the same key is used to both encrypt and decrypt content. Public key cryptography is asymmetric – using a key pair that are mathematically related such that information encrypted by one of the keys can only be decrypted using the other key, and vice versa. Public key cryptography is often used by child pornographers to distribute contraband. In public key cryptosystems, an individual makes their public key openly available. When someone wants to send an encrypted file, they use the public key of the recipient. The recipient then decrypts the file using their private key. Individuals will frequently keep the public keys of others that they trade with on a digital keyring. Any individuals on the keyring of a child pornography subject should be looked at as possible trading partners.

Encryption can be difficult to handle when encountered by investigators. Strong encryption, freely available in packages like TrueCrypt, can be impossible to crack directly if a strong passphrase is used. The problem is not necessarily insurmountable, however. There are multiple approaches an investigator can take when they encounter encryption:

- **Ask For the Password.** While this seems obvious, many investigators fail to ask the subject if they use encryption and what their username and password are. If subjects are asked before the interrogation gets tense, as part of an initial questioning or immediately after the investigator has built good rapport with them, this can be an effective approach. Finally, the subject can be tricked into providing their password if they believe their device can be hacked into anyway, often by implying the government has capabilities to decrypt anything if given enough time (which is technically true, but enough time may be the age of the universe).
- **Catch Them When the Device is Logged In.** If you can execute a search warrant when the subject is logged into their system, or if the investigator can pretext the subject into logging in, the device can be seized while already decrypted and can be maintained in that state until it can be imaged or live forensics can be done. If a logged-in device is seized, the contents of its memory can be scanned for possible decryption keys.
- **Install a Keylogger.** If the subject's device is accessible either remotely or hands-on, or the subject can be convinced to run a software package, a keystroke logger can be installed. A hardware keystroke logger generally requires a standard search warrant, whereas a software keystroke logger requires a Title III warrant.
- **Catch Them on Camera.** Similar to a keystroke logger, the subject can be caught logging in on camera. This can be through a hidden camera in their house that is installed with a sneak-and-peek warrant, through a camera in the interview room, or by requesting the camera footage from a local Starbucks where the subject regularly logs on. Similar to the camera, the old standby of surveillance on the subject and then "shoulder surfing" their password works as well.
- **Subpoena an Alternate Source.** Many subjects will re-use the same password in multiple places. The investigators can subpoena online services for the passwords, or hashes of passwords, associated with the subject's account, or request that the subject's employer provide a copy of the subject's network password or hash if available. Alternatively, the subject's web proxy log files from their ISP or from their work can be subpoenaed - some sites still put the password into the query string of an HTTP request.
- **Catch Them at the Border.** Border searches, both outgoing and incoming, can be done without a warrant. If the subject is expected to make an international trip, Customs and Border Protection or Homeland Security Investigations can assist in performing a border search on the subject's devices. While the subject may still refuse to decrypt a device, they are likely to be more cooperative due to a desire to either continue their travel plans or to re-enter the country.
- **Subpoena the Password from the Subject.** The issue of whether or not a password can be subpoenaed, or if the subject can be subpoenaed to unlock the device, is still being played out in the courts. If your jurisdiction permits it, subpoena the subject directly.
- **Crack Another Password.** Not all passwords are stored using the same degree of protection- some applications may store passwords in a less secure fashion. Older Windows networks, for example, store easy to crack hash values, and many networks still use these passwords for backwards compatibility. If you can obtain the hashes for an easier-to-crack password, that may be a better target for guessing

than the location of the suspected contraband.

- **Build a Custom Dictionary.** Because users tend to pick passwords containing words and phrases that are meaningful to them, a custom cracking dictionary can be created from all of the subject's personal info. Additionally, a full list of text strings present can be obtained from all digital media associated with the subject and used by the password cracking program.
- **Crack the Encryption.** There are password crackers commercially available like DNA or Passware that can be run on multiple machines at once to try all possible passwords, starting with those that have fewer characters. If the user has chosen a simple password or a shorter password, these tools are very effective. Additionally, using the custom dictionary and the intelligent guessing algorithms they offer, the encryption can be attacked directly. This can be time consuming and may not be possible in a reasonable amount of time if the user has a long, complex password that they never re-used.

Digital Technologies

The child pornography investigator is likely to encounter many different types of technology that may be of forensic interest in a child pornography case. The technologies may be encountered while executing a search, during a Terry stop, or as part of a knock-and-talk. While the myriad of technologies that can be encountered change on an ongoing basis, an understanding of the general forensic value of each technology can lead to intelligent seizure decisions. The technologies noted below are meant to be a representative but not comprehensive list of currently popular devices. Additionally, because each category is evolving, the guidance has been generalized and specific expertise, if available, should be sought when a specific device is encountered.

Desktop Computers

In 2005, laptop computers outsold desktop computers for the first time. In 2013, tablets outsold desktops. While they are no longer the first in sales, new desktops are being sold to niche markets – high end gaming, graphic design, and other high horsepower users. Additionally, older desktops may be encountered in the homes or offices of child pornographers.

Modern desktop computers generally have one or more internal hard drives, an optical drive (Blu-Ray or DVD), and may have other attached storage. The computer itself may be networked via wireless or wired connection, and may be always-on. Because they are meant to be tethered to a monitor, mouse, and keyboard, desktop computers are not highly portable and are most likely to be encountered within a home or office, which may be a consideration if using a border search or a vehicle stop to arrest a subject.

Some child pornographers engaged in distribution will use desktops as peer-to-peer servers, and may be attracted to the increased storage capabilities. Desktops generally have the largest hard drive capacities available, though external hard drives have somewhat nullified this. Smaller form factor desktops may also be used as high end digital video recorders (DVRs) or as media devices attached directly to a home network or to a television. When a desktop is encountered, it should almost always be searched for child pornography

- even devices not currently in use may have evidence of legacy child pornography activities still present.

Enterprise Servers

While any computer can be made into a server based on how it is used, corporations still utilize rack-mounted hardware, including storage, to run enterprise systems. Despite the growth of virtual computing and outsourced cloud services, all of these systems still require underlying hardware. It is rare to encounter enterprise servers in a home, and if they are encountered the subject may be engaged in commercial distribution or other enterprises of interest.

In general, if the subject is storing their child pornography on systems where they work, the investigators will not seize the corporate assets. There are always exceptions (e.g. the business itself is providing services to child pornographers), but in the case of an individual bad actor in a large enterprise, the forensic team is more likely to work with the corporate systems administrators to obtain copies of the online storage space used by the subject, corporate email records involving the subject, and any relevant log files. The investigator can additionally request copies of the same records from the corporation's backup systems to get older data that may have been recently deleted. While the investigators can make copies themselves as part of executing a warrant, the data is frequently requested via subpoena.

If enterprise-class servers and storage are going to be seized, the investigator must engage with technical experts and will need to evaluate the ability to house and search the systems post-seizure. Unless the target is a commercial distributor or producer of child pornography, this is an infrequent occurrence.

Laptops

Laptop computers and variants such as convertibles are one of the most common items seized in child pornography cases and one of the most fruitful. Although tablet use is growing, laptops are still the mainstay of child pornographers due to their increased storage capacity, flexibility in managing media, protections available, and diversity of child-pornography related software that they can run.

Laptop computers come in all shapes and sizes, from 11" ultrabooks that may have a small solid state storage device inside and no optical drive to large-screen gaming laptops that have multiple hard drives, an optical drive, and various media readers present. Some child pornographers may even own multiple laptops - one with a large screen for home viewing of movies and a smaller one for road trips.

Laptops are the device of choice for peer-to-peer exchanges, IRC chats, digital movie processing, and other activities of interest in most child pornography cases. Most laptops encountered will be running either a Windows operating system or a Mac OS X operating system, and investigators should have a basic familiarity with both.

Tablets

Tablets, whether Android, Windows, or iOS-based, are almost tailor-made for child pornographers. They are primarily a content consumption device, as opposed to content creation, and feature high resolution screens with always-on network connectivity. The limiting factor in their use in child pornography to-date has been the availability and usability of tablet-based peer-to-peer, IRC and content viewing software (including codecs) favored by subjects.

While tablets may not be the primary acquisition mechanism for many child pornographers, they are frequently used as a viewing platform. Subjects will load their child pornography collections onto their tablet, and take it with them as a portable viewer for their illegal content. Because of this, tablets are generally paired with another computing device. When encountered, the investigator will want to find out what other devices the tablet has been connected to or synced with, and acquire those devices as well, even if child pornography is not readily found on them.

Because the tablet market is only expected to grow, these devices will be encountered more often in every type of search. The smaller 7" tablets can be carried in a pocket, and the larger tablets are easy to carry in a backpack or in the car. Because tablets are increasingly password protected, and even encrypted in some cases, the investigator will want to request the password before or during their seizure to increase the chances of successful forensic exploitation.

Cell Phones

Originally, cell phones were used exclusively for making phone calls, and examinations consisted of extracting contact lists and call logs. In the United States, now even low cost "feature phone" devices can contain digital camera pictures, text messages, and other forensically interesting content. The days of the feature phone are numbered, however, and smartphones are close to ubiquitous.

As smartphone cameras improve, they are increasingly used by child pornography producers to create high definition image and video content. The resultant images can be shared via a cloud account, or via MMS (multimedia message service) as part of the texting stream. While prosecuting sexting minors who take "selfies" is generally not occurring, the images they take may be sent to less discriminating friends or relatives and end up as part of the collection of a child pornographer.

Some child pornographers are using the larger screens on cell phones as portable content viewers. As with tablets, the content is frequently side-loaded using a microSD card or as part of a sync process to a desktop or laptop. Because of integrated hardware encryption on newer phones that complicates, and in some cases makes impossible, their analysis, the investigator should seek to obtain cell phone passwords from subjects whenever possible.

Game Consoles

Everything from the PlayStation 4 to the Wii U is a potential content viewing platform for child pornography. While the consoles were not originally created to view child pornography, they are essentially fully functioning computers. In the extreme but rare case, child pornographers have been known to install a custom version of Linux or other operating system on the devices and use them as traditional computers, albeit connected to a large screen television.

In addition to their co-opting as computers, game consoles have onboard storage, allowing them to be used as a networked media hub that may contain child pornography. Unless they are rebuilt with a custom operating system, the child pornographer is likely to have downloaded any contraband found on the consoles from another networked device.

A final note on game consoles is their use in grooming and potential contact with minors. The subject's gamer ID may be helpful in finding other Internet accounts with the same ID, and it may have been used by the subject on the console to engage in voice chat with minors. This may be of particular interest if the subject is a repeat offender and has restrictions on contact with children.

Media Hubs

While game consoles, desktops, and laptops can serve as media hubs, there are also dedicated media hubs in widespread use. These include wireless-connected Blu-Ray players, with widgets to allow for connections to Netflix, web browsing, and other Internet activities. More fully featured devices, like Apple TV and Google TV devices, are fully programmable and contain on-board storage. Finally, smaller form factor devices such as Chromecast allow for the connection of another device like an iPad or smartphone to a television for easy viewing.

Media hubs with minimal onboard storage, such as Blu-Ray players and Chromecast devices, are less likely to have child pornography on them but may have been used as a viewing mechanism by subjects. Because there are likely to be fewer items of forensic interest on them, the investigator should carefully consider if their seizure and analysis are worth the effort.

Media hubs with substantial on-board storage, however, are essentially special-purpose computers. They can contain the same content that any other device has on it, and may be used as the central storage location for the subject's full collection. The limitations on their usage by child pornographers tend to be driven by family dynamics – if they are living with others that have access to the device, they may shy away from using it to store and view their collections.

Flash Drives

Sometimes called thumb drives or USB drives, referring to their connection and not the underlying storage mechanism, these are now ubiquitous as a method for physically transferring files between systems. In many new systems without optical drives, the USB port, or lightning adapter on Apple devices, may be the primary mechanism for the non-networked transfer of files. Flash devices come in all shapes and sizes, ranging from Swiss Army Knives with an integrated flash drive to stuffed animals with an embedded USB connection. Because they are inexpensive, readily available, and can come in so many shapes and sizes, it is rare to not find at least one flash drive at a child pornography subject's residence.

Flash drives vary greatly in capacity, but affordable terabyte-sized drives are on the horizon. Child pornographers may carry parts of their collection, often their favorite parts, around with them at all times on a keychain device. Likewise, they may use flash drives at home to transfer images and movies between their acquisition and viewing platforms. As a result, any flash drives found should be seized and their identifiers searched for on other devices to determine if they were plugged in at any point and if any child pornography was transferred.

Digital Cameras

Digital cameras are decreasing in general popularity, commensurate with an improvement in the cameras integrated into cell phones and tablets. Subjects who are producing child pornography, especially for distribution or commercial purposes, are likely to possess high-end digital SLR cameras and other devices that may make it easier to record high definition images and movies. Additionally, because the increase in quality of cell phone cameras is a relatively new phenomenon and their resale value is limited due to rapid technological progress, child pornography subjects are likely to have retained older digital cameras and their associated media.

When a digital camera is encountered, it should always be seized, even if no digital storage media is present. The camera itself may have on-board storage, and newer cameras place unique identifiers such as a model and serial number in the Exif information of the images they have generated. Seizing the camera can assist in conducting a search for that camera's identifiers to determine if any of the child pornography found was created by the subject.

Hard Drives

Hard drives come in two main categories, with multiple variants under each category based on size and connectivity. The two major variants are solid state drives (SSDs) and traditional magnetic media drives. SSDs are newer, and have a higher cost per gigabyte, though they have lower power consumption and generally higher performance capabilities. Traditional drives have higher capacities, lower costs per gigabyte, and are still more frequently encountered. Although SSD sales are expected to take over the majority of the market in the near future, traditional drives still outsell them in desktops and laptops. Tablets almost exclusively use SSDs.

Both SSDs and traditional drives can be either internal or external. Internal drives are meant to be installed within another device, though they may or may not be installed when encountered. External drives have connectivity through USB, Firewire, or eSATA connections that allow them to be connected without installation to a computing device. External magnetic media hard drives tend to be the medium of choice for child pornographers to back up large collections due to their low cost, portability, and ease of use.

Any hard drives found by investigators should be seized. Although the devices they were originally installed in may be long gone, the drives themselves will still have information of forensic interest. Many child pornographers will not bother to wipe old drives still in their possession, and even if they do make an attempt to do so their contents are often recoverable.

Network Equipment

Network equipment is a general category encompassing everything from wireless Ethernet cards to access points and routers. Because most network equipment does not have a large storage capacity (though there are integrated media hubs and wireless routers with USB attached storage), it is often overlooked when seizing the kit of child pornographers. In practice, network equipment should almost always be seized, and analyzed on-site if possible, to confirm devices present at the location, tie IP address activity to specific devices, and refute the "drive-by" SODDI defense.

Most modern routers and access points provide some degree of logging. By reviewing their log files and routing tables, investigators can identify current and prior devices that have connected through that network. This can serve as a checklist of items to seize, and the MAC addresses, the unique addresses of Ethernet adapters, can uniquely link the IP addresses found to be acquiring child pornography to a specific device. Additionally, if the subject claims to have had an unsecured access point that someone else connected to and used to download child pornography, having the network equipment for analysis can refute or confirm that assertion.

Storage Media

Storage media is a general class of device that ranges from 5.25" floppy disks that store 360KB of data to Blu-Ray disks to 1TB microSD cards. Because child pornographers likely to make backups of their collections, and may retain copies of older images for years or even decades, any storage media encountered should be seized with one exception - commercially pressed and printed media.

CD's, DVD's, and Blu-Ray disks are manufactured using one of two technologies. Commercially mass-produced disks are "pressed" - the pits are generated by a glass (or other substrate) "master" that is physically duplicated onto new disks. Media that is made at home is generally "burned" - a laser is used to heat a phase-changing dye to create zeroes and ones. Although there have been instances where commercially pressed disks with professional, misleading silk screening have been used to hide child pornography, they are rare enough that the investigator should not generally seize commercial media. That does not mean that the investigator should not open all CD/DVD/Blu-Ray cases and ensure that the subject has not hidden their collection on DVD in the case for "The Little Mermaid", it just means that if the front of the DVD is professionally created and it is not a burned disk, it is not generally worth taking.

Electronic Files

Increasingly, seizure of physical devices is taking a backseat to the seizure of logical files. Subjects that are using cloud storage, or use an Internet email provider to trade child pornography, will require electronic search warrants to obtain the necessary data. In these cases, the investigator will be "seizing" a copy of the information and not the physical devices that they are housed on. For evidentiary purposes, the seized records are generally treated as business records from a third party.

When analyzing networked devices or when conducting a subject interview, special attention should be paid to any potential online storage locations. If a device has a Google Drive mapped to it and that device contains child pornography, it may be sufficient probable cause to obtain a warrant for the current and historical information on the networked drive. Additionally, some network storage, such as iCloud from Apple, may house backups of encryption keys and device settings that would otherwise be unavailable in an investigation.

Other Digital Media

By the time this book goes to press, any discussion of the "latest" digital media formats will be outdated. Digital media is increasingly being integrated into every aspect of our lives. Digital photoframes sit on desks, GPS units have online storage, intelligent car navigation systems have integrated flash memory and can display photos, and DVRs and televisions are networked media centers.

Because no treatise can cover every possible electronic device that may be encountered, search warrants should be broad enough to allow for the seizure of any equipment that can process, store, transmit, or display digital information. The investigator must then be judicious in what to take – the pocket calculator with a green LED screen and 32KB of storage may technically qualify under the warrant, but it is not likely to be a valuable item to seize. Similarly, it will likely make more sense to do a live review of the integrated LCD on a refrigerator than to seize the entire device. On the other hand, the vehicle of a subject who has been known to drive around and to use open wireless access points from their car may be worth seizing if it has a USB port and built-in storage. The bottom line is that any item seized is now the responsibility of the investigator to have analyzed – if you don't plan on doing a forensic analysis of a device, don't take it.

7 LIVE FORENSICS

Better three hours too soon, than one minute too late.
William Shakespeare, *The Merry Wives of Windsor*

The traditional approach to executing a search warrant is not the most effective in child pornography cases. Encountering digital evidence is treated as a special case for the purposes of item collection, and is focused on finding and processing computers (desktops and laptops). The standard approach to executing a warrant for traditional criminal offenses is as follows:

1. Perform basic reconnaissance of the physical location where the warrant is to be executed. Examine threats to safety and possible methods of entry/egress.
2. Create an ops plan for the execution. Identify team membership and develop a strategy for the specific situation.
3. Perform entry and clear the location. The entry team announces the warrant, clears the premises, and secures the area.
4. Perform a physical search. After executing entry, split into teams, break up the house into zones, and look for the evidence enumerated in the warrant.
5. Bag, tag, and document the items identified.
6. Examine the physical evidence at the appropriate forensics facility.

While this is a simplification of warrant execution, it is representative of the approach in place at law enforcement organizations around the country. Where digital evidence is expected, a bolt-on approach is taken. In step 2, a digital forensics team may be assigned to the case, frequently without consultation about the execution. In step 4, any personal computers encountered will be shut down. These machines will be placed in anti-static bags in step 5, and analyzed by a digital forensics laboratory in step 6.

With the proliferation of non-PC hardware, the increase in the use of encryption, the miniaturization of storage technology, and the presence of a "digital ecosystem" as opposed to discrete devices, the need for a framework that incorporates digital evidence into all aspects of the search is required. Child pornographers are likely to have many potential evidentiary items, ranging from digital cameras to game consoles. Some of the items will contain transient information and may need to be examined immediately. Others will need to be triaged to determine if they should be taken back for further analysis or left at the scene. Still others will have to be immediately secured to prevent ongoing destruction of evidentiary information.

To more effectively serve warrants on child pornographers and perform live analysis of relevant digital information, a better approach is needed. One approach that may be useful is the PRESENT (Plan, Reconnaissance, Entry, Search, Examine, Notify, and Take) framework. Geared toward search warrants where large amounts of digital gear are likely to be encountered, the framework provides a tool that incorporates digital evidence as a prime concern in all aspects of the search, from planning through execution. PRESENT is meant to provide context to existing methods for searching and seizing digital evidence, and is presented in the context of the United States legal system consistent with the rest of the book, though the approach is applicable to any search with digital evidence, even with differing legal tools available.

Current Challenges

Changes in technology and the evolution of digital ecosystems have greatly increased the difficulty in successfully executing a search warrant in child pornography cases. Over the course of the past decade, the approach to individual aspects of digital forensics has changed. Today, most digital forensics teams will do a live analysis of devices encountered, and acquisition of volatile memory is routine, whereas five years ago a "pull the plug" approach was the norm. Additionally, digital forensics expertise is now more widely available and accessible to search teams in many jurisdictions.

Though the expertise is available and the individual techniques have moved forward, there is still the lack of a framework in which to place these advances. Additionally, while procedures have advanced, their ability to address several areas of technology has been outpaced. Several of the challenges detailed below are not well addressed in current approaches:

Miniaturization

A decade ago, by far the most common digital storage devices encountered in child pornography cases were desktop and laptop hard drives and CD-Rs. The drives were 3.5" or 2.5" in size, and were found in desktop and laptop computers. The sum total of available storage could be found with reasonable accuracy by searching for the physical computers, and by removing the drives from the cases. Older drives were likely to be found in close proximity to existing computers, and the devices were generally found in an "off" state, lending them to an approach where they would be seized for later static forensics. Floppy disks could be hidden, but were limited in how many images they could store. CD-Rs were generally stored in jewel cases. Although child pornographers might mislabel CD-Rs containing contraband, the risk of scratching them and their fairly large comparative size made hiding them difficult, though not impossible.

Executing a warrant in 2014, the size of storage media has greatly decreased. At the small end, MicroSD cards measure 15x11mm in size (approximately the size of a dime) and are becoming the small form factor storage standard. Currently, 128GB MicroSD cards are readily available, with larger cards on the horizon. 1TB MicroSD cards have been announced, though they are cost prohibitive at present. Child pornographers may use these cards in tablets, digital cameras, smartphones, or other devices. Because of their storage capacity and ability to be easily concealed, they may even be used to house the subject's collection, and may be carried on the subject's person at all times.

The new nano-SIM standard for cell phones has an even smaller form factor – 12.3x8.8 mm. Physical searches for devices of this size are nearly impossible, making identification of their likely presence through other means a necessity. There is a benefit to investigators with the shrinking form factor, however – the small size of these devices can be used in writing the application for a search warrant to justify searching in containers of just about any size.

Encryption

While not in ubiquitous use, child pornographers are more likely to encrypt their collections than other users. Both full disk and file system encryption have increased in prevalence on devices ranging from Android cell phones to traditional laptops. Hardware-based full disk encryption, as well as easy-to-use software-based encryption such as BitLocker and TrueCrypt, uses algorithms that cannot be broken by brute force techniques. Side-channel attacks, as described in the previous chapter, are much more likely to be successful. This makes the identification of written passwords and acquisition of unencrypted devices critical. Strong passwords may be written on documents that are physically secured, and unencrypted devices may have forensically recoverable text that can be used to build a custom dictionary as highlighted in the dead box forensics chapter.

When systems are on and unlocked, there is generally a short window for starting the acquisition of data before the systems lock and become the forensic equivalent of a brick. The ability to quickly lock an encrypted device makes planning critical for when and how a warrant is executed. While cold boot attacks and subsequent memory analysis are possible in some circumstances, they rely on the preservation of the current power state of a device and expertise not generally found in field digital forensic examiners.

SSD Devices

Solid state drives (SSDs) are, on the surface, smaller and faster versions of traditional magnetic media hard drives. SSD drives are now standard on MacBook laptops and on most tablets, and are commonly found in use by child pornographers. While their smaller size may mean that collections are offloaded to cheaper magnetic media-based USB storage, they are likely to be used as part of the primary device used to acquire and view child pornography. The difference forensically comes with the introduction of two specific commands unique to SSDs – the OS level FORMAT command and ATA hardware TRIM command. Both have the potential to rapidly make recovery of data, both in unallocated space and on the entire drive (in the case of FORMAT) impossible.

Traditionally, the FORMAT command is run at the operating system level. Most operating systems when they format the disk only delete the data blocks that contain meta information on the files present (for example, the primary $MFT on NTFS file systems). The data could historically be recovered through carving or reconstruction of the file system structure information. With SSD drives, doing a FORMAT from the OS may delete the entirety of the drive data (again at the hardware level), providing a rapid way to wipe content that wasn't available with spinning media.

The TRIM command is used in the background by the SSD to erase unallocated space. Based on the deletion information provided by the OS, the SSD queues up requests for deletion for when there is minimal drive activity. Because of this, a drive that is identified during a search may be actively deleting content. Additionally, because this is done at the hardware level, a write-blocker will not help stop the deletion – only removing power will cease the operation, and even then it will not stop any queued deletions from occurring when the drive is powered back on.

Terabyte Storage Devices

On a standard floppy disk, forensic analysis could be performed using a hex editor with the analyst manually reviewing all sectors. With the advent of gigabyte-sized hard drives, additional automation from forensic tools was required for effective analysis. Now, with terabyte-sized hard drives (the current largest single drives available at retail top out at 4TB), even automated tools are not practical for full disk, on-scene analysis. While they may not have piles of 4TB hard drives lying around, child pornographers are likely to have a mixture of media devices, and encountering multiple terabytes of total storage is fairly common.

The time required to image a single drive, or read every sector for analysis, is limited by the maximum transfer rate on the drive and can take several hours. Because of this, selective review of key areas is necessary for on-scene efforts. Additionally, even if the file system is crawled and features extracted (e.g., images), reviewing a gallery on scene, as is the case with tools like ImageScan, likewise becomes too time consuming. If a 4TB drive stores 1 million images, reading them and reviewing them without more intelligent processing cannot be done in the time spent on-scene executing a typical warrant or during a knock-and-talk. Unfortunately, processing those same images fully to prioritize their manual review may take even longer.

Cloud Storage

Storing data in the cloud, using services such as Google Drive, iCloud or Dropbox, can make the acquisition of on-scene hardware meaningless. Traditional search warrants are location-limited. If information is sought that is stored off-site at a cloud storage provider, a secondary warrant is needed. While the speed limitations due to bandwidth, fear of monitoring by the provider, and (relatively) small amounts of storage freely available have prevented their widespread adoption by child pornographers for their entire collections, they may contain system backups (especially of Apple products) with encryption keys, personal documents of evidentiary value, or encrypted archives with key portions of their collection. Additionally, they may serve as distribution platforms for trading child pornography with select individuals, making the acquisition of both the contents of the drive and the permissions important.

Rapid identification on-scene of cloud storage providers is a must. Because cloud storage can be accessed from anywhere by anyone, a subject or their confederate can be actively removing evidence remotely while the scene is being processed. Additionally, any device the subject has access to can be used on-scene or afterward to delete data stored remotely before it is even identified by forensic teams in the lab.

Digital Ecosystems

The era of the standalone computer is over, and most digital devices encountered are likely to be part of an ecosystem. The Xbox One in the living room may be connected to stored media on a desktop in the basement. The iPad is equipped with 4G capability and its data may be stored using the iCloud service. The iPod in the dining room been synced with the MacBook Pro in the bedroom. The microSD card found in the desk drawer may have originally been in an Android phone, then a digital camera, and finally inserted into the laptop in the office. The photos found on the digital picture frame may also have been uploaded to the navigation system in the Ford Explorer in the driveway.

Because devices are connected via networks, both wired and wireless, and because a house can have multiple external connections to the Internet, understanding the connectivity can be as important as examining the stored information. This means that on-scene forensics are not complete until all of the Internet connections have been identified, and the possible links between devices, and links that are missing devices, are found. Additionally, articulating the ability to connect digital devices in an ecosystem that includes a vehicle using technologies like Ford Sync, can justify seizure of these non-traditional sources of digital evidence.

Digital devices in a child pornographer's residence should be viewed not only as storage devices but as to their potential function in committing child pornography offenses. Digital cameras are used to take pictures of victims. Laptops are used to engage in peer-to-peer trading of movies. Chromecast devices are used to view illicit content on a large screen television. USB flash drives are used to backup key parts of the subject's collection to carry on the subject's person. All of these devices should be viewed as interacting with each other, and the identification of those interactions may uncover new devices and lead to an understanding of the possible inbound and outbound digital roads that child pornography may have travelled.

PRESENT Approach

The PRESENT approach to executing a search warrant in child pornography cases attempts to address the challenges that occur when processing the modern IT environment within a home. By incorporating the identification and acquisition of digital evidence into every stage, from planning through execution, the approach is more likely to yield rapid results and the built-in feedback is designed to assist in concurrent interviews on-scene.

The success of the approach relies on the inclusion of a digital forensics team in every phase. The team can consist of a single individual or multiple teams of specialists, depending on digital evidence likely to be encountered. If information is obtained in the early phases of the framework that requires additional expertise, that expertise should be brought in as soon as possible.

In addition to the digital forensics team, the PRESENT framework assumes the availability of an adequate digital forensics kit. At a minimum, the kit should include the ability to review and process hard drives, removable media, cell phones, and tablet devices.

Additionally, a laptop with a wireless Internet connection and an on-scene printer and scanner are necessary items.

Planning

The planning stage of a search warrant is generally well documented for safety and security (e.g. identifying nearby hospitals, determining a method of entry, etc.). Most planning overlooks the digital forensics needs of the investigation, and is relegated to "add a forensic specialist to the search team". By removing the digital forensic specialist from the planning process in a child pornography case, investigative teams handicap themselves.

The digital forensics planning process should involve a review of all open source and easily obtainable commercial information available on the subject. Child pornographers tend to have multiple personas, with some personas associated with their real name and background and additional personas with fake information that they use to view, download, and share images and movies. Though some less savvy subjects may use their real name even for their illicit activities, even the more savvy subjects are likely to inadvertently cross-pollinate between their real and alias activities. Linking the two can frequently be done prior to warrant execution as part of the planning phase. Areas to focus on in evaluating a child pornography subject include:

- **Technical Acumen.** Does the work/education/usage profile of the subject indicate they are highly technical or a pure Luddite? Articulating a high degree of technical skill or an information security background can assist in justifying no-knock, after hours, or sneak-and-peek warrants. If the individual is known to use encryption, the installation of a keystroke logger or hidden camera with the appropriate warrant may be a necessary course of action.
- **Identifiers.** Building a list of online identifiers for an individual will assist in question development, identification of possible targets for electronic warrants/subpoenas, and later forensic analysis. The chapter on static forensics provides pointers to online resources to submit the identifiers below for the purposes of identifying other child pornography activity they are associated with. These sources should be checked as part of the search warrant planning phase. Identifiers to look for include the following:

    - **Usernames.** Individuals tend to use the same username or permutations of the same username on multiple systems. Identifying a Skype username may lead to an individual's Amazon.com profile and then to postings on a message board. The ID used on a peer-to-peer network may be the same as (or similar to) the username the subject employs on a web forum trading illicit images.
    - **Email Addresses.** Email addresses provide a target for electronic search warrants, and are frequently used as unique search identifiers when issuing a subpoena to online (or even offline) entities. Because many entities, both public and commercial, solicit emails from an individual the possibilities for obtaining addresses from corporate or government sources is almost endless. Subjects using alias email addresses will frequently include their real email address as one of their recovery options for lost passwords.

- **Passwords.** Obtaining passwords or personal questions/answers used by a subject from other sources can assist in password guessing attacks against encrypted systems encountered later. It is rare for an individual to not reuse a password or permutation thereof on multiple systems.
- **Phone numbers.** Phone numbers may provide additional subpoena targets, which may lead to other identification information. Mobile phone subpoenas, in addition to providing basic subscriber information, will almost certainly provide an email identifier if asked for. Additionally, knowing the level of data plan on a mobile phone and features available (such as tethering) are critical for identifying the subject's methods of Internet access and for identifying device targets for the physical search. Call detail records (CDRs) can provide location information on where a subject was as a particular time.
- **IP Addresses.** Finding the IP addresses that a subject has used, especially if they are static, can be useful in both geolocating where they connect from (e.g. does the IP return to a Starbucks in De Pere or a Marriott in Spartanburg) and for determining if an individual is openly sharing child pornography (by connecting to the IP they are currently using).

- **Online Activity Profiles.** The trap-and-trace is a frequently overlooked investigative tool in child pornography cases. Aside from the basic connection information provided, using a trap-and-trace on the ISP can show when an individual is online, which in turn can be used in planning when to execute the warrant. Showing a subject connecting to a child pornography website that uses GET requests may even provide evidence of search terms used or images downloaded, and any SMTP records may provide pointers to other individuals the subject is trading with.
- **Technology Purchase History.** Finding where an individual shops allows their technical purchase history to be obtained via subpoena. If an individual leaves reviews of products on Newegg.com, it's likely they purchase their computer hardware from there. Additionally, if they are asking questions on an Apple message board, they likely have an iTunes account. By issuing subpoenas to these merchants, the search team can identify products to look for during the search, and ensure the appropriate forensics expertise is available.
- **Social Network Information.** Publicly available information on the social networks the subject belongs to is useful in obtaining additional details on the items noted above. An iterative Google search on permutations of the person's name and other identifiers as they are found can lead to the development of a full profile on an individual in a completely non-invasive manner. Subpoenas for records from Twitter, Bebo, or Facebook can provide early context on an individual's digital activities.

Because the PRESENT framework relies on a team approach to investigative planning, any information obtained by the analysts performing the open source research should be shared with the rest of the team. Information on group memberships, associates, friends, and interests can assist an interview team and may help draft approaches in other areas of the warrant execution. It is also the responsibility of the digital forensics analyst to create a list of unanswered technical questions for the interview team to address with the subject.

This list will be revised and updated in later stages.

The products of the Planning stage for digital evidence purposes should include the following:

- A list of known products containing digital evidence to be seized.
- Identification of the appropriate expertise to bring for on-scene forensics given the list above and the technical profile of the subject.
- A determination of the best times, based on usage, to execute the warrant.
- All of the potential usernames, passwords, and biographical information available on an individual to assist with later forensic review.
- A list of interview questions related to the usage of the items identified above.

Reconnaissance

Standard reconnaissance for any warrant is iterative with the planning stage. Reconnaissance activities are differentiated from planning activities in that doing recon has the potential for discovery. For the purposes of a child pornography search warrant, recon can be divided into two phases - physical and logical.

Physical Reconnaissance

As with all search warrants, a thorough visual inspection and digital photography of the subject's residence is needed. Standard recon photographs cover possible approaches for entry and exits, potential threats to the team, and details of the location for the warrant application.

For digital evidence purposes, additional relevant information can also be gathered at the time of the physical reconnaissance. The presence or absence of cable boxes can give an indication of Internet connectivity at the home, and information on the subject's ISP. The demarcation point for any physical access (the place the coaxial or fiber cable, or satellite dish connection, enters the house) should be noted.

Wireless access can and should be enumerated as part of the physical recon stage as well. Use of a laptop and wireless card with Netstumbler (or similar tool) will provide a view of local wireless access points. Any open or secured access points present at the home, including their SSIDs and manufacturer, should be identified. Additionally, any open wireless access points in range of the home should be identified. The use of a directional antenna can help to associate specific access points with a specific residence. Enumeration should end at the identification of the devices and care should be taken not to capture any data packets to avoid potential wiretap concerns.

Because access to children is a concern with crossover offenders, any indications of children nearby should be noted. While an elementary school across the street is obvious, there may be other less obvious indicators present. Children's bicycles left outside, a swing set in the back yard, school bumper stickers on vehicles, or a basketball hoop either at the subject's residence or next door may be indicators of children the subject has physical access to.

Logical Reconnaissance

Logical recon is an attempt to ascertain relevant warrant execution information using semi-invasive online techniques. These involve connecting to devices owned by the subject or engaging with the subject in an undercover fashion in ways that may reveal the presence of the investigation. As with physical recon, the value of the information obtained should be weighed against the risk of the investigation being revealed prematurely.

A low-risk preliminary step in logical recon is the attempt to engage the subject over social networks. If the subject has a Facebook, Google+, LinkedIn, Bebo, or other social networking profile, viewing that information with an undercover account is considered non-invasive. As users become more privacy conscious, it is becoming increasingly necessary to be a member of a person's network to view much of the profile information of investigative value. Creating a profile that would likely be friended by the subject, and even approaching people in the subject's network in an undercover fashion online, may be warranted for search purposes. Once accepted into the network, the interest profiles, employment history, and education presented by the subject may provide clues as to their tech savvy and digital activities. Additionally, photos posted can be analyzed for search planning purposes, and the Exif information on them exploited to identify devices and locations to search. Finally, minors that the subject has "friended" may be potential victims, and groups the subject has joined (e.g. the local Boy Scout troop) may provide additional avenues for contact with children.

If the case involves file sharing, connecting to any shared files and obtaining evidentiary copies of them can be done at this point. US courts have held that connecting to an individual's machine that is publicly sharing files over peer-to-peer does not require a warrant, and obtaining digital evidence in this fashion can be used to support planning or probable cause, as outlined in previous chapters. Additionally, any child pornography that the subject shared publicly and is downloadable by the investigator becomes evidence for a distribution enhancement. Since child pornographers may only keep their connections open when they are online, the investigator should be ready to connect at any hour that the subject may power up their computer.

Case-specific logical interactions may be necessary at this point as well. Engaging in an undercover chat with a subject to trade images or sending the subject targeted emails to elicit behavior may be done depending on the specifics of the case.

The products of the Reconnaissance stage for digital evidence purposes should include the following:

- A list of likely ISPs and an annotation of where they physically enter the location.
- An assessment of the subject's potential contact with children.
- An enumerated list of potential wireless access points, both inside the residence and nearby.
- An updated list of items to be seized inside the residence, based on online profiles.

Entry

Entry is concerned primarily with obtaining access to the residence and securing the scene. In a typical warrant, the entry team stacks up on the door, knocks and announces their presence, then enters the location, either when the subject opens the door or when the door is forced. The warrant is served during daytime hours, and there is a small delay between knocking and obtaining access to the interior.

There are two primary considerations with child pornography evidence in the entry plan. First, the need for a non-traditional entry should be evaluated if the subject is likely to have encryption or the subject is likely to quickly destroy evidence. Second, the entry team should be trained to recognize systems that may go into sleep and/or hibernation mode or lock if not immediately secured.

Approach

Ideally, all digital media will be encountered up-and-running and unlocked. With creativity, the entry team can enhance their chances of this occurring. First, by articulating the likelihood of encryption and a technically sophisticated subject, a no-knock warrant can be sought. Based on the information obtained in the planning and recon stages, a no-knock can be executed at a time when the subject is likely to be using target systems of interest. If the subject is acquiring or sharing child pornography actively over peer-to-peer networks or participating in chat sessions with investigators, the team can wait until the subject goes live before executing.

If a no-knock warrant is not available, the entry team should consider a ruse to bring the subject out of their home. Making a pretext phone call, which has the benefit of the subject potentially possessing an unlocked and active cell phone, to bring the subject outside the location is preferable, as the subject may lock their systems when answering a knock at the door. If neither of these is possible, the entry team should be trained to identify any active digital evidence immediately after securing the location.

Physical Entry

Many current digital devices have a limited amount of time before they become inaccessible without the use of a password. Cell phones may lock in a matter of 30 seconds, whereas a laptop may go into sleep mode after 5 minutes. Because of this, rapidly securing and maintaining the state of a device takes precedence over everything except safety and security. Traditionally, digital devices were treated like any other piece of evidence. Once the search teams found the evidence during the normal course of the execution, the devices were shut down, bagged and tagged. The delay for active devices, given the current state of encryption and the volatility of information, justifies a more immediate approach.

First, the entry team should ensure the subject and others present do not have access to any digital devices that may allow them to initiate the destruction of information. This includes cell phones, computers, tablets, and other digital equipment. Second, any active devices encountered by the entry team should be immediately identified and the necessary steps taken to ensure they remain active. For a cell phone, this may mean touching areas of the touch screen that are unlikely to impact the underlying data. For a laptop or desktop, it means moving the mouse or using a tool such as the Mouse Jiggler™ to maintain the active state. While there is the small possibility of altering evidence with this approach, including physical evidence – e.g. fingerprints and swipe patterns on a touch screen, it is outweighed by the exigent need to avoid complete data "destruction" through its unavailability.

After the active electronic devices are secured, a means of ensuring constant power should be the next priority. The may range from asking the subject for the location of a charger to prioritizing the finding of power adapters to using charging tools from the digital forensics toolkit.

In terms of household residents, the subject will generally be sequestered to prevent alteration of evidence and ideally to participate in a voluntary interview. Any other individuals present, including the spouse or roommates, should be interviewed contemporaneously if they consent, and if they have potential remote access to the subject's information should also be detained until the information can be secured. Finally, if the investigators know that children will be present, arrangements should be made ahead of time to interview them offsite at an appropriate child advocacy center or other neutral location, per local protocol and in coordination with child protective services.

The products of the Entry stage for digital evidence purposes should include the following:

- The subject and others present are separated from digital devices.
- Any readily identifiable, active digital equipment is stabilized and powered for further analysis.

Search

The PRESENT framework Search step is iterative with the Examination and Notification steps, and encompasses both physical and logical searching procedures. In a typical search, the digital evidence is identified exclusively as part of the physical search procedures. The PRESENT approach allows the search teams without digital specialization to proceed with the physical search, permitting the digital evidence specialists to focus on identifying items that they can exploit on-scene to provide the physical search teams with the immediate results of exploitation. The steps presented do not preclude following standard evidence handling procedures (photographing, documenting, and handling appropriately) and chain of custody requirements.

Network Identification

Instead of beginning the search blindly for physical storage devices, a more effective approach is to identify connectivity equipment and then find those devices that they interact with. If a physical Internet connection is identified in the Recon step, that should be the first stop for the digital forensics specialist. The connection is likely to terminate at a router (with a modem or other translation device in between) which can be used as a starting point for identifying network devices. If the router has physical connections, these can be traced to connected devices. If it is purely a wireless device, exploiting it to obtain connection logs can be performed to identify machines for which to search. The exploitation mechanism will be device-specific, and is covered in the Examine step.

After identifying the wired Internet connection, wireless connections should be identified. This may consist of cell phones, 3G/4G network access cards on computers, or tablets with built-in wireless connectivity. These devices are most likely to be found by a physical search, and should be the next priority for the Examine phase.

Device Identification

Device identification should focus on items found during the physical search which may have digital storage capabilities. Once a device is found, it should be triaged to ensure the expected digital storage is present. Any digital storage that is missing, for example a computer without a hard drive or a camera without an SD card, should be listed on the potential seizure list and provided to the search teams as items to seek out. Similarly, storage devices without any associated processing unit, for example a SIM card without a phone, should also be noted.

Because of the small size of digital devices, search teams should open all available containers and pursue all reasonable hiding spots. While searching for the devices, any papers that may contain passwords should be collected, and any manuals or paperwork for devices not present should be noted. Any chargers or cables found should be seized, and if the associated item has not already been found it should be added to the list of missing items for the search teams.

The investigative team may also want to consider a preserve-for-prints approach to key pieces of evidence. Though cumbersome, preserving the prints on items that are believed to contain child pornography and showing that the only prints present belong to the subject can be as effective as digital evidence in showing the subject was the exclusive user. Additionally, for items that the subject may have used to display child pornography, the investigative team may want to consider examining the devices for other bodily fluids such as semen. Although it applies to any search, nitrile gloves are a must for searches in child pornography cases.

The products of the Search stage for digital evidence purposes should include the following:

- A checked-off list of digital evidence items seized and digital evidence items yet to be found.

Examine

Because of advances in digital forensics, many search teams now have the capability of doing live analysis of devices found on-scene. This analysis should focus on items that will be of immediate value – both for preservation of evidence and for feedback to the search and interview teams. Preservation should focus on the most volatile information first, generally RAM and activity logs, and should be performed consistent with sound forensic practices.

With standard hard drives, connecting to a hardware write blocker was the accepted practice for many years in digital forensics. Because of the inability of a write blocker to avoid data alteration on SSDs, and because of the diversity of digital items encountered, write blocking may not be possible. As such, in-situ analysis is becoming necessary more often, and is a valid and accepted practice. In-situ analysis may include running tools off a known-good CD, manually navigating a smartphone menu, or mounting an SD card as read-only to a Linux laptop. As with most forensic techniques, every analysis should be well documented and ideally observed by a second individual.

Due to the large amount of storage that is frequently encountered, exhaustive on-scene forensics is not likely to be possible. For the purposes of PRESENT, the priorities in examination should be set to preserve the most volatile data first, and to analyze for the following:

- **Network Connections.** Identification of any networks that a device was attached to will show where it fits into the digital ecosystem. Additionally, the networks themselves can then be connected to and enumerated, identifying additional devices of interest. Network connections should also include cloud storage services, social networks and email connections. Identifying these will be helpful in the Notify step below.

- **Devices.** Any devices that have been recently attached to a digital evidence item should be enumerated. Devices may be found by looking at everything from USB mass storage devices shown in the Windows registry to an iPhone profile found on a MacBook. Because any devices not seized while on-scene are subject to later alteration or destruction, it is critical to identify possible targets for seizure before ending the search.
- **Recent Activities.** Showing what an individual was doing just prior to the search can provide pointers to other pieces of volatile information. Most-recently-used (MRU) lists and activity logs provide the most valuable insight into recent actions. This is most critical if the activity is still ongoing at the time of the seizure - active peer-to-peer uploads of child pornography may not be logged, but may be viewable on-screen while the device is active.
- **Child Pornography-Specific Activities.** Identifying specific evidence of child pornography is generally the first thing done, but once seized and appropriately secured, the evidence will remain for future analysis. Any searches for evidence of elements of the crime should be focused on finding things that will be helpful to the interview team in the Notify step, or to form the basis for an immediate arrest as needed. Physically confirming the presence of a handful of child pornography images or movies will generally suffice for both purposes, negating the need for full on-scene cataloging of content.
- **Barriers to Access.** Encrypted files, inaccessible areas, and locked devices encountered can be fed to the interview team as questions to be addressed. Specific access controls may require additional Search actions - finding a login that looks for a SecureID token number or encountering an Android phone with face locking features may require additional searching or taking a digital photograph of the subject, respectively.

The products of the Examine stage for digital evidence purposes should include the following:

- An updated list of devices not yet found.
- A list of questions to ask the subject based on identified activities or obstacles encountered (e.g. an encrypted drive).

Notify

Notification is a two-way process between the interview team and the forensics team. Interview preparation and conduct is covered extensively elsewhere in the book, but the actual on-scene interview requires re-planning to accommodate new information on the fly. Notification can be done at a set time, where the interview team takes regular breaks to consult with the forensics team, or on-demand, where the forensics team interrupts the interview with critical information. With either approach, the rules for that particular search should be agreed upon beforehand by the entire team. If the forensic team believes that child pornography can be found in a reasonable amount of time, the interview team may want to wait before starting the interview.

Interview Team

The confrontational interview of the subject should occur simultaneously and in close proximity to the search, but be physically separated from the activities of the search team. Ideally, the interview can occur inside an already-cleared room at the location of the search. Alternatively, a simultaneous offsite interview can be coordinated though active communication between the search and interview teams.

In addition to the questions relevant to child pornography and the interview in general, which are covered in later chapters, the interview team can obtain several pieces of information that are relevant to the search team. Questions that can be asked include:

- How do you connect to the Internet?
    - What do you do when you are online?
- What cell phones/computers/tablets/digital cameras do you own?
    - Do you password protect them?
    - With what password?
    - Where are they?
- How do you backup your data?
    - Where are those backups located?
- Do you use encryption?
    - What password did you use to encrypt your devices?

The answers to these questions should be provided to the digital forensics team for confirmation and corroboration. Additionally, the subject should be asked about any digital items identified during the search, any passwords or usernames encountered, and any items on the list created that have not been found by the search team.

While it should be part of an overall interview strategy, informing the subject that a top notch digital forensics team is actively reviewing their devices and asking if there is anything that the team may find that, when taken out of context, may be misunderstood is often an effective technique in search warrant interviews.

Digital Forensics Team

The digital forensics team, in coordination with the search team, should prepare a list of questions during the Examine stage above and provide them to the interview team at the appropriate time. Any usernames/passwords, unusual devices, or barriers to entry encountered should be fed to the interview team as required information to be obtained from the subject.

Any information that is obtained during the above phases or by the interview team regarding online accounts should be used to generate preservation notices to send to the appropriate providers via fax or email. By generating and sending the notices immediately, any confederates that have access to the subject's online information, or the subject themselves if the interview is non-custodial and is terminated, will not be able to destroy existing digital evidence.

In addition to preservation notices, the digital forensics team should generate consent forms for access to all of the online services enumerated above. The consent forms should include a space for the username and password used, and should be provided to the interview team for signature by the subject at the appropriate point. The consent should give the digital forensics team the ability to access and obtain any and all information stored in the account. Ideally, the information provided can be verified before ending the search. If the case involves other subjects - if the subject is the member of an access controlled child pornography distribution forum for example - consideration should be given to obtaining consent to take over the account in lieu of just accessing it.

The products of the Notify stage for digital evidence purposes should include the following:

- Current locations and/or disposition information on all digital forensics items identified but not found.
- Preservation notices sent to all identified online providers.
- Signed consent forms for all online services.
- Usernames/passwords for all protected devices.

Take

Generally speaking, any items explicitly called out in the search warrant can be taken. Additionally, any contraband or other items that are found in plain view during the search and may be evidence can be seized as appropriate under exigency and a second warrant sought either telephonically or in person for them. Although the warrant may give the team the right to seize the items, the team should triage digital evidence items on-scene into several categories before deciding what to remove:

- **Items to Seize.** Items that either have been found to contain child pornography or are likely to contain evidence of child pornography activities and cannot be examined on scene should be seized.
- **Items to Clear.** Time permitting, items which can be easily reviewed and cleared on-scene should not be seized. Stacks of CD/DVDs, digital cameras, memory sticks, and other items that can be quickly reviewed on-scene should be examined and cleared.
- **Items to Ignore.** Items predating the criminal activity or that are not likely to be used to store relevant data can be ignored. Older gaming systems without network connectivity and commercially stamped, as opposed to burned, DVDs are examples of items that can generally be ignored.
- **Items to Image.** Items to image include items that will remain and not be seized as well as items that require imaging of their volatile areas before being packaged for seizure. In a corporate environment, where the subject is using the resources of a third party company to store child pornography, there may be a reason to image storage devices in place and leave the physical devices behind. Similarly, a laptop without a charger may need to have its memory rapidly imaged, even though the

device will be seized for full analysis at a later point.

Once the items identified have been bagged-and-tagged, they can be entered into evidence and processed in the lab environment. Packaging of the materials is item specific and may include anti-static bags, Van Eck shielded storage, or portable power supplies depending on the item.

The products of the Take stage for digital evidence purposes should include the following:

- All digital items requiring further processing or found to contain evidence of criminality are seized.

By thinking about digital evidence as a core component of searches in child pornography cases, law enforcement maximizes their ability to successfully solve both computer and non-computer crimes. With the further integration of digital evidence teams, evidence that may have been previously left behind or overlooked will, in the future, be seized and assist in prosecuting (or exonerating) subjects of criminal inquiries.

The PRESENT framework provides a specific method of organizing and executing a search warrant tailored to digital child pornography cases. It is meant to supplement and not supplant existing search warrant procedures, and is flexible enough to change as the digital landscape changes.

8 STATIC FORENSICS

People are good at intuition, living our lives. What are computers good at? Memory.
Eric Schmidt

Static analysis, sometimes called "dead-box" forensics, refers to any examination that is not performed on-site on a live device. Because there is an assumption that the data at rest on a seized device is not going to be altered, the examination can take place under the conditions most favorable to the examiner in terms of time and location, generally in a dedicated digital forensics lab by a specialist in that particular technology. Static analysis lends itself to thoroughness not possible with live analysis, but resource availability must still be a consideration

The particulars of a static analysis are highly case dependent and specific to the media being analyzed. For configuration data alone, the possibilities are numerous:

- Windows-based systems rely on a series of binary files called the registry.
- OS X systems use property list files, or .plists.
- Linux systems utilize configuration, or .conf files.

To further complicate matters, each operating system version may introduce changes in the location and formatting of configuration information. When mobile devices are added into the mix, the picture gets even cloudier.

There is no universal tool to analyze devices, though both Guidance Software's EnCase and AccessData's FTK products come close. Every device analyzed may require specific technical expertise, but a general methodology can still be put in place for all child pornography cases. This chapter provides a general set of procedures for analyzing devices seized from child pornographers. It does not provide operating system-specific guidance, nor does it provide details on tool usage. Because of this, it is assumed that the analyst working with the investigate team has basic digital forensics training and is using a tool suite that they have experience with.

The methodology below can be applied to just about any device. Depending on the type of digital evidence being analyzed, some of the techniques may not be applicable, for example finding the installed software on a seized microSD card. Additionally, every examination should have a cost-benefit analysis performed. In production cases, a deep-dive to identify all possible victims may require a more comprehensive analysis than the cataloging of DVDs containing known images that can be tied to a specific download mechanism in a possession case. These decisions will be resource driven and the methodology below is meant to be flexible enough to cover each area in whatever depth a particular case demands.

The primary goals of digital forensics analysis in child pornography cases are as follows:

- **Find All Images and Movies Containing Child Pornography.** Identifying all of the visual depictions of child pornography on a particular device is generally the highest priority. Prosecutorially, there may be a reason to stop once the maximum number of images that count toward sentencing are found, and identifying additional images may not be the best use of resources.
- **Identify Victims.** For production cases, identifying victims may be a predominantly local matter. For possession or distribution cases, identifying known victims can be done through NCMEC. Identifying unknown victims may require extensive research and resources not available to a particular law enforcement agency and may need to be coordinated with other organizations. Either way, identifying the victims may help rescue them from further abuse and obtain restitution for the acts committed against them, while bringing contact offenders to justice.
- **Show That the Subject is Associated With the Child Pornography.** Although a device may be seized from a subject's residence, showing that device belongs to the subject and that the child pornography present was created or acquired by the subject are necessary steps in defeating the SODDI defense should it be attempted.
- **Rule Out Future Legal Defenses.** The defense bar has multiple strategies they can employ when a case goes to trial. These range from blaming mysterious viruses to using a "pop-up" ad defense to attacking the procedures of the forensic team. Several steps in the methodology are performed to proactively preclude these potential defenses from being successfully employed.

All of the above digital forensics analyses should be done in coordination with the prosecutor. While the analysis is ongoing, communications of the interim results with the prosecutor should happen on a routine basis, but should be done in person or verbally on the phone. The creation of written records from incomplete analyses should be avoided.

For any digital forensic analysis performed, there are some baseline factors that are necessary for a successful examination that is both thorough and will hold up in court. The four primary factors are as follows:

- **Trained Personnel.** Digital forensics analysts should have baseline training in digital forensics, ideally from the Department of Defense Cyber Investigations Training Academy, Quantico, the Federal Law Enforcement Training Center, or other recognized government training academy. This baseline knowledge will ensure that widely accepted best practices are used in handling evidence, documenting an analysis, and presenting the results in court. Additional training on the specific tools used in the lab environment is necessary as well, with certifications in the tools a plus.

- **Documented Procedures.** The first step in ensuring that examinations follow documented procedures is to ensure that the lab actually has documented procedures. Everything from the acquisition of images to their storage and handling should be in a lab manual. This does not mean that there cannot be a deviation from procedures when the case demands it, but there should be an established baseline and any deviations from that baseline should be documented.
- **Solid Case Documentation.** The old court adage noted earlier also holds true here – if it isn't documented it didn't happen. All forensic actions taken, and the results of those actions, should be documented contemporaneously with the analysis. Additionally, the primary analyst should sign off on any documentation, with a secondary sign-off by another analyst for quality control purposes. In child pornography cases, any images should be kept in a separate appendix from the primary case report and controlled as contraband.
- **Impeccable Evidence Handling.** The handling of evidence of any type is an often-attacked area when the remainder of a case against a subject is strong. This is doubly true for digital evidence. The chain of custody for digital evidence should be firmly established from seizure through destruction or return. Additionally, any hash values generated during imaging should be recorded and maintained for later use in proving evidence was not altered.

While having the proper tools available is also important, these will change over time and may not be the same from one analysis to the next. A large triage project may require bulk_extractor to identify drives of interest, while an Apple-heavy analysis will want BlackBag's BlackLight suite. A lab that deals primarily with mobile devices is likely to have the Paraben tool suite and a UFED device, while a custom chip-off lab may have custom hardware and write bespoke code that is not commercially available. Whatever tools are used, the methodology below will ensure the critical points in an analysis are covered.

Digital Forensics Methodology

It is rare that the digital forensics examination of a device takes place in a vacuum, with a single item being seized and searched. In practice, most seizures involve multiple items, with potentially terabytes or tens of terabytes of data to analyze. A solid process will ensure that each item gets appropriately triaged, imaged, and processed to the greatest degree possible given time and resource constraints. The first step in the methodology is triage – the identification of which devices to analyze and in what order.

Triage

While smaller cases may lend themselves to imaging all of the items that were seized and processing them at once, limitations in forensic software tools and storage space make this impractical for larger investigations. Additionally, external time constraints and personnel resource limitations may require that the analyst review the most probable devices first.

This may be needed to get a search warrant to seize additional items before they are destroyed, or to obtain an arrest warrant for a subject that will flee the country or potentially cause harm to themselves or others. Triage, from the French word trier, which means to separate, is the process of prioritizing which devices to analyze and it what order. Triage involves making educated guesses based on the probable offenses, the information known about the item seized, and the level of effort needed and resources available to analyze the item.

The first step in triaging items is to understand as much as possible about the likely offense(s) committed by the subject. If the subject is under investigation for distribution of child pornography over peer-to-peer networks, priority would be given to computers that are capable of running the software used in the offense. In a sexting case, the cell phone associated with sending the MMS message would be prioritized. For a subject involved in production, the digital camera is likely to be the first target. Because all of these factors require knowledge of the subject's alleged crimes, the analyst must sit down with the investigator to understand the details of the offense. This may include reading interview reports, reviewing log data, or going over the subject's criminal history to understand their modus operandi in past offenses.

The next step is evaluating the digital items for their potential value to the case. If a distribution charge is being sought, items that are too old to have been involved in the current act can be de-prioritized. If the subject has been downloading digital movies, the 3.5" floppy disks seized from their home aren't likely to contain the expected evidence. A computer purchased a week prior to the seizure will likely have less data of evidentiary value than their previous computer for a long-term offender.

Once items have been excluded, then the remaining items can be reviewed for likely value. While storage of child pornography on the hard drive of an Xbox 360 is possible, it is less probable than the subject storing the information on an external USB hard drive attached to their desktop at the time of seizure. Similarly, the DVD labeled "Misc Pix" is more likely to contain items of interest than the DVD labeled "Windows 7 – Home Professional".

The third factor in triage is the time and effort required to analyze and clear an evidence item. Analyzing a 1GB SD card is likely to be significantly less time consuming than reviewing the hard drive of dual-partitioned MacBook Pro. Similarly, while reviewing a single DVD may be rapid, reviewing a stack of 500 DVDs will require extensive person-hours and machine hours. Finally, certain items seized may require special training that is not readily available given current analysis resources to be properly analyzed. If a seized Android phone is going to require chip-off forensics and the only analyst that does this has a six month case backlog, that piece of evidence may need to be placed at the bottom of the priority list.

The above procedures will allow the investigative team to produce a list of items, in order of priority, to be subjected to the remainder of the steps in the methodology. In some cases, however, there may not be enough information available to differentiate between devices for prioritization and a forensic preview may be needed. The method for doing a forensic preview will depend on the devices and their status.

If the devices have already been imaged, using bulk_extractor to identify drives with keywords associated with child pornography or email addresses and URLs of interest can be the most effective technique. Additionally, using image carving tools (e.g. scalpel) and child pornography detection tools (e.g. Netclean Analyze) can help with rapid previews of the images and movies carved from the disks. This can help direct analysis resources toward devices of interest.

For devices that have not been imaged, they can be connected to a write blocker and reviewed using older versions of EnCase (as of this writing, version 7.x is not effective at rapid previews). Other tools like Internet Evidence Finder Triage can also be utilized for quick snapshot reviews. Finally, the FBI makes its ImageScan software available for free to law enforcement for knock-and-talk situations. Because carving content generally requires imaging a drive and may be too time consuming, a rapid preview should consist of the following:

- Identify all images (and movies) on the drive through the file system.
    - Review the most recently opened images and the largest images.
    - Search image and movie filenames against a list of child pornography terms.
- Browse recent Internet history.
    - Review the list of the most recently and most frequently visited sites.
    - If you have a tool that can extract Internet searches, review those searches.
- Identify relevant, installed programs.
    - Any peer-to-peer or chat software should be reviewed for the presence of log files or stored content.

Any indicators of child pornography activity found above will put the device higher on the priority list for a full analysis. The rapid preview conducted as part of a triage effort is different from that performed as part of an on-scene live analysis. The purpose of the triage is to determine the likelihood that evidence of contraband exists on a device to prioritize analysis. The main goals of a live preview are to identify factors that can be immediately used on-scene and to preserve transient data.

Imaging

Following the triage stage (or before it, depending on resource availability and the quantity of data seized), forensic images should be created of all storage devices to be analyzed. Once the image is created, the original device should be returned to the evidence room. Because forensic images are best-evidence copies of the data, analysis can and should be performed on the image and not the original device. Ideally, two copies of the image files should be created – a working copy that is processed with the forensic tools and a pristine copy that can be used to overwrite the working copy if it becomes corrupted.

Where possible, devices should be connected to hardware write blockers and a physical image taken of their contents. If hardware write blocking is not possible, software write blocking should be employed. There may be circumstances where write blocking is not feasible – some backup drives, for example, have firmware-based unlocking that requires custom software to be installed on the analysis machine. In these cases, the analyst should take the appropriate procedural precautions to ensure data is not altered and should document the reasons for not using a write-blocking device.

There are two categories of images that can be created – raw images and structured images. Raw images, traditionally created using the Unix dd command, are a single file that contains a bitwise copy of the device. They are the easiest to work with and in some cases the fastest (though on higher performance forensic workstations, decompression is faster than disk access, resulting in faster processing of compressed images), and almost every tool is compatible with raw images.

Structured images, including the Expert Witness Format (.e01) images used by EnCase and Advanced File Format (AFF) images that are open source and compatible with most tools, add additional features to the imaging. The four primary features in the structured files are data labels, segmentation, compression, and encryption.

Data labels allow the analyst to include meta-data with the image, including the hash value of the image, the name of the analyst, the date and time of the imaging, the tool name and version used to do the imaging, the evidence description, and case identification information. If raw imaging is performed, the analyst should document these items in a separate file.

Segmentation allows for an image to be broken up into multiple files. Originally designed to allow large images to be copied to CDs or DVDs for storage, this has become increasingly less practical, though images can still be copied to external hard drives. Segmentation is still valuable for selective decompression and decryption operations, however, and intelligent tools will make use of this factor.

Compression allows an image to be stored in less space than the size required by a raw image of the original drive. On media where the majority of the storage space is not used, there may be large areas of zeroed bits that will compress to a very small size. Conversely, if the subject has filled their device with child pornography images and movies in already-compressed formats (e.g. JPEG or MPEG), further compression may slightly increase the storage space required.

Encryption gives the analyst the ability to protect the image from unwanted disclosure. In child pornography cases, there is an assumption that contraband will be present on a device until it is cleared through analysis. Because of this assumption, many labs will encrypt images associated with child exploitation cases to prevent other analysts from seeing their contents, either intentionally or inadvertently.

No matter what image format is used, a hash is performed on the resultant image file, either as part of the imaging process or at its completion. The hash value should be copied down immediately into the written report, and will later serve as verification that the image has not been corrupted or altered.

When an image is loaded into the forensic software, the logical device size, any partitions present and their associated size, file system, and name, and any unallocated space should be recorded.

Hash Analysis

The first step in automated analysis on the devices that have been triaged for further review is to perform a comparison to hash values. This is generally done as part of the basic case processing when loading a new device image, and both positive and negative hash analysis should be performed. Ideally, the investigator will obtain the latest hash sets from the FBI, HSI, NIST, and other providers prior to performing the analysis.

All files on the device, including carved files, should be hashed. While negative hashes can be used as part of a filter to exclude files from manual review, positive hashes require manual review to confirm their contents. There are two positive hashsets of general interest in these cases – child pornography and malware. Malware analysis is covered in a separate section below.

Hashsets of known child pornography are maintained by both the FBI and HSI. Positive hits on child pornography hashes are becoming less frequent, as the volume of images and movies increases and the number of variations of known-bad content grows. Changes that add logos, resize, compress, or crop images will completely change the signature values for traditional hashing. Even a single hash hit, however, can point investigators to a location on the device or timeframe of interest, and the hashing process itself is completely automated. Any hits should be manually reviewed, and, if confirmed, should be documented in the report. If the images are part of a series, the name of the series should be included in the list of search terms used in later steps.

Two additional hash analyses can be performed - PhotoDNA hashing and online hash submission for suspect images. PhotoDNA uses histograms of regions in images to find matches to similar content. While extensive databases of PhotoDNA hash values are not readily available, each investigator should add identified content in a particular case to their own PhotoDNA hashset. This will allow them to identify similar content on other devices (or elsewhere on the same device). By using this technique, investigators can often identify thumbnails of the illicit material, which may provide insight into to how the content was acquired. Additionally, for images in a series, PhotoDNA hashsets may identify similar images taken in the same location with the same victim.

Online submission of hashes for images that appear to be child pornography but are not matching known series from the analyst's hash set is also useful. The two submission locations, CPS and LESP, both provide useful services in this area.

CPS, or Child Protection System, is part of Gridcop and provides a hash submission service where investigators around the globe can submit suspected child pornography images. Even if the victims are not known, hits through Gridcop can link investigators to other law enforcement organizations that are seeing the same images, or can help in excluding images if they have been confirmed to be over 18 by other entities.

LESP, the Law Enforcement Services Portal, is run by NCMEC and provides online submission services. Details about general NCMEC submissions are covered in a separate section, but investigators can submit hashes of their suspected child pornography images through the portal and receive an automated response almost instantaneously. Because of this, all suspect image and movie hashes should be submitted.

Image/Video Analysis

Following the hash analysis, an image and video review should be performed. Because the volume of images and movies to be reviewed may be large, using a methodological approach and automation can greatly assist from a throughput and accuracy standpoint. Although there may be a tendency to stop cataloging images once the maximum sentencing guidelines have been reached (with some buffer space), it is still valuable to identify all of the potential child pornography on a system to identify previously unknown victims and to find evidence of additional crimes beyond receipt and/or possession.

The first step in image analysis is identifying all of the images present on a device. This starts with a crawl of the file system, where all of the files identified as images by their extension are flagged. Next, all of the existing files with other extensions are analyzed to see if they may be images that were mislabeled. Finally, images are carved from unallocated space or from other files (such as SQLite Databases).

Videos are processed the same way as images with one additional step - thumbnail generation. To enhance the ability to review video content, the major automated tools now generate thumbnails, allowing the investigator the ability to preview movies without extracting and opening the original files. To ensure videos can be processed, the analysis machine should have a comprehensive installation of the common codes encountered. The K-Lite codec packs provide excellent coverage in this area.

Following the initial image and video extraction, the images are placed in thumbnail galleries for review. Generally, the entire device is reviewed all at once by manually reviewing all of the extracted thumbnails. While explicit image detection software may highlight likely pornography (and even child pornography), the false positive and false negative rates are still high enough to require manual review. These tools make excellent assistants when doing a preview, but are not a substitute for performing a comprehensive manual analysis.

Where possible, a single analyst or investigator should review the content for a single case. As the analyst becomes more familiar with the contents of the devices, he or she will be able to more rapidly rule out non-child pornography images, and will be able to identify trends in the subject's collecting habits. Images of the subject's children, or any children the subject has close contact with, should be made available to the analyst to aid in their review.

In general, one of the most effective ways to review all images on a drive is to sort them by size and start with the largest files. The analyst can set a lower threshold past which identification of the contents of an image becomes problematic for evidentiary purposes, and stop the review at that point (generally between five KB and ten KB in size). While very small images may be missed, they are not likely to lead to identifications due to the low resolution present. If time and resources permit, the remaining images can be reviewed after completing the other analysis steps.

When doing a thumbnail analysis, the analyst should have a large screen monitor available. Larger monitors can display more thumbnails at a time, requiring the analyst to do less scrolling and spend more time on viewing the image contents.

Pictures should be flagged and cataloged when they are identified as being in one of three categories:

- **Suspected Child Pornography.** These images appear to be of minors engaged in sexual activity or lascivious display of genitals that meet the legal definition of child pornography.
- **Suspected Child Erotica**. Child erotica are sexualized images of minors that do not meet the definition of child pornography but may be useful indicators of the subject's sexual interests in children or pointers to how the subject acquires images of interest. Child erotica can also assist in showing a pattern and practice of behavior and refute defenses of the subject "accidentally" downloading child pornography while viewing legal, adult pornography.
- **Potential Evidentiary Images.** There may be images identified that do not show child pornography or child erotica, but may be useful in proving the offenses. Examples include images from a location that place the subject there at a particular time, Safari preview images showing search terms used, and screenshots of software programs of interest.
- **Non-Erotic Images of Children.** Any images of children that were potentially

produced by the subject, even if they are not sexualized, should be identified. These may represent potential victims, and can be matched against the child pornography and erotica present to assist in victim identification. They may also be used to identify potential interview targets.

In addition to noting any files of interest, the investigator should note the dates and times of the files and their location on the drive. These will be used later in the location and timeline analyses.

While adult pornography should not be cataloged, the analyst should note any trends in its presence on the device. This can include the volume, the percentage of images that are adult as opposed child pornography, and any differentiators in how the subject stores or accesses the adult pornography compared to the child pornography.

Finally, the Exchangeable image file format (Exif) information should be obtained from any of the flagged images of interest. Exif information may point to a particular camera that took the images, to a location where the images were taken (based on GPS coordinates), or to the date and time the images were taken. All of these pieces of information can assist in victim identification, and in tying the images to a subject in production cases.

Device Protections

The protections that might be present on a device include passwords, encryption, anti-malware software, system security settings, and other security software. Identifying the protections in place is essential in combating the SODDI defense, in proving that malware did not cause the child pornography to be downloaded, and, in the case of encryption, that the subject attempted to hide illegal content.

The simplest device protection, but the one most likely to prevent unauthorized usage from others with physical access to the device, is the presence of passwords. The strength of the password, whether or not the subject ever shared the password, and the password settings (e.g. the screen lock time) can be used as evidence against a SODDI defense, and can prevent the defense from even raising one if done as part of the forensic examination. Passwords may also be placed on individual files or folders, indicating that their contents are of investigative interest because the subject took actions to protect them from viewing. This may assist in showing that the subject was aware of the contents of the files and folders that are protected, and differentiated them from other illicit but not illegal content present.

Following the identification of any password protection, encrypted files and encryption programs should be identified. If whole drive encryption is used, this may preclude further analysis until it is dealt with (see chapter five). Otherwise, the investigator should identify any encryption applications that have been installed, and review the most recently used files for those applications. Additionally, PGP keyrings or the presence of other encryption keys of potential co-conspirators should be noted.

Once the encryption software has been identified, the subject should look for encrypted files. These may be identified based on file extension, determined by the software installed. They can also be identified by their location on the device, using the most recently used lists above, or by performing an entropy test.

An entropy test looks at the randomness of characters in a file. Compressed and encrypted files both have very high entropy, and the major forensic packages include the ability to identify these files. Once identified, these files can be exported and the process of cracking them can be done in parallel with the more manual forms of analysis. As with password protected content, encrypted content provides evidence that the encrypted files were differentiated from the other files on the device by the subject.

Following the identification of encrypted content, the analyst should note any anti-malware present on the system. If multiple software packages are present, for example if the subject is running separate anti-virus and anti-phishing software, all of them should be noted as potentially relevant. The settings for the installed software should be obtained as well – this includes showing that the software runs automatically at system startup, that it is set to automatically update definitions, that it is configured to scan downloaded files on the relevant drives, and that scheduled scans were set. If possible, the logfiles showing updates to the software should be identified to be able to show that it was up-to-date at the time the contraband was acquired.

More difficult to identify are the general security settings present on the system. These can include built-in operating system settings, such as disabling services or locking the screen after inactivity, or custom settings present in other security software, such as third party firewall applications. Whether the patch settings are configured for automatic or manual update and the current patch level of the system should be noted in the report as well. Any additional settings above-and-beyond the default may provide evidence that the subject applied advanced security procedures and was less likely to have been infected with malware.

Malware Analysis

The logfiles associated with the anti-malware software should be reviewed to find any evidence of infections that were identified on the system during scanning, and the source and disposition of the infections. Additionally, any hash values associated with known malware should be recorded.

Because anti-malware definitions are updated regularly, the investigator should be running at least one anti-malware package on the analysis system. The device being reviewed should be scanned, through mounting the image or through the write blocker, by the anti-malware software in "notification" mode, and a copy of the log saved. Ideally, a second, scan-only software package should be run against the machine as well. Scan-only packages such as Malware Bytes do not provide protective services, but can do an on-demand analysis and the results of that analysis should be noted.

If any malware is found, the investigator should research the particular virus/worm/Trojan Horse and determine what impact it has on the underlying machine. Frequently, low-impact malware, including many types of spyware, will be present but will be well characterized and have behavior that would not include downloading child pornography. In addition to identifying the behavior of the malware, the investigator should attempt to find and document the vector by which the malware was acquired. A time analysis (see below) can often show the source of the infection.

Previously unknown malware can be installed on a standalone device and a dynamic analysis performed, if the lab has the requisite capabilities. Alternatively, it can be submitted to the major anti-virus software vendors and their teams may be willing to analyze it for inclusion in their signatures.

System Settings

There are several key system settings to note, depending on the type of device being analyzed. While the security settings were noted previously, other system settings can provide pointers to information that is forensically relevant.

The first system setting to review is the user list. Any user accounts present on a system, even those that have been disabled, should be noted. The default directories for each user should be identified, and any globally unique identifiers (GUIDs) associated with the user account should be logged.

Following the enumeration of users, the basic system information should be identified. The operating system present, its patch level, and its installation date should be recorded. If the installation appears to be an upgrade from a previous version, that should also be detailed. The system name (and network name, if different) should be identified and recorded. In the case of non-operating system devices, the device name (if any) and serial number should be noted.

Because child pornography needs a physical or virtual vector to be placed on or removed from a system, any devices associated with the system should be identified and recorded. These can include virtual services like iCloud or Google Drive, or they can include physical devices like USB flash drives, external hard drives, and digital cameras. The identifiers for physical devices should be compared to the other devices seized from the subject, and the usernames associated with logical devices should be recorded.

Paging and hibernation file settings should be noted, and the associated files flagged for later analysis if time and expertise are available. Similarly, any system restore points should be identified for similar analysis.

Almost every device that is used for anything other than basic storage has some level of networking capability, and network settings can be very relevant to proving possession or distribution of child pornography. Frequently, subjects are initially identified by an offending IP address, and tying that address to a device can assist in linking illegal activities to a particular user. Any network connections, past or present, should be recorded. The MAC addresses should be noted, and any IP address information, current or previous, should be noted. This can include the host IP addresses, gateway IP addresses, cached IP addresses for network connections, and proxy server IP addresses. If VPN software is present, any IP addresses associated with that software should be recorded.

Any network connections or device connections should be considered potential vectors for either importing or exporting child pornography from the device under examination, and the associated identifiers correlated with those present on other devices seized.

Software Installed

Any relevant software that is currently installed, as well as software that has previously been installed, should be cataloged. The relevant items to document are specific to the type of software but can include the following:

- Installation dates and times
- Usage dates and times
- Sharing settings
- Upload and download directories

- User IDs and passwords
- Buddy lists
- Cache information, including in-progress actions
- Activity logs
- Favorites or bookmarks
- MRU file or connection lists

Determining what software is relevant is case-specific. Outside of the security software above, applications that should be commonly documented include the following:

- **Web Browsers.** Child pornography subjects may have multiple web browsers installed on their system. The detailed browsing history, including bookmarks, cache files, cookies, and history files should be extracted and analyzed. Specific URLs identified can be visited by the investigator on a separate computer, and the resultant pages documented as evidence. Additionally, search terms and usernames can be extracted from the query strings on GET requests or from certain cookie files. The dates and times of all relevant activity should be noted, and the sites visited just prior to and just after the activity should also be noted.
- **Peer-to-Peer Software.** Any peer-to-peer software, including both legacy software like Kazaa and more recent software like Limewire, Ares, Vuze, Shareaza, or Bittorrent should be identified. It should be determined whether the subject had file sharing turned on, if they subject designated a custom upload/download directory (which goes toward intent to share), and if there are partial files still in existence for each program. The Global Unique Identifier (GUID) associated with each client identified can be extracted and run through CPS to link it to prior distribution activities.
- **IRC/IM Software.** Internet Relay Chat and Instant Messenger applications include single protocol clients like Yahoo! Messenger and ICQ, multi-protocol clients like Pidgin and Trillian, and video clients like Skype. With IRC/IM clients, the analyst should note the usernames used, the subject's contact lists, any logs of times connected, any biographical profile information saved (real or fictitious) and any chat rooms, forums, or servers that the subject has connected to. Forums with names associated with child pornography (e.g. "Boy Lovers Forum") or servers known to be associated with child pornography (e.g. motherless.com) should be noted. Additionally, the log, upload, and download folders for the client should be identified and searched for relevant content. Any User ID's found, including the subject's own IDs and those in the subject's buddy lists, should be run through CPS for possible matches.
- **Email Software.** The functionality available in email clients varies greatly. Similar to IRC/IM clients, there are fully featured programs like Outlook that may connect multiple accounts. On the other side, there are also single provider mail applets with minimal features developed for use on smartphones. Any email accounts used by the subject should be noted, and the mail should be reviewed for any content related to child pornography through keyword searches (see below) or through manual review. Any email addresses in the subject's address book and any email addresses used by the subject should be run through CPS. Additionally, any

relevant information in other mail client features should be noted. These can include task lists, calendar entries, or messages placed into folders with unusual names.

- **SMS Clients**. SMS messages, including MMS messages, should be searched for keywords and the images and movies associated with MMS manually reviewed. As with the clients above, any identifiers for individuals that the subject communicates with regularly, including phone numbers and friendly names assigned by the subject, should be run through CPS.
- **Media Players/Image Viewers**. To be able to view child pornography, the subject must have the appropriate viewing software installed. The subject may use built-in viewing options like the iOS Videos player and Android Gallery, or custom players like VLC and IrfanView. The operating system's file associations can be used to identify which player the subject uses with which media type. Within the player, the analyst should note any albums created and the most recently opened files. If the player automatically generates thumbnail images, the location of these thumbnails should be searched for residual content.
- **Codecs**. Movie files may require specific audio and video codecs to be viewed on a system. The investigator should confirm the relevant codecs are (or were) installed. A system that does not have the proper codecs may indicate the subject was not able to view a particular movie, or that the movie was viewed on a different device and moved to that system.
- **Digital Camera Software.** Integrated camera software (for cell phones, webcams, or tablets) or custom software for external digital cameras may include evidence of the production of child pornography. The model and serial numbers of associated cameras should be noted, and the default directories into which images are copied should be recorded.
- **Other Software**. While the above-mentioned software represents the major areas of interest, specific cases may require the analysis of other software packages present. If a large quantity of DVDs is found, the CD/DVD burning software may be relevant. Similarly, a backup client specific to an external hard drive or a custom proxy agent like TOR may be relevant in a particular case. Finally, a subject may use virtualization software such as VMWare to conduct their illicit activities within a virtual machine.

In addition to noting all of the relevant software installed, the analyst may need to acquire copies of specific software to analyze the contents of unusual files. If the client was producing child pornography for profit and used QuickBooks to maintain purchase records, the relevant software may need to be procured. If the subject has numerous movies that are encoded using an unusual codec, that codec should be identified and installed on the analysis machine. Ideally, the analyst will maintain several virtual machines on their analysis device that are capable of loading software for a multitude of environments without impacting the core analysis build.

NCMEC Submission

The previously mentioned LESP allows the submission of the hash values associated with movies and images for comparison to the database of known victims. This is only one of the services that NCMEC can provide, however, and many investigative agents either do not know of or do not utilize their other services.

First, any images or videos that do not generate hash matches but appear to be child pornography can be submitted. NCMEC will attempt to do manual matching against their image database. For images that cannot be matched, NCMEC will try to do victim identification through image features such as logos and background details. These will be used to provide leads to local law enforcement around the globe and to assist in rescuing children currently being exploited.

Second, any identifiers associated with an individual should be submitted. NCMEC maintains details on the usernames and other identifiers associated with previously submitted content. This can link your investigation to other law enforcement agencies that may represent the other side of a distribution or production charge, and may have information and evidence to assist you in your case.

Finally, NCMEC can provide guidance and expertise in handling victims that you may have identified. While production cases are less frequent than possession cases, providing the victims with the appropriate support and information may be beyond the capabilities of local resources.

Even if it does not immediately benefit your case, submission of the evidence of child exploitation to NCMEC should be done on every child pornography investigation.

Keyword Searches

Many investigators perform keyword searches as their initial analysis step. Because many of the keywords that are to be searched may not be known yet, the initial searches may be a shot in the dark, whereas searches performed at the end of the initial analysis will be informed and targeted. Although running the keyword searches and analyzing the results should occur later in the forensic examination, indexing can be performed as part of the initial processing to speed up later searching.

The terms that can be effectively searched will depend on the size of the image and the type of term used. Terms like "PTHC", although closely associated with child pornography, will randomly occur numerous times on terabyte-size images due to the short length of the search string. Similarly, identifiers that have other meanings may occur frequently and generate large numbers of false positives – terms like "parent" and "child" have a programming meaning as well as a physical meaning and make poor search terms. There are still several things that can and should be searched for to identify targets for review for other potential child pornography evidence:

- **Child Pornography Terms**. Any terms that the subject has used in searches or appear in filenames associated with the subject's collection should be searched. Strings with more than five characters are preferable. If nothing has been found prior to the keyword searches, the investigator can try common terms uniquely associated with child pornography. Lists of keywords are available on GridCop and through the ICAC taskforces.
- **IP Addresses**. Any IP addresses found above as being meaningful should be searched. Additionally, IP addresses not found during the review but present as part of external evidence (e.g. a CPS capture of an IRC session) should be searched. IP addresses can also be geolocated, and the resultant locations searched for further

results.

- **Names, Addresses, and Phone Numbers.** The names of individuals, including the subject and potential victims, should be searched. Additionally, any addresses where criminal activity allegedly took place (city or street names), or where IP addresses or image Exif information resolved to should be searched. Finally, phone numbers of any potential contacts associated with child pornography should be searched.
- **Usernames and GUIDs.** Any usernames associated with the subject, either through open source searching, through a database hit on CPS, or identified through forensic analysis should be searched. Similarly, any GUIDs identified should be searched.

Other terms may be searched based on the results of the initial search or based on case-specific details. They may include the names of websites, chat forums, or other string identifiers that were uncovered as part of the initial investigation.

Temporal and Spatial Analysis

The final step in analyzing the device image is a review of the file system contents in light of the findings noted above. Temporal and spatial analysis looks to expand upon the initial findings and identify files and activities that have occurred close to the time and in the same folder locations as the evidence already found. This can assist the investigator in providing context to child pornography activities, and can be crucial in rebutting later defenses at trial. Timeline analysis can include log entries, file times, and Internet activity records. Some of the analyses that should occur during this step are as follows:

- **Content Transfer Analysis.** For each image of child pornography identified, the analyst should try to determine how the content was acquired. If there are duplicates of an image or movie, then both the initial transfer and the copying should be analyzed. This can be done spatially – the directory the content is in may be related to the download directory of an application - or temporally – the file time on the content may correlate to a chat session, browsing session, or other activity. Additional files located in the same folder or acquired at the same time may provide further clues as to the original source of the content and the application used to acquire it. The file and folder names identified can be used as keyword search terms to determine if they appear in any logfiles, as part of any cache, or as part of an email message.
- **Bookend Analysis.** Similar to a transfer analysis, a bookend analysis looks for non-offending behavior that occurred immediately before and immediately after acquiring, creating, or viewing illicit content. Showing that the subject checked their email immediately before downloading child pornography, and logged in to Facebook immediately afterward can help to show that the download was not due to malware or attributable to another individual at the keyboard.
- **Image and Folder Name Analysis.** The names that a subject puts on folders can provide direct evidence that they were aware of the folder's contents. Names like "Good Pixxx" or "CP Movies" are indicators that the subject selected specific images and movies to store at a particular location. Sometimes, subjects may even break

down their images by age or preference – there is no limit to the taxonomical lengths subject may go to in cataloging their collections. On the other hand, subjects that are trying to conceal their collection may put it in a folder that is labeled innocuously – "Misc" or "Personal Stuff" are common choices. This is more likely to occur on shared machines or on external labels on devices that are accessible to others in the household. Image names should be reviewed as well – renaming images is fairly common, especially with the lengthy image names present on many peer-to-peer downloads. The choices the subject makes in renaming images can provide insight into what they consider the important feature of each image. Subjects may label them by perceived quality, by age, or by the series name. Each provides a different insight into the subject's personality and should be noted.

- **Most Recent Files.** The most recent file times will show the activities that the subject was conducting just prior to their device being seized. The times may show the last time a device was accessed (or shutdown), the activities that the subject was conducting, and the content that they viewed. Logfile times can be correlated with the file times to show what network activities and users are associated with a particular piece of content. In addition to general file times, all MRU lists, including folders containing shortcuts to recent documents, should be reviewed.
- **Session Analysis.** Session analysis looks at a particular computer usage session, from the time the subject logs on to the time the subject shuts down. It can also look at an application-level session, reviewing the progressive browsing history of a subject or the flow of a chat session. Looking at a discrete session can show how an individual transitioned from one application to another, for example a subject that went from an IRC chat room to a private conversation over IM. Additionally, it can show how a subject acquired content and what content they were interested in. For subjects that are primarily viewers of child pornography, the last content viewed in any particular session is likely to be the content that they masturbated to.
- **Largest Files.** As a final analysis step, the investigator should sort the file system contents by logical file size and review the largest files present. These may be hidden encryption containers, virtual hard disks, large archives, or other content of interest. Although many of these should be picked up by automated forensic software, a double check of any unusually large files is a quick step and generally warranted.

While many procedures involve obtaining the system time for devices that have processing power at the time of acquisition, this may not always be possible. Showing in the system logs that the system time has not changed, and correlating activities on the device with known times from subpoena returns can provide corroboration of times, as can fragments from the Internet cache that store server times. If it is possible to do so without altering the evidence, the system time can be obtained from a computer after the drive has been removed, and on other devices upon startup as part of the imaging process.

Dictionary Generation

As a final step toward breaking encryption, the analyst may need to generate a custom dictionary of all of the strings present on a device, or on all devices belonging to the subject. This can be done in a manual fashion using Linux commands like *strings*, or by using automated tools like bulk_extractor. Once the custom dictionary is generated, it can be used with the Passware suite or with packages like DNA and PRTK from AccessData to generate permutations on the custom wordlists to attempt to break more complex passwords associated with encrypted volumes.

Final Steps

The basic analyses above will provide a thorough forensic review for most child pornography cases. Obtaining the information that is forensically available is only one step in the process, however. A decision must be made regarding the disposition of the evidence, and the results of the analysis must be mapped to the elements of a criminal statute to prove (or disprove) the allegations. Finally, the information must be put together in a format that can be effectively presented in court as needed.

Disposition of potential evidence is decision that needs to be made in conjunction with the prosecutor's office. There are generally three categories that evidence can be placed into following analysis – irrelevant, potentially relevant, and relevant. The determination and disposition guidance varies based on what category the evidence falls within:

- **Irrelevant Evidence.** Evidence that, following analysis, provides no information that is either inculpatory or exculpatory, is irrelevant. This can include drives that have never been used, devices that belong to another individual but were present when a search was executed, or computers without storage devices. Additionally, devices where the analysis shows no evidence of child pornography activity nor ties the subject to other relevant activity (e.g. showing the subject accessing an email account that was later used to trade child pornography) are irrelevant. These should be returned to the subject as soon as possible.
- **Potentially Relevant Evidence.** While any evidence has some potential of being relevant "in the future", potentially relevant evidence is evidence whose relevance may not be able to be immediately determined. This includes encrypted drives, damaged media, and devices that require specialized skillsets not readily available to analyze fully. The determination about whether or not to retain potentially relevant evidence will depend on the likelihood of ever analyzing the evidence and the strength of the case without the evidence. In a strong case, or in the event that resources are never likely to be available for an advanced analysis such as rebuilding a damaged drive platter, the evidence should be returned. The exception is encrypted devices – these should be retained as a "closed container" until the subject is willing to provide the decryption key or the case has been fully tried and appealed.
- **Relevant Evidence.** Relevant evidence is information that is directly used to support a criminal case. In general, relevant evidence must be retained throughout the trial and through any appeals period. Investigators should request written permission from the prosecutor to dispose of this evidence. Because any devices containing contraband cannot be returned to the subject, disposal may include asset forfeiture, abandonment (if part of a plea agreement), or wiping of a drive (if possible) and returning it to the subject or their designee.

In non-child pornography cases, drive images can be retained in lieu of the physical hardware and still meet the requirements of best-evidence. This is frequently done when business computers are seized and innocent parties are disadvantaged as a result. Unfortunately, contraband cannot be legally turned over to a third party, precluding the image-and-return option in most child pornography cases. A key exception is the scenario where a subject consents to imaging and not seizure and a warrant is not readily obtainable. In these cases, the investigator should make reasonable efforts to carve out files identified by the third party as relevant to their business and return copies to them.

Drive images may also need to be made and placed on an analysis machine for the defense to view as part of discovery obligations. Most jurisdictions will not permit defense attorneys to retain contraband, even temporarily, and appropriate procedures for their own experts to conduct a review will be negotiated between defense counsel, the prosecutor, and the judge.

In many child pornography cases, the subjects will make special requests to return their devices or to obtain access to specific files on a device. Whenever possible, the investigator should endeavor to return copies of files or data from devices that are not contraband. Doing so generates goodwill with the subject as well as the court, which may be helpful if there is a suppression hearing. Additionally, the subject's criminal activities have likely made their life very difficult – assistance in providing tax information, telephone contacts, or business documents is a small price to pay to keep them from becoming desperate and causing harm to themselves or others.

In addition to the technical reports generated by forensic analysts, the investigator may be required to put the information in context for the purposes of writing a criminal complaint or obtaining a follow-on warrant. Putting information in context may require the analyst to perform additional forensics work, or may require taking the analysis and putting it together with other non-digital evidence. Examples of contextually meaningful data points to show may include:

- Showing that the most frequent websites the subject visits are those dealing with child pornography (requires analyzing non-relevant web activity).
- Identifying the percentage of pornography in the subject's possession that is child pornography (requires estimating the amount of adult pornography using a repeatable methodology).
- Showing that the subject explicitly encrypted, secured, or hid their child pornography collection (requires showing that they did not take similar actions with other content).
- Linking statements the subject made in an interview to the forensic analysis to confirm or refute them.

Finally, court presentation must be considered as part of the digital forensics process. While most subjects in child pornography cases opt for a bench trial if available, jury trials do occur. Most courts will not permit actual images of child pornography to be shown, both because they are prejudicial and because they potentially victimize jurors. In these cases, detailed physical descriptions of the contents of key images and movies may be worthwhile to generate. In other cases, booting an image of the subject's drives in a virtual machine environment may be helpful in generating screenshots of directory structures, filenames, or chat sessions that can be shown as court exhibits. Even though the forensic report may detail the same information, a picture can be worth a thousand words.

Part

3

Interviewing and Interrogation

9 INTERVIEWING CHILD PORNOGRAPHY SUBJECTS

The only winning move is not to play.
John Badham, *War Games*

There are many techniques for interviewing available, and multi-volume book series dedicated to the subject interview, sometimes called an interrogation or a confrontational interview, have been written. This book is not a replacement for an in-depth interviewing course, and an interviewing course is not a replacement for on-the-job training. Reid offers an excellent nine-step framework for interviewing, while the Federal Law Enforcement Training Center (FLETC) provides a five-step process that covers both subject and non-subject interviews. This book incorporates many of the concepts from these techniques and applies them to the specific area of child pornography subject interviews.

While many child pornography cases are made based on digital forensics, obtaining a confession from the subject is always advantageous. In addition to providing details not available forensically, the confession can show intent and preclude future defenses, such as the previously noted SODDI defense. To obtain the greatest chance of success, extensive preparation by the individuals involved in the questioning is necessary. Using information obtained while planning for the interview, the successful investigator will build rapport with the subject, and elicit both behavioral and informational responses to questions about the offense. Following the questioning, the investigator will use a series of themes to obtain an admission, which will then be expanded into a confession.

Conducting a subject interview is broken down into five separate chapters. These are not meant to be discrete steps. Instead they are general components of the interview process. The chapters are as follows:

- **Planning.** Planning is the process of obtaining all information possible about both a subject and their alleged criminal actions prior to the interview. The information gathered may include everything from general background on the subject to psychographic details that will be used to develop themes to in-depth information on the specifics of the criminal behavior. Planning will ultimately inform the setting, players, and structure of the interview, as well as define a set of goals for what information needs to be obtained. Additionally, planning involves making a threat assessment of the subject.

- **Rapport**. Building rapport with a subject is critical in obtaining a confession. Setting the tone for a situation where a subject is willing to share details about their most intimate and embarrassing activities is not easy, and requires both time and dedication on the part of the interviewer. Rapport building begins with the introduction and continues throughout the interview. In a good interview, the interviewer obtains a detailed confession. In a great interview, the interviewer obtains a confession and the subject shakes their hand afterward.
- **Questioning**. Questioning is the elicitation of behavioral and informational actions from the subject. Behavioral analysis looks at both verbal and non-verbal responses to questions. Informational analysis looks at the content of the responses to establish factual details about the crime and to obtain data that can be used to further build rapport and develop likely themes.
- **Theme Development**. Inbau and Reid identify themes as attempts by the investigator to Rationalize, Project, or Minimize (RPM) the subject's actions. More simply, themes are stories the investigator tells the subject in an effort to provide them a reason for their actions that they are comfortable with and can agree to for why they committed a criminal act. Unlike questioning, where the interviewer is mostly listening, theme development consists mostly of the interviewer talking and can require the interviewer to sustain an extensive monologue. Ultimately, theme development seeks to obtain an admission from the subject based one or more of the scenarios presented by the interviewer.
- **Confession**. Many interviews stop with an admission, which is an acknowledgement of an action and may be as simple as a head nod to a question. A confession is a detailed account of a subject's actions, and uses multiple techniques to expand upon the initial admission. In a successful confession, details that map to all elements of a particular criminal statute and corroborating information on the subject's actions are obtained, preferably in writing.

Child pornography subject interviews differ from interviews of other criminal offenders. Because of the technology components inevitably involved, planning becomes very important. Rapport building is even more essential than other interviews, and may require additional time commitment. Developing questions specific to the offense for both the identification of likely themes and the locking in of the offender's actions requires technical and subject matter expertise. The rationalizations that are used tend to be viewed incredulously by the novice interviewer, and may require a suspension of disbelief when first theming subjects to understand that they work. Finally, confessions require elements unique to the individual statutes to be effective in court.

10 INTERVIEW PLANNING

Plans are worthless, but planning is everything.
Dwight D. Eisenhower

Preparing for the interview involves building questions around the information already obtained forensically. It also involves determining the time and place of the questioning, the individuals that will be involved in the questioning, and the tone and atmospherics of the interview. While some of the factors noted below may be pre-determined – for example, an individual who is stopped by Customs and Border Protection when entering the country potentially limits the location and time to prepare – thinking through the additional factors will greatly increase the chances of obtaining a confession.

Forensic Information

Forensic information includes information obtained as part of the initial complaint, information obtained during the digital analysis, information obtained from forensic interviews of witnesses, and any information obtained concurrent with the questioning. The information obtained forensically prior to (and during) the questioning should be used in three ways – as part of building an offender profile, as a driver to obtain the answers to questions that have arisen during the analysis, and as corroboration for any statements made by the offender.

Offender Profile

Building an accurate profile of the offender is critical in determining the interview approach. The profile should include both demographic and psychographic information, and will drive several of the decision points noted in the following sections.

Demographic Information

The bulk of the information for the demographic profile of the offender will have been obtained from research performed prior to the interview. Information obtained from DMV records, NCIC reports, Choicepoint/Lexis-Nexis reporting, reconnaissance of the residence, and similar sources will provide information on the offender including the following:

- **Sex and Gender**. While the overwhelming majority of child pornography subjects are male, there are both solo female offenders and female co-offenders. One possible consideration for female subjects may be the use of a female interrogator and/or a co-ed team.
- **Age**. As with sex and gender, the age of the offender may introduce considerations with respect to the age of the interviewers. While young offenders can be interviewed by either youthful or more mature investigators, possibly with two different approaches, having a more mature investigator present may help in developing rapport with older offenders.
- **Marital Status.** Potentially the single most important factor in deciding on an interview approach is the subject's marital/relationship status. If the offender has a significant other, the key decision point is whether or not to interview the offender when the significant other is accessible. There are generally two possibilities - doing a simultaneous interview or setting the interview for a time or place where the significant other is absent. Barring a specific reason for doing a simultaneous interview (e.g. co-offender possibility), separating the offender is generally the better approach.
- **Family Situation**. The presence of children or other family members is generally a detriment to the interview. If children or non-significant-other adults are present in the household, the interview should be scheduled for a time when they are not in the residence, or if possible the offender should be removed from the residence for the interview.
- **Employment Status**. Whether or not a subject is gainfully employed effects the hours of the day that they are likely to be home and online. If the goal is to catch a subject while they are actively engaged in criminal activity, individuals with full daytime employment may be better targeted during the mid-evening, whereas the afternoon may be better for those who are unemployed. Psychosocial concerns related to employment are noted below.
- **Socioeconomic Status**. The socioeconomic standing of the offender has a direct impact on the questions asked regarding the scope and nature of their crimes. Indigent individuals using a library system to access child pornography are unlikely to take frequent sex tourism trips to Thailand. Conversely, the wealthy individual with high end computer equipment is more likely to have access to digital production capabilities that are not available to the library browser.
- **Past History with Law Enforcement**. Offenders who have been arrested for child pornography offenses in the past are more likely to take steps to hide their collection and/or employ countermeasures such as encryption. The outcome of their past charges may change their level of immediate cooperation, and an early hardline approach may be more likely to yield an early request for legal representation.

Psychographic Information

The demographic profile is closely intertwined with the psychographic profile of the offender. While less empirical than the demographic profile, information obtained in emails, chat logs, usage history and from other forensic interviews can help build rapport and drive the sophistication level of questions and the types of questions asked.

Information obtained for rapport building can include religious affiliations, places lived, favorite sports teams, hobbies, or just about any other information of personal interest found in the forensic research. This can be ascertained from the websites visited by the subject, postings to online forums, and information from those who know the subject. The use of rapport building information can be as direct as asking an avid gamer about their online gaming preferences, or as subtle as wearing a necktie with the insignia of a favorite sports team. If a subject exhibits true expertise in an area where the investigator has little knowledge, the subject may "see through" any superficial knowledge the investigator may have obtained with basic research. In these cases, simply professing no knowledge and asking the subject about a topic of interest may be an effective strategy. The use of this information is covered extensively in Chapter 11.

Equally important to psychographic information obtained to build rapport is the identification of potential hot-button areas to be avoided. If the subject posts to a chat room bemoaning the outsourcing of positions to other countries after losing his job to a foreign worker, extolling the virtues of globalization is unlikely to win any rapport points. Similarly, if an individual exhibits strong views in an area that is not likely to be useful in the interrogation phase, the risk of raising tensions may outweigh the benefits of using that topic for rapport-building.

The psychographic information may also be used to formulate specific interrogation themes. If the subject is exceptionally proud of their military career, themes surrounding "What would you do if one of your soldiers told you they made a mistake?" may be relevant, whereas an individual with strong religious convictions may warrant the use of a theme surrounding sin and forgiveness, though a distinction must be made between moral and legal "forgiveness".

One piece of psychographic information that is critical to obtaining a confession is the opinion of the subject toward child pornography. A subject that is a member of NAMBLA or bemoans the unfairness of age of consent laws in emails is unlikely to view their actions as "wrong". Themes regarding mistakes or uncontrollable urges are unlikely to be successful in these cases. On the other hand, sympathetic themes will be more likely to resonate with a subject that believes the views that most of society has regarding sex with children are wrong.

A final piece of psychographic information to be obtained is the sophistication of the subject in terms of general computer expertise, existing laws, and the child pornography subculture. The levels of sophistication should will drive the level of questions asked and may impact the interrogation themes utilized.

Computer expertise may be one of the easiest characteristics to assess based on online profiles. A poor assumption is that a subject who uses a computer to obtain child pornography is knowledgeable about computers and/or networks in general. The level of expertise present in subjects varies tremendously from barely computer literate subjects who are able to browse and view child pornography without any deeper understanding to the technical wizards who may run custom software and employ the latest-and-greatest encryption. Assessing computer expertise can be done by looking at the software used, the content of any postings on forums or message boards, and the level of online presence and specific sites visited.

The software the subject uses can be indicative of expertise-level – an individual who is using an obscure Linux build with a less common browser is likely more sophisticated than the user utilizing the default version of Safari on Mac OS X or Internet Explorer on Windows 8. Additionally, a subject who downloads hardening scripts for their operating system, anti-malware scanners, and whole drive encryption software is generally more sophisticated than a subject using an iPad with only the default applications installed.

Postings to message boards and forums can give a good indication of an individual's abilities – specifically if they are technology-related. An individual posting to the iTunes message board is likely to be using an Apple ecosystem. Similarly, a posting to a forum asking about tweaking the registry in Windows 8 is likely to indicate a Windows ecosystem user. The level of expertise in the post and/or questions asked will provide a rough estimate of the computer experience of the subject. Likewise, the age of the oldest post found may indicate the number of years the subject has spent online.

The breadth of the subject's online presence is a good indicator of their ability to navigate cyberspace. Does the subject have multiple profiles on Facebook, Twitter and Google+? Is the subject frequently posting to message boards and running a blog? Does the person have a Second Life account and play multiple online games? While not necessarily indicative of computer expertise, online presence may indicate the likelihood an individual is making virtual contact with children.

Assessing computer expertise will drive the phrasing of questions and the level of technical questions asked. Asking questions that are too complex may confuse novice users. As an example, consider the following three ways to ask a subject about their home network:

- **Novice**. Do you connect your computer to the Internet over your cable, over the phone line, or wirelessly? Who do you buy your Internet from?
- **Average**. Do you have a wired Ethernet network at home, a Wi-Fi network, or do you still use dial-up? Who is your provider?
- **Expert**. Do you run 802.11n or are you still on 802.11g? Do you also have a wired switch for high-speed transfers or gaming? Do you have your own router or use the one your provider gave you?

If the level of computer expertise cannot be determined a priori, questions to assess the level of expertise can be employed during the informational questioning stage of the interview.

Similar to technical knowledge, the legal knowledge of the individual being questioned can drive the questioning approach used and the themes presented.

First time offenders may not even realize that downloading child pornography is illegal. They may believe that producing it is illegal, or that selling it is illegal, but may not be aware that simple access or possession is against the law. Additionally, they may not realize the legal age limit is 18 years old and may believe it is younger, consistent with state-specific consent laws. Finally, they may not realize that actions performed overseas may have legal implications domestically, for example the fact that bringing into the United States a computer that they used in another country to download child pornography constitutes an importation offense. A low level of legal knowledge can suggest themes such as "If you had known it wasn't allowed, your wouldn't have downloaded those images" or "It wasn't like you were selling the images, you were just giving them to a few friends at their request" or "You never downloaded any of the images in this country – you only downloaded them when you were overseas where it is culturally acceptable".

Any individual who has been previously convicted of a child pornography offense should be assumed to have at least a modicum of knowledge about the offense for which they were convicted, but not necessarily other offenses. They are more likely to ask for a lawyer up-front. Because they have had at least one prior experience with law enforcement, their previous interaction may reduce their likelihood of signing a consent form to search their systems. With any prior convictions specifically for child pornography offenses, the investigator should assume the subject has taken at least minor steps to obfuscate their actions, to include the use of encryption and the physical hiding of their collection.

Question Formation and Statement Confirmation

Generally, information obtained during the preparatory stages will generate more questions than answers. The questions developed from the preliminary work should be used to drive informational and behavioral questions and to provide confirmation of known facts to solidify any confessions obtained.

Informational questions will include a positive confirmation by the subject of all accounts and activities identified in the preparation, starting with the innocuous – "Is xyz@mail.com your email address?" and going through to the direct – "When was the last time you downloaded movies depicting minors from xyz.com?". A list of all relevant accounts and activities can be generated from the preparation material, then used to elicit further detail during the interview.

Behavioral questions generated from the preparation work should include an assessment of the subject's response to information gathered. This can be as simple as asking the subject what PTHC means, assuming they used that search term, or which adult sites they believe are most likely to contain child pornography.

Confirmation information is data that is withheld during the questioning for the purpose of assessing the veracity of the subject's statements. If the subject has half a dozen known handles on a teen chat board, asking the subject to list his accounts will provide two pieces of information. First, it will provide behavioral clues, based on whether or not the subject lists all of the already known accounts. Second, it will confirm the quality of the information obtained. Are all the accounts identified by the subject? Do they identify more? Fewer? Having the subject identify a specific account without prompting provides the interrogator confirmation of ownership and may be helpful in the event of a suppression hearing further along in the legal process.

Interview Setting

The setting of the interview is likely to be one of two locations – the site of the offense, whether a residence or an office, or an interview room at the investigating agency. The choice between the two will generally be dictated by the decision to concurrently execute a warrant, the desire to catch the subject in the act, and the safety of other parties that may be present.

Knock-and-Talk

The most common scenario for a home-based interview is affectionately known as the knock-and-talk. When a subject is identified, but the identifying information is stale or otherwise unusable in an affidavit for a search and/or arrest warrant, the investigators will frequently arrive at the subject's home and request an interview and to do a consensual search of the premises and any computer equipment therein.

The knock-and-talk is best executed when the subject is expected to be alone. If there are other family members in the household, they represent additional barriers to the subject being candid. Fear of their family discovering their crimes may be greater than the fear of going to jail, and as such the likelihood of a confession diminishes. Additionally, other members of the household present logistical and security concerns for investigators and require additional investigative personnel to handle.

If a knock-and-talk cannot be arranged when other household members are not around, consideration should be given to approaching the subject outside the home. Asking the subject to accompany investigators to a neutral but private location such as a nearby hotel room may yield a successful outcome. In all likelihood, the subject will not want their family to hear the allegations, and will go willingly. While a simultaneous preview of digital media is largely precluded in these situations, consent can frequently be obtained off-premises if the investigators are willing to be discrete when entering the subject's home and flexible in avoiding familial conflict. A basic approach of telling the subject that investigators would like to discuss a "sensitive issue" regarding their Internet usage in private will appeal to and be successful with many subjects.

Home Interviews

There are both advantages and disadvantages to interviewing a subject in their home. When interviewing the subject at their home, they will be on "their turf" and will generally feel slightly more confident during questioning. Additionally, in the case of a knock-and-talk, the situation may dictate the use of certain rooms of the house based on the subject's comfort and not that of the investigators. On the advantageous side, evidence of the subject's actions may be immediately at-hand, and consent can be easier to obtain. Finally, though both an advantage and a disadvantage, the subject may feel they are working against the clock if a spouse of other household member is expected to return at a later point.

Safety is of a higher concern in home interviews. Home interviews should always start with a confirmation that the subject is the only one at home. Especially in a non-custodial knock-and-talk scenario, clearing the home and doing a pat-down on the subject may not be options. At a minimum, investigators should note the possible entrances and exits to the area of the home where the interview will take place, and know the outside entrance locations from prior reconnaissance. All home interviews should be conducted with at least two investigators present. If possible, having an additional investigator stationed outside will provide a measure of protection from unintended entrants for safety purposes and help to avoid unwanted interruptions.

The location of the interview in the home is not as flexible as that in an office. Depending on the layout of the home, investigators can ask to talk in an area where both parties can sit in private, with the added benefit of seeing more of the home when navigating to that area. In addition to safety-related concerns, investigators should note any visible digital devices when walking between rooms. Investigators may be able to have the offenders show them more rooms in their home by requesting to use the restroom or to be provided a glass of water. If these steps are taken, the investigators should always ensure the subject is not left unaccompanied at any point.

Office Interviews

Interviews conducted in an investigative office should be performed in a private room with minimal distractions. Clocks, paintings, and other wall-hangings should be removed as they provide something for the subject to focus on instead of the interviewer. If monitoring equipment is used, it should be unobtrusive and not provide a distraction to either the subject or to the investigator.

In an office interview, it will need to be established directly whether or not it is a custodial interview. If the interview is custodial, or could even potentially be perceived as custodial, a Miranda warning must be given. If the interview is non-custodial, the investigator should establish clearly with the subject that they are free to leave at any point. Ample restroom breaks should be offered and a drink provided to the subject in either case.

The office interview will likely have a higher tension level for the subject than a home interview. Additionally, the office interview will allow the interrogator to leave the subject alone at strategic points before and during questioning with relative safety, and to control the subject's access to electronic resources.

While the environment is controlled in the office interview, care must be taken to ensure the subject does not bring anything into the interview which may be either disruptive or dangerous. The subject should be searched for weapons prior to the interview, and if the subject has a cell phone or other mobile device they should be asked to turn them off and place them in a secure location outside the room, ideally in a locked cabinet to which the subject is provided the key. Mobile devices have the potential to disrupt the interview with incoming calls or may cause inadvertent recording of the proceedings. The devices that are secured can be provided back to the subject at any time if the investigator wants to provide the subject with a means of making a phone call. Any digital equipment found on the subject should be fodder for a consent search later in the interview.

If there is no convenient office for the investigator to conduct the interview near the subject's location and other investigative agencies are unable to provide space, a hotel room can be used. If the budget permits it, a small suite with a sitting area is ideal for the interview setting, and the room should be staged prior to the subject's arrival. Under no circumstances should the room be the same room the investigator is actually staying in when conducting an out-of-area interview – ideally it should not even be located in the same hotel.

Ideally, the primary interviewer will sit closest to the door in either setting to provide for officer safety. The second interviewer, if two are present, should sit outside the line of sight of the subject. Despite the presence of a table separating the interviewer from the interviewee in most television crime dramas, anything between the investigator and the subject presents a symbolic barrier separating the two parties. One of the primary goals during the interview is rapport building, and anything contributing to an "us v. them" implied separation, such as tables or desks, should be avoided.

Interview Participants

The use of a single interviewer or two interviewers is almost always a matter of policy. If given the option, there are benefits and drawbacks to both setups.

The single interviewer provides a more intimate environment, and is more conducive to the subject making admissions – it is easier to admit a crime to one person rather than multiple people. Given the sensitivity of the subject matter in child pornography cases, this can be a distinct advantage. Additionally, a single interviewer provides fewer distractions for the subject, and prevents a more seasoned subject from playing the interviewers against each other.

Having a second interviewer enhances the safety of the situation. The second interviewer is able to take notes, allowing the primary interviewer to focus on behavioral cues. In the event that the primary interviewer cannot build rapport with the subject or needs a break in the session, the second interviewer can take over. A seasoned primary interviewer can use the second interviewer for confirmation in themes as needed, but this requires the interviewers be experienced in working as a team. Finally, the second interviewer may see or hear something the primary interviewer might have missed, allowing for a more thorough interview. For non-recorded interviews, a second interviewer can provide corroboration in court of any statements made by the subject. If there are two interviewers present, they should confirm ahead of time the protocol for taking notes – ideally only the second interviewer takes notes for the record and the primary interviewer only makes notations for use in the interview itself.

Many of the advantages of both setups can be achieved through the use of active monitoring of the interview. This can be through two-way glass or through a CCTV setup. Having a second, or even a third, investigator monitor the interview remotely allows for the intimacy of a single interviewer scenario while providing the safety and situational benefits of a two person interview.

In a two person interview, the team must discuss roles and responsibilities beforehand. Ideally, the interviewers can bounce ideas off each other for potential themes and approaches before the interview. If a single person interview is planned, the interviewer should seek out another experienced investigator to bounce ideas off of. Even if the interviewer is experienced, the act of verbalizing an approach can generate additional thoughts that lead to improvements to the plan.

Both interview participants should have familiarity with child pornography cases and know the modus operandi of child pornography subjects. The interviewers must be comfortable talking explicitly about the subject matter, and maintain a calm appearance no matter what the subject confesses to.

Ideally, department policy permitting, the interviewers should dress casually but professionally for the interview. The use of the black suit and white shirt or the wearing of an official uniform serves as a reminder to the subject of the criminal justice system and creates the us v. them atmosphere that interviewers want to avoid. A good target for dress code would be that of a professional therapist or a social worker. Visible firearms, badges, raid jackets and other reminders of the law enforcement status of the interviewers should be avoided where the situation allows.

Interviewers should be well hydrated, and not be taking any medications that may interfere with their cognitive state. Getting a good night's sleep beforehand, and freeing up sufficient time for the interview are also necessary for success – an interviewer that is "watching the clock" because of a later engagement will not be as effective.

11 RAPPORT

The secret of success is sincerity. Fake that and you're in.
Unknown, but frequently attributed to Groucho Marx

If there is one area that novice interviewers have the most difficulty with, and spend the least time on, it is rapport building. Rapport building is a critical skill for achieving successful interview results. Rather than being a discrete stage in the interview process, rapport building starts before the interview and continues after the interview is concluded. If the investigator achieves rapport successfully, the subject will shake their hand at the beginning of the interview and then shake it again at the end of the interview – even after confessing to serious violations of law.

Rapport building is a gradual process. Like any other interpersonal interaction, allowing the subject to feel comfortable enough to discuss intimate sexual details with the interviewer takes time and patience. A subject that comes in wanting to confess still needs to feel comfortable, and a reticent subject needs to be brought to the point where they are more comfortable sharing the details of their criminal actions with the interviewer than they are withholding them. This is not to imply that the interviewer attempt to become friends with the subject – only that they show understanding to the point necessary for the confession.

Pre-interview

In the preparation phase, everything that can be learned about the subject that will help build rapport should be explored. This includes any life stressors, areas of commendation, interests and hobbies, or areas of prejudice.

Life Stressors

Life stressors include financial hardships, changes in relationship status, loss of a job, death of a loved one, or any other proximal event that could cause the subject to experience stress. These should be noted for use in theme development, but are also important for building rapport. If the interviewer has had or can relate to a specific life stressor that is commonly known about the subject, that can become an early topic of conversation. If the life stressor isn't commonly known, for example gambling losses that the investigator finds out about through FinCEN checks, it can become a question in the interview to allow the subject the chance to provide the information. It can also become the topic of a theme the interviewer uses - "I was interviewing another guy who had made all of the right choices in life, then got in a bind due to some bad luck..."

Life stressors may also provide areas and/or topics in which the subject needs reassurance before an admission will be made. A subject that is going through relationship problems may be more concerned about a spouse finding out about their child pornography issues than about going to prison. A skilled interviewer can make use of these issues and build rapport with the subject at the same time - "What you tell me I write down and provide to the decision makers. What you tell your loved ones is between you and them."

Finding the Good

A frequently overlooked but critical step in building rapport is finding the good in the subject. This is often the most difficult step for the interviewer. It is very easy to vilify a person producing child pornography and molesting their own children. Though a monolithic view of a subject is easy to take – that the subject is wholly evil – even the most horrific subject has some good aspect or good deed they have performed at some point in their life. Finding positives in a subject that they can be proud of is one of the most important steps in rapport building. Not only does it provide theme material, it allows the interviewer to see the subject as a human being and find common ground on which they can relate to them.

Areas to look for in finding the good include family life, work history, military service, and community service. The investigator should look for things that the subject may perceive to be positive aspects of their life and personality – the truth of whether they are or are not is irrelevant. As an example, an employee with mediocre performance reviews at their job that cites their laziness may view themselves as underappreciated – the interviewer should go with their perception and not the reality.

For family life, the subject may be taking care of a spouse, an elder, a child, or another family member. This can be both a stressor and an area of commendation - "I know how hard it is to take care of an elderly parent – I don't know how you do it." The commendation need not be based on the current situation either. Successfully raising children or caring for long-dead parents can be areas of pride. Any family member that loves the subject is an additional source of pride and can be exploited. Any time a subject swears on their mother's life, that is a clue for the interviewer that their mother's opinion of them is important.

Work history can include paid work, education, or volunteer work, depending on the circumstances. Any significant time spent at a particular organization is a matter that can be brought up as a positive – "25 years at the same firm is commendable – you don't see that kind of loyalty in this generation". Awards received or recent promotions can be highlighted. Even an employee with a lackluster record may view themselves as undervalued, and any positives from performance reviews can be pulled out, even if surrounded by negatives. Statements such as "Several of your co-workers had positive things to say about you" or "It looks like they may not have utilized your talents to their fullest – everyone talks about your high potential" will appeal to just about anyone's self-image. Alternatively, any indication that an employee has not been promoted recently, has not received a raise, or was passed over for a position can be used later during the interrogation phase.

Military service is almost always something an individual will be proud of, and something they should be commended for. If the subject had a military record, unless there was a dishonorable discharge, that can be used in the rapport phase. A skilled interviewer should always thank a subject for their service to their country at the outset if their military record is brought up. If the interviewer has served in a similar capacity, that can be the basis for forming a bond as well. Although bluffing is a viable strategy in other interview phases, an interviewer should never bluff about their military service.

Community service can take just about any form, from being a scout leader or organizing a neighborhood watch to running blood drives. The act of giving back to the community should be highlighted as a positive, even if the interviewer believes the subject took the position for less-than-admirable reasons (e.g. to obtain easier access to children). Any public commendation should be highlighted when going through the positives in the subject's life.

In addition to the review of material from the planning stage, there are a few items that can be done immediately prior to the interview to assist in rapport building. First, the interview room should have an adequate supply of tissues for potential later use. Second, the interviewer should have a bottle of water ready to provide to the subject. Finally, the interviewer should have funds available to use in the interview for the vending machine or for a cup of coffee for the subject as needed.

Interview

First impressions are said to have a lasting effect in social settings, and interviews are no different. The introduction of the interviewer to the subject and the first questions asked depend on the setting of the interview. There are four primary scenarios that are likely to be encountered:

- **Scenario 1.** The interview occurs at the subject's residence or place of business as part of a knock-and-talk.
- **Scenario 2.** The interview occurs at the subject's residence or place of business as part of a search warrant execution.
- **Scenario 3.** The interview occurs in a law enforcement interview room where the subject has come in voluntarily.
- **Scenario 4.** The interview occurs in a law enforcement interview room where the subject is under arrest.

For all of the scenarios, the interviewer will greet the subject, shake their hand, and ask after them. The specifics for each scenario differ based on the environment – it does not make sense to thank an individual for coming in if they have just been arrested in a forceful manner, nor does it make sense to offer a drink to a subject during a knock-and-talk. The initial greeting should not include any questions regarding the case, as the appropriate rights warnings have not been given.

Scenario 1

In the first scenario, the primary interviewer should be the first person that the subject sees, and if a second investigator is present they should introduce themselves after the primary. The key first step in a knock-and-talk is getting the subject to allow you into their residence or place of business, and to begin a dialog. The primary interview should always introduce themselves and not wait for the subject to say anything, and should pace the dialog so that the subject is not provided an opportunity to jump into the conversation until after the initial statements are made. An ideal dialog would go something like this:

- **Primary**: Is Mr. Jones at home?
- **Subject**: I'm Mr. Jones.
- **Primary**: Good afternoon Mr. Jones, my name is detective Bishop <shows credentials in left hand>, <offers right hand while talking> and this is detective Carter <offers right hand>. We are looking into some issues with open wireless access points in the area, and were hoping you could help us out. Is there someplace we could talk in private?
- **Subject**: What is this all about?
- **Primary**: We just have a small matter related to some wireless Internet traffic coming out of this area, and are talking to people in the area looking to rule out potential homes as the source. Hopefully this won't take more than a little bit of your time. Are you willing to help us out?
- **Subject**: Sure.

The opening dialog plays as a mini-theme, and serves to accomplish four things. First, the interviewer establishes who they are for the subject and why they are ostensibly there. Second, the interviewer sets the tone by asserting control in a non-confrontational way. Third, the interviewer offers up the questions as a way of "ruling out" homes - who wouldn't want to be ruled out? Finally, the interviewer solicits help from the subject – requesting their cooperation and obtaining the first affirmative response. While the interviewers are there primarily to determine the subject's involvement in child pornography, providing the details of what the wireless network misuse consists of can and should wait until the questioning begins in earnest.

After the interviewer enters the home, they should be on the lookout for anything that indicates a hobby or interest of the subject. Paying a compliment to the subject's home or furnishings can go a long way. Even better, asking about a piece of art, a classic car, or an unusual plant can be a way of getting the subject talking about something positive. Most people like to hear themselves talk, and if the interviewer appears interested and engaged it can start the interview on the right foot. This should always be used lightly, however. Nothing comes across as more insincere than a "How 'bout them Mets?" question that comes from out of the blue.

Scenario 2

Building rapport with a subject who just had their house entered as part of a search warrant is an uphill battle. Generally, breaching a door and restraining a subject is not getting things off on the right foot, but it may be an operational necessity. Despite the less-than-ideal situation from a rapport standpoint, there are a few things the interviewer can do to set the stage better.

First, on any search warrant, the interviewer should not be part of the entry team and should not be one of the individuals that initially secure the subject. Individuals on the entry team should limit their questioning of the subject to three things – announcing the warrant, establishing their identity, and identifying any immediate threats to the team executing the warrant such as other people in the house, weapons, or logistical security issues. Once the house is secure and an area cleared for the interview, then the interview team can introduce themselves.

If operational security permits it, the interviewer should remove any restraints that are on the subject, and apologize for the abruptness of the entry – blaming standard operating procedures is a common approach. The interviewer should tell the subject that they are investigating Internet activity that originated from the subject's home, and that they would like to ask for the subject's help in doing so. A typical starting dialog may go as follows:

- **Primary**: Good morning, Mr. Jones, I'm Detective Bishop. Officer Anderson, can you take those handcuffs off of Mr. Jones? Thank you.
- **Subject**: Why was I put in handcuffs?
- **Primary**: I'm sorry about that – its standard operating procedure. I apologize if we caught you by surprise – I know that it's not pleasant to be woken up to all of this.
- **Subject**: I don't know what you are doing in my house – I didn't do anything wrong. I want all of you out. You break down my door then you put handcuffs on my like I'm a criminal - I don't understand this. Am I under arrest?
- **Primary**: Mr. Jones, you are not under arrest. Our goal is to get out of your hair as quickly as possible. To do that, I'm going to need your help. We have a warrant to look through your house for evidence of some Internet activity of interest. If you are willing to help us understand a few things, the folks out there can be on their way a lot quicker. Can I get your help with a few questions we have so that we can be done here as fast as possible?
- **Subject**: I guess so.

If the subject is initially handcuffed or otherwise secured, the interviewer will need to establish clearly with the subject that they are not under arrest, unless, of course, a simultaneous arrest warrant was issued. The subject is likely to be more confused than in the other three scenarios, and to be overwhelmed and upset by the intrusion into their residence of business. The first goal of rapport building in this scenario is to calm the subject down and to get them talking. Establishing a deeper rapport will take additional time, and requires a more patient approach. After the introductions, the interviewer can begin by asking routine questions about the location, and by asking after the welfare of the subject.

Scenario 3

The easiest scenario for the interviewer is the voluntary interview in a law enforcement interview room. The operational security concerns are lower, though the subject should still be frisked prior to the interview, and the interviewer has control over the environment. Additionally, the subject has shown a willingness to come in – indicating they are at least interested in hearing the interviewer out. Most subjects will come in with the mindset that they are going to try and find out what the interview is about and what the interviewer knows about their activities. Fortunately for the interviewer, this motivates the subject to engage in conversation and by the time the issue of child pornography comes up in earnest, the subject has ideally lost their original resolve and is responding to the interviewer's cues.

When starting an interview in this setting, the primary interviewer should greet the subject, shake their hand, and thank them for coming in to help. The secondary interviewer should additionally shake hands and introduce themselves. The primary interviewer should offer the subject something to drink, at least water, and can volunteer that they would like some as well to increase the likelihood the subject accepts. Offering a restroom break is also advantageous. In addition to helping to build rapport, the offers of a drink and a restroom break help in establishing that an interview is non-custodial. The drink also provides a possible indicator of stress for later in the interview – subjects tend to get dry mouths when they become stressed about a particular question or topic area, and may increase their water consumption during those questions.

The primary interviewer should guide the subject to a particular seat, and sit down after the subject. Showing appreciation again for them coming in a second time never hurts. A typical dialog would be as follows:

- **Primary**: Good morning Mr. Jones, I'm detective Bishop <offers right hand when talking> and this is detective Carter. Thank you very much for coming in today and agreeing to help us. Before we get started, did you need to use the restroom?
- **Subject**: I'm good.
- **Primary**: The restrooms are right around the corner if you do need them. Can I offer you a cup of coffee or some water? It's a bit dry in here and I think I need a bottle myself.
- **Subject**: Some water would be great <secondary retrieves water>.
- **Primary**: Let's move into our discussion room where we can talk. Please, have a seat <secondary hands water bottle to primary, who provides it to the subject>
- **Subject**: Thank you.
- **Primary**: We really appreciate you coming in like this on short notice. Did you have any trouble finding us?

The primary providing the water instead of the secondary is a small detail but important in establishing direct rapport. Once the introductions are complete, asking a simple question that will cause the subject to start talking in a non-confrontational manner will start off the rest of the rapport building. A good opening question for rapport in this scenario is to ask if the subject had any difficulty getting there. If the subject says yes, the interviewer can apologize for the difficulty, beginning to show empathy. If the subject says no, the interviewer can move on to further rapport building.

Scenario 4

Perhaps the most difficult scenario to build rapport is when a subject is under arrest and has been brought to the interview room in handcuffs. If possible, the arrest should be performed by officers not involved in the interviewing and interrogation.

The interviewer should introduce themselves to the subject, and similar to Scenario 2, should remove their handcuffs if safety allows. After shaking hands with the subject, the interviewer should inquire as to how they are doing. The interviewer should offer the subject the opportunity to use the restroom, and should offer to bring the subject something to eat or drink.

Unlike the first three scenarios, though it may apply in Scenario 2 depending on the specifics of the operation, an individual in custody who is going to be questioned needs to be read a Miranda warning, or even requested to sign a waiver of rights form, depending on local policy. While the Miranda warning is a tip-off to the individual that things are serious, the large amount of attention it is given in television shows and on the big screen has largely desensitized the public to the warnings. Because a significant portion of the individuals arrested for child pornography have no prior criminal history, it may be more confusing to them than to others. A typical Miranda scenario might be as follows:

- **Primary:** Good evening Mr. Jones, I'm detective Bishop. I don't think we need those cuffs on – I'm sorry they had to put them on you for transport <removes cuffs>. How are you doing, given the circumstances?
- **Subject:** I'm in a police station, how do you think I'm doing?
- **Primary:** I know this isn't easy, but I wanted to talk to you about an allegation that you had downloaded some illicit pictures of minors to see if we can't clear things up. I know they had you in here a while, do you need to use the restroom at all?
- **Subject:** I need to get out of here – this is all a big misunderstanding.
- **Primary:** I understand your frustration, sometimes things are misunderstood if viewed in the wrong way, and I want to get your help to ensure things aren't being misconstrued. Because we've brought you here, our department requires I advise you of the rights you have. More specifically, you have the right to remain silent, and anything you do or say can and will be used against you in a court of law. You have the right to be represented by an attorney. If you cannot afford one, one will be provided by you. Do you understand these rights?
- **Subject:** Do I need an attorney?
- **Primary:** I'm sorry, I can't advise you on that. I wanted to ask you a few questions to avoid any misunderstandings. I have some very basic informational questions before we get to the issue at hand.

The question about needing an attorney should be answered according to local policy, but if there is no governing regulation it is generally safe to decline to provide guidance in either direction. If the subject asks for an attorney, the questioning is over until they are provided access to counsel.

In addition to the scenarios above, if this is an internal affairs investigation the subject may need to have their Garrity rights read to them. Because their job may require them to cooperate with internal administrative investigations, the investigators must make it clear to the subject that this is a voluntary interview and that they have the right to remain silent and retain counsel, and to leave at any time. Unlike Miranda warnings, Garrity warnings apply in both custodial and non-custodial situations when the interviewer is part of or acting on behalf of a government employer.

Setting the Stage

Following the introduction, the investigator will need to set the stage for the remainder of the interview. There are two effective techniques for setting the stage that are easy to employ in any child pornography case. First, the investigator can explain to the subject what is going to happen in the interview to reduce their anxiety. Second, the interviewer can ask innocuous background questions before getting to the substance of the interview.

For many subjects of child pornography investigations, their interview will be their first real contact with law enforcement. Because of this, their anxiety level will be very high due to several factors. The subject's only view of what happens in an interview may be based on television shows. If that is the case, once they see that no one is going to pull out the phonebook they may relax a bit. Even if their procedural fears are reduced, the subject will likely retain some latent anxiety over the acts they committed and the possibility of getting caught. To combat this, the investigator can explain in general terms what will happen in the interview. A typical explanation might be:

- **Primary**: We talk to lots of people about their Internet habits. We'll be talking about some sensitive areas, and will be asking you some pointed questions. You will have every opportunity to explain any answers, and I will work with you resolve things as quickly as possible. First, I need to ask a few basic background questions, but before we get started, do you have any questions for me?

Following the explanation of what is going to happen, asking background questions will get the subject in the habit of answering questions, and allow them to bring down their guard when they see there is no hostility or judgment being reflected by the interviewer. Questions should be either biographical or relate to the subject matter at hand. Irrelevant question such as which football team is the subject's favorite or where they would like to go on vacation will be seen as a waste of time at best an a blatant attempt to curry favor at worst.

Biographic questions can include items that will help with a later risk assessment, but should not touch on the subject at hand. Typical questions might be about the marital status of the person, their living arrangements, or their employment. Because of the nature of child pornography offenses, asking about any kids the person has, or grandkids, as the situation dictates, at an early stage and before the child pornography issue is introduced can be advantageous. Additionally, asking the subject about their work history and any volunteer work may provide additional details about contact with children. If the interview takes place at the subject's home, asking how long they have lived there is a relevant and innocuous question. Similarly, asking how long they have been at their present job in a workplace interview can be helpful. Any biographical information that can provide identifiers can be asked here also. Asking how the interviewer can get back in touch with the subject following the interview not only shows the subject that the interviewer does not intend to arrest them immediately, but allows for the acquisition of cell phone numbers and email addresses.

When asking questions, the interviewer should be observing body behavior to ascertain if the subject is becoming more relaxed. Indicators that the subject is relaxing include less unnecessary body movement (e.g. fidgeting), less grooming behavior, uncrossed arms, and a comfortable posture. Once the subject has relaxed, the key informational and behavioral questions from the interview can be asked. Additional biographical questions can be included as necessary to reduce agitation, but any more that 15 or 20 biographical questions will likely have the opposite effect.

In addition to observing their body language for signs of relaxation, the investigator should note their verbal and non-verbal behavior in answering questions. This will serve as a baseline for other behavior later in the interview. Things to note include the following:

- **Non-Verbal**
  - Body Position
  - Body Rigidity
  - Posture
  - Hand Position/Movement
  - Eye Movement
  - Eye Contact
- **Verbal**
  - Speed of Speech
  - Timing of Speech, Including Pauses
  - Loudness
  - Emoting
  - Word choice
  - Verbosity

Frequently, individuals talking together will exhibit subconscious mirroring – the matching of the posture and demeanor of the person they are conversing with. The investigator should be aware of this during the rapport building and keep a calm, open demeanor in both body posture and speech.

Post-Interview

Even the best interviewer is not likely to get every single detail of all offenses the subject has committed on the first try. Further interviews of the subject may be necessary, and follow-up questions may need to be asked. Additionally, if a subject is being released or is free to go following the interview, the interviewer can ensure they leave in a mental state that would make them less likely to hurt themselves or others.

To leave the interview and maintain rapport, the interviewer should always thank the subject, even if they only provided answers that were half-truths. The interviewer should note their helpfulness and candor, and acknowledge the difficulty of talking about the subject matter of child pornography. The interviewer should set the stage for follow-up interviews by asking the subject if they can call again if they have any need for clarification. Finally, the interviewer should inform the subject that the interviewer believes they are basically a good person who may have made a few mistakes.

Before dismissing the subject, the interviewer can ask them where they intend to go, and what they intend to do immediately after leaving. If the subject appears distraught, the interviewer can assist them in identifying someone they can talk to. If the subject appears to be a threat to themselves or others, the interviewer is ethically obligated to obtain help for them, for their own good and for the good of society. A typical post-interview might go as follows:

- **Primary**: I want to thank you for answering all of our questions – I know this subject is a difficult one and we appreciate your candor. Thank you for helping us understand this matter. Your honesty tells me that you are basically a good person who may have made a few mistakes, and it's natural for good people to feel a bit drained and to beat themselves up unnecessarily. Now that you've helped us, where do you think you'll head to?
- **Subject**: I don't know. I don't know.
- **Primary**: We generally recommend you think of someone you can go talk to - a trusted friend, a relative, or even a counselor. What you tell them is up to you, but it sometimes helps to be around others after a stressful experience, and sometimes telling the truth can be stressful. I think you'll find that ultimately it may take away some of the hidden guilt you've been feeling in the long run.
- **Subject**: What's going to happen now?
- **Primary**: We are going to write this up and present it to the decision makers, but this is a bureaucratic system and paperwork takes time to get through the process. You know how the government can be. Can we call someone for you?
- **Subject**: No, that's okay.
- **Primary**: What's the best way to contact you in case we need to clarify anything from our notes?
- **Subject**: My cell phone, I guess.
- **Primary**: Thank you again, Mr. Jones <shakes hand>.
- **Secondary**: Thank you <shakes hand>.

12 QUESTIONING

All we want are the facts, ma'am.
Jack Webb, *Dragnet*

Although Sergeant Joe Friday in Dragnet was only concerned about the facts, a good questioning session is about more than just factual items. In a good interview of a child pornography subject, the investigator asks behavior provoking questions and makes observations, identifies key information relevant to the alleged child pornography offense, and prepares the subject for later interrogation as necessary. Basic biographical questions are covered in the rapport phase, but questions related specifically to the offense under investigation are asked in the questioning phase. The questions can be broken up into four categories:

- **Informational.** Informational questions are the basic facts necessary to prove or disprove an allegation, or to elaborate on the details of an area of interest.
- **Blocking.** Blocking questions are used to cut-off avenues for excuses that may be provided by the offender, either later in the questioning or interrogation phases, or in court. These are frequently innocuous-sounding and can be asked prior to the more stressful questions later.
- **Assessment.** Assessment questions are intended to assess some aspect of the subject beyond just information gathering. These can include threat assessment questions or skill assessment questions, and can be used to modify future question asking.
- **Behavior provoking.** Behavior provoking questions are designed to elicit a response that is likely to be different between innocent and guilty subjects. Additionally, behavior provoking questions are used to elicit theme information for the interrogation phase.

The grouping of questions is for taxonomy purposes only, and does not imply a specific order or grouping. Questions from one group can and should be interleaved with questions from another group, and some questions may cover multiple categories.

Prior to interviewing the subject, the interviewer should prepare a detailed list of questions. Whether or not the list is used by the primary, held by the secondary for follow-ups as a checklist, or just done as a mental exercise is up to the primary interviewer based on their particular style. Whatever method is used, the questioning should be flexible enough to allow for a change in direction if the subject's answers or behavior warrant doing so during the interview itself.

During the questioning phase the interviewer should maintain a calm, even demeanor when asking questions. The answers should be recorded and followed up on where appropriate, but not initially challenged, even if they are deliberate falsehoods. If the subject becomes agitated and raises their voice, the interviewer should intentionally lower their own voice and speak slower and calmer until the subject loses steam. Both the primary and secondary interviewers should avoid any facial expressions beyond a neutral expression, and should never comment negatively on anything the subject states, no matter how reprehensible it may be to their sensibilities.

The primary interviewer should ask the questions and focus on the behavior of the subject and the formulation of follow-up questions while the secondary takes notes and provides focused observation of the answers. If there are follow-up questions or a detail that the primary interviewer overlooked, the secondary interviewer should be given a chance to ask them under the direction of the primary. This can be done with a simple nod to the secondary, or with a directed question such as "Kristen, did you have any follow-ups at this point?"

Newer interviewers frequently make several mistakes when asking questions in a subject interview. The most common mistake is not providing enough time to the subject – if they don't answer right away, there is a tendency for the novice interviewer to "fill the dead space" by talking. As awkward as the interview may be for the interviewer, it will be even more awkward for the subject, and waiting through an awkward silence is a core interviewing skill. Additionally, there are several types of questions that are frequently asked that can provide sub-optimal responses. While every interviewer will eventually ask a question in a way that could have been phrased better, interviewers should strive to avoid certain wordings, including:

- **Polite Questions.** We are taught from an early age to ask permission, and management training teaches us to ask politely rather than to tell ("Would you mind coming in this weekend to cover the duty desk?"). Polite questions generally have no place in a subject interview – they allow the subject the ability to say "no", and send the message that answering questions is optional. Instead of asking "Would you mind telling me if you've ever been at the Rolling Hills Elementary School?", the interviewer should just ask "Have you ever been at the Rolling Hills Elementary School?", or, alternatively, "When was the last time you were at the Rolling Hills Elementary School?" The exception is the first question soliciting the willingness of a subject to help in knock-and-talk situations.
- **Compound Questions.** Nervous interviewers may put multiple questions together in one. This is called a compound question, and can lead to confusion in interpreting an answer. A typical compound question may sound something like "Have you ever

downloaded child pornography or viewed it online?" The subject will have a tendency to answer to the most favorable section of the question based on their actions. If the subject answers "no", the interviewer doesn't know if the subject answered "no" to the downloading, the viewing, or both. The interviewer must then ask the follow-up questions they intended to ask in the first place.

- **Leading Questions.** While there is a place for leading questions in the confrontational interview, it is generally not during the questioning stage. Questions like "You never had sex with your daughter, did you?" are almost certainly going to elicit a "no" response, no matter what the truth is. The subject believes that is what the interviewer wants to hear based on the way the question was phrased, and the wording doesn't make it appear that the interviewer would look favorably on a "yes" answer.
- **Complex Questions.** The subject is likely under a lot of stress during the interview. Because of that, the interviewer should avoid questions that involve complex legal terms or detailed explanations. If the subject were asked "Did, at any time, you purposefully receive any pictures of minors that contained a lascivious display of the genitals?", the likely response will be "I don't know" or "I'm not sure". These are not indicators of deception in this context - instead they are a potentially honest misunderstanding of the question.

Informational Questions

Informational questions are the primary tool for the elicitation of basic facts. They are used to identify potential mechanisms of obtaining child pornography including Internet access methods and devices, document online identifiers, and establish times and locations of activity to corroborate available evidence. Informational questions are non-confrontational, and are simple fact-based queries. Where possible, open ended questions should be used first - e.g. asking "How do you access the Internet?" instead of "Do you use your laptop to browse the Internet?". Follow-up questions can be directed and specific, depending on the answer or lack of an answer to the initial question.

As with the rapport-building biographical questions, the informational questions can be used to observe baseline behavior in the subject. In addition to observing the same items noted in the rapport section, the interviewer should begin to assess the sophistication level of the subject in terms of computer savvy with the informational questions. This will drive the need to use specific assessment questions later in the questioning. If the answer provided in response to an informational question is not consistent with the information obtained in the planning stages, the investigator should attempt to follow-up in a non-specific and non-confrontational way. The subject should not be confronted with direct evidence at this point, however, as that may shut down the interview and prompt a request for legal counsel. By way of example, here are two approaches to the scenario where the investigator knows the subject has used an email address of child_lover@doesnotexist.org:

Preferred Approach

- **Primary**: What email accounts do you use?
- **Subject**: I use my name, jondoe@doesnotexist.org for my personal email and I have a business email account at jdoe@doesnotexist.com.
- **Primary**: What other email accounts do you use?
- **Subject**: I think that's all of the accounts I use.
- **Primary**: What other accounts have you used?
- **Subject**: I don't really remember any other accounts. I think I had one at my old college, jdoe@whatsamattau.edu, but I haven't used that for years.
- **Primary**: What other accounts have you signed up for in the past, even if you didn't use them?
- **Subject**: Umm... I think that's it. Yeah, that's it.
- **Primary**: Thank you, that's very helpful.

Alternate Approach

- **Primary**: What email accounts do you use?
- **Subject**: I use my name, jondoe@doesnotexist.org for my personal email and I have a business email account at jdoe@doesnotexist.com.
- **Primary**: Can you remember using any other email accounts?
- **Subject**: Not really.
- **Primary**: What about child_lover@doesnotexist.org?
- **Subject**: That doesn't sound familiar.
- **Primary**: We have the email address registered in your name. Why would that be?
- **Subject**: I'm not sure. Maybe someone else has the same name.
- **Primary**: It was coming from the IP address at this house.
- **Subject**: I don't know too much about IP addresses, but I've heard those things can be faked. How do you know it was coming from the IP address at this house?

The preferred approach follows up on the initial question to obtain any other email addresses the subject is willing to provide. The initial question is open ended and two direct questions are needed to round out the answer, but the subject never mentions child_lover@doesnotexist.org. This should be noted for follow-up during a later phase. It can be asked as a behavior-provoking question, which has the benefit of letting the subject know the interviewer has more information than they realize. Alternatively, it can be ignored and brought up during the interrogation or confession as appropriate. Although not a behavioral question, the use of the phrases "I think that's it", "I think that's all", and "I don't really remember" are potential indicators of deception and should also be noted by the interviewers.

The alternative approach shown above has a few problems. First, the phrasing of the question "Can you remember" is using a memory qualifier. The subject is provided an immediate "out" to not answer the question – that they do not remember. Second, the interviewer engages in a back-and-forth with the subject, ending with the subject obtaining more information than the interviewer wanted to provide at that point, and taking control of the interview by questioning the interviewer.

Several common questions that will likely be asked of every child pornography subject:

- **Question**: How do you connect to the Internet?
- **Discussion**: The question of Internet connectivity is left open to obtain all of the possible methods. The person may have a home Internet connection through a traditional ISP. They likely have a connection at work, and they may have devices such as tablets or smartphones that have LTE or similar connectivity. Follow-up questions on the home, mobile, and work side can be asked if the answers are not satisfactory. For mobile devices, the subject can also be asked where they connect to the Internet from. This may provide details on their movements or other locations they frequent.

- **Question**: What computers or other devices do you use to connect to the Internet?
- **Discussion**: The subject may need prompting regarding smartphones, tablets, gaming devices, televisions, and other non-computer devices. All of the computers in the home/workplace should be detailed. Older devices that are not used any longer but are still owned by the subject can be asked about at this point also. The investigator should note likely additional questions based on the responses. As an example, users of Android smartphones will have Google accounts. Similarly, iPad users are likely to have iCloud accounts. If a cell phone is not explicitly mentioned, the interviewer should ask if the subject has any cell phones and obtain their phone numbers.

- **Question**: What are your email accounts?
- **Discussion**: The email accounts associated with a child pornography subject can be used as identifiers in systems such as Gridcop and searched for related investigations through NCMEC. Email addresses are frequently associated with registration on websites, and provide fodder for subpoenas and electronic search warrants. In addition to the accounts provided, the lack of candor regarding accounts already known to investigators but not mentioned is a potential behavioral clue. A common follow-up question would be to ask the subject what they use each of the accounts for.

- **Question**: What social networking sites do you use?
- **Discussion**: Social networking sites are a treasure trove of information on subjects. Posted photos, friend lists, and activity logs provide insight into the offender and, occasionally, even direct evidence of an offense. They can help with victim identification in production cases, and with mapping out networks in distribution cases. If the subject does not explicitly provide information on accounts, the interviewer can ask about accounts on specific services – e.g. Facebook, Twitter, Pinterest, and Google+. As with emails, the exclusion of accounts in the subject's response that are known to be associated with the subject is also of behavioral interest.

- **Question**: What online/cloud storage sites do you use?
- **Discussion**: Cloud storage is popular for both backups and for file sharing,

especially in child pornography cases. While not commonly used for primary storage on entire collections at this time, the advent of portable devices with limited on-board storage will make cloud storage more prevalent in the future. Google Drive, iCloud, and Dropbox accounts all provide remotely accessible storage, and can be enumerated with individual questions. Specific accounts should also be enumerated for each of the sites.

- **Question**: What photo sharing sites do you use?
- **Discussion**: The photo sharing sites can be sites that the subject has accounts with, or open photo sharing sites the subject visits. Sites like Flickr have good monitoring for child pornography, but may have relevant personal or non-explicit victim photos. Sites like imgsrc.ru are well known for hosting password-protected content and are popular sites for sharing child pornography.

- **Question**: What web browsers do you use?
- **Discussion**: The specific web browsers used will determine the targets for initial forensic analysis. This question is an informational question, but also provides assessment value. The difference between "I click the little "e" on my computer" and "I used to use Firefox, but recently moved to Chrome for the more streamlined interface" provides insight into the amount of technical savvy possessed by the subject. If the subject mentions a browser other than the default browser for their device (e.g. Internet Explorer on Windows or Safari on OS X) a follow-on question of why they chose that browser can be insightful.

- **Question**: What peer-to-peer software do you use?
- **Discussion**: The peer-to-peer question is not asked as a yes or no question intentionally. Peer-to-peer software clients and networks, including BitTorrent, eMule, and eDonkey, are used for transferring files. Many of the files transferred are copyright violations in the form of movies, music, or software, but both child and adult pornography are frequently traded via these networks as well. If the subject uses peer-to-peer networks, their IP addresses and identities should be checked through Gridcop to determine if they have been actively sharing child pornography. Specific inquires related to the sharing functions of peer-to-peer can be elicited during the confession.

- **Question**: What instant messaging clients do you use?
- **Discussion**: Instant messaging clients are used to communicate with others as wells as to transfer files, including photos and movies. Individuals that are suspected of communicating with minors, or of distributing child pornography, may have used instant messaging as one mechanism to do so. As with the other questions above, if instant messaging applications are used the interviewer should ascertain any and all accounts used with the clients. Frequently, child pornographers will maintain multiple accounts for different personas, depending on who they are contacting.

- **Question**: What credit cards do you have?
- **Discussion**: Credit cards can be used to tie individuals that purchased child

pornography to the purchase. The investigator can ask to confirm the answer by seeing the wallet of the offender, or by searching the wallet pursuant to an inventory search as appropriate to the circumstances. Credit and debit card statements can also be subpoenaed to identify cell service providers, adult services, online vendor purchases, or other relevant procurements. In addition to credit cards, the investigator should elicit any Paypal accounts and associated eBay accounts, or the use of any other online payment mechanism, such as Bitcoin. Past credit cards can be asked about as necessary.

In addition to the above questions, if there is a concurrent or future forensic examination of the subject's devices, or a concurrent warrant being executed, the phrasing of the questions can be changed or secondary questions asked which leverage the situation. Generally, the questions can be prefixed with a statement of confidence. A follow-on where the subject's computer has been seized might be as follows:

- **Primary:** John, I don't know too much about computers, but I have one of the best forensic teams anywhere working on your machine. They will tell me everywhere you've been, everything you've done, and recover everything you may have thought you hid or deleted. When they come back with their report, what other email accounts are they going to find on your computer?

For any accounts the subject mentions, the investigator should have previously prepared consent-to-search forms at the ready. These can be presented to the subject during the questioning phase, but are generally best presented at a later stage. When they are presented, they should request the subject provide their password in addition to the account name. If distribution or solicitation offenses are suspected, the subject can be requested to provide not only consent to search their accounts but also consent to take over their accounts by impersonating the subject for the purposes of identifying and investigating co-conspirators.

One time to use consent forms after the informational questions is on a knock-and-talk. After getting answers to the questions above, the investigator can present a consent to search form to the subject to have an examiner do a live preview of their computer. This can be done before the subject has made any denials regarding the possession of child pornography.

Aside from issuing search warrants for content, a frequently overlooked investigative step is the issuance of trap and trace orders (prospectively) or subpoenas (retrospectively) to determine access to online services. These logs can provide evidence of distribution or assist in the identification of other access devices or locations, and add additional information to corroborate subject statements during the interview.

Blocking Questions

Blocking questions cut off or "block" future avenues that the subject may try and lead the investigator down. They are intended to combat the known excuses frequently provided by child pornography subjects, both during the interrogation and in later court proceedings. While the investigator may use additional blocking techniques for a particular situation, the key questions are noted below.

The most common defense put up by individuals accused of child pornography offenses is the infamous SODDI ("Some Other Dude Did It") defense. This defense can take on many forms, depending on the devices being looked at and the location the offenses took place. The blame may be placed on another individual in the household, on an unknown virus, or on an interloper on an open wireless network. To prevent these later defenses, the subject can be asked about their information security practices. The questions can be interspersed with general informational questions to make them less obvious, but should be asked early in the interview before specific questions about child pornography are brought up. Blocking questions can be prefaced with basic theming material, depending on the question. Specific questions are as follows:

- **Question**: You mentioned you used Verizon FIOS as your Internet connection. Did you keep the wireless security that came with the service?
- **Discussion**: Most ISPs now provide encryption as a default setting when providing a wireless router for home use. By determining the wireless router does have encryption present, you can show that it is unlikely anyone else used the network. While it is fairly easy to determine if there is WEP or WPA security currently in place and doing so should be done as part of the forensic analysis, locking the subject into having never changed the settings ensures that they cannot claim they recently turned it on.

- **Question**: You mentioned you have a laptop, and I see one on the desk over there. Do you need to enter a password to get into it?
- **Discussion**: If the situation is a knock-and-talk, having the subject show you their computer or other relevant device is an excellent time to ask or observe if there are multiple accounts or if they have a password. You can ask if they choose a strong password, and if they use encryption - this is an assessment question as well. An additional question that can be asked is whether or not the subject uses the same password for multiple accounts.

- **Question**: What antivirus software do you run?
- **Discussion**: What antivirus software is running is largely irrelevant – it is the fact that they are running antivirus software that is important. Once it is established that antivirus software is running and for how long it has been installed, the interviewer should ask if the subject's computer has ever had an infection. The interviewer can provide details if the subject is unsure with a simple narrative like "You can tell if you are infected if there is software you didn't install that suddenly appears, if your computer slows down for no reason, or if there are files you don't remember downloading that are present."

- **Question**: Sometimes people visit sites with questionable content, such as illegal file sharing sites. Some of these sites will generate pop-ups with illegal content. Has that ever happened to you?
- **Discussion**: The pop-up defense has been heard repeatedly by every veteran child pornography investigator. There are two main tactics to dealing with it. The first,

using the question above, is to cut it off before it starts. The second tactic is to allow the subject to claim they had a pop-up with child pornography appear during the interrogation, then to work them down the path of having clicked on the pop-up out of curiosity. The approach used will be dependent on the comfort level of the investigator in getting a confession. If the investigator believes the subject will not provide any admissions, locking them in to never having a pop-up appear is more valuable to bolster later forensic analysis. Otherwise, it can be more advantageous to let the pop-up defense become a theme later in the session.

- **Question**: One of the big things that we see in the computer crimes squad is identity theft. Have you ever been the victim of identity theft?
- **Discussion**: There is a possibility the subject has been the victim of identity theft online, especially if they have engaged in risky behavior. The investigator should document any instances of identity theft, and specifically ask about how the subject identified it, who they reported it to, and what the ultimate outcome of the theft was. If the subject claims to be a victim of identity theft and the thieves used their information to register for or purchase illicit material, this will be raised later as a defense, either during the interrogation or in court.

- **Question**: Have you ever had anyone compromise any of your online accounts?
- **Discussion**: Compromise of social networking or email accounts does occur. As with identity theft, any compromise could be used to misattribute illegal activity to an unknown individual. If an email account or social network account was compromised, the investigator will need to subpoena records showing password changes or other actions to verify the compromise occurred. Alternatively, the investigator can contact that provider and obtain evidence that no compromise likely occurred by showing no password changes, unusual activity, or IP addresses from unknown sources accessed the servers.

- **Question**: Has your credit card ever been lost, stolen, or compromised?
- **Discussion**: A stolen credit card can be claimed to have been used by a third party to purchase illicit material and not by the subject. This leaves the investigator with the task of showing the activity or the accesses were consistent with the subject's history. If their credit card has never been stolen, the investigator can ask if unusual or unwanted charges have ever appeared, and if they were disputed. Any prior disputes of charges related to the purchase of child pornography can be validated through the credit card company.

When being asked the blocking questions, the subject may try and outmaneuver the interviewer and claim they have had infections. There may be legitimacy to the claim – viruses do infect computers, connections are not always secured, and password choices are not always the best. If the subject claims they were compromised in any way, the interviewer needs to get every detail possible about the compromise. This should include when the compromise happened, for how long, how the subject noticed and confirmed the compromise, and what they did about it. Specific to child pornography, the investigator can ask if any illicit material was downloaded or found as a result. If the subject says no, any material found is the result of their own actions. If the subject says yes, the investigator should quantify the material and ask what actions the subject took following the discovery. Detail about what files were accessed, moved, deleted, or altered should be gathered.

Assessment Questions

Assessment questions are used to evaluate the subject in three specific areas - technical acumen, child pornography involvement, and threat of committing a contact offense. The interviewer should be looking to establish a picture of the subject in each of these areas throughout the interview, and the answers to these questions can be used to supplement any prior knowledge. Questions such as whether or not the subject has any children should be known to the investigator a priori, but others such as hobbies that put them in contact with children may not be. Like the other categories, assessment questions can be combined with informational, blocking, or behavioral questions.

Technical Assessment

First, the technical competence of the subject should be assessed. Their technical proficiency will drive the phrasing of later questions and of interrogation themes. Contrary to intuition, it is frequently more valuable to play opposite the strength of the subject skill-wise. If they have a PhD in computer engineering and work at Google, the investigator should not get into a technical "whose is bigger" situation. Alternatively, if the subject has no technical knowledge then showing confidence can often result in a successful admission.

For a technically proficient subject, a statement like "I don't know much about computers, but we've recruited folks that go to years of training at the FBI, at the Federal Law Enforcement Training Center, and even at the Department of Defense who know a lot more. They are using their magic on your systems right now, and tell me that there are always ways to find information, even if the person thinks they deleted it. I don't understand half of what they do, but I do know that I had a person in here last week who thought everything was deleted and they were able to recover just about everything he did." If the subject is not proficient, the other side of the theme can be used, "I have a team of some of the best digital forensic specialists anywhere reviewing your system right now. They tell me that pieces of your activities remain in unallocated space, in cache files, and as fragments in the computer's memory. The team is combing through the data as we speak and we both know what they are going to find." Technical proficiency can be established mainly through follow-on questions to the informational questions. While it is a good open-ended approach for all questions, asking technical assessment questions with the "Tell me about" qualifier keeps the interviewer from revealing too much of their own level of expertise.

In addition to the basic assessment, technical acumen can drive the forensic analysis strategy. Expect a technically astute subject to use encryption and to have obfuscated their activities to a greater degree. Example technical assessment questions are as follows:

- **Question**: Tell me about how you search for things of interest on the web.
- **Discussion**: The searching techniques described will provide insight into technical proficiency, and will let the investigator know the search tools the subject uses.

Depending on the point in the interview, and if the subject has admitted to viewing adult pornography, the investigator can ask the subject how they find adult pornography. This can be matched with the general search question response above for consistency. Additionally, if the pornography question is asked later, the investigator can bring up the search answer above. The search engine used will also provide a potential avenue for later subpoena requests, if the searches were logged, or for forensic review if they were not. The way the subject describes how they constructed their searches will provide further insight into their technical competence. If they mention detailed Boolean operations on Google, they are likely somewhat sophisticated. If they use search terms with unnecessary words in the default search box that their ISP installed on their home screen, they are likely less sophisticated.

- **Question**: Tell me about what peer-to-peer software you use.
- **Discussion**: An unsophisticated subject will likely look confused by this question. An individual with technical savvy will at least understand the question, and may provide answers like “BitTorrent” or “eMule”. If the subject mentions a particular technology, ask why they chose to use that technology. The subject can then be asked what types of things they download using the peer-to-peer software. If the subject admits to using peer-to-peer software, the investigator should try to ask about the most popular peer-to-peer clients at the time. BitTorrent, eMule, eDonkey, and Frostwire are all current market leaders. For historical cases, tools like Bearshare, Limewire, and Kazaa can be asked about, with the added advantage of knowing how long the person has been using peer-to-peer by their response. While not strictly peer-to-peer in the sense of the tools above, Gigatribe offers similar functionality and is a favorite of those sharing child pornography due to the relative difficulty in obtaining law enforcement support from the host country, France, and its use can likewise be queried at this point.

- **Question**: Tell me about how you backup your data.
- **Discussion**: Individuals that have a greater technical acumen are more likely to backup critical data. Additionally, the method of backup will provide technical and psychological insight into the offender. If they have their backup with them at all times, they are potentially treating it as a trophy. If it is stashed away inside a wall, they may be technically savvy and afraid of discovery. If it is in plain sight with no barriers to access, their technical controls may be taking second place to their need to view the content it contains. In addition to potential insight into the offender, on a concrete level the locations of the backups and when they were performed can be used to direct search activities.

- **Question**: Tell me about your use of TOR.
- **Discussion**: TOR is the predominant onion routing software. Onion routing hides the identity of the provider of a service, including hosting providers for child pornography websites, and of the customer of the service. Freely available, TOR software makes it difficult to identify the parties in a communication through traffic analysis. Subjects using TOR likely have a high technical acumen, and are likely using source

encryption. Additionally, because the use of TOR hides traffic, their activities are not likely to directly show up on HTTP logs or other traffic-based areas of analysis, including trap-and-trace returns.

Child Pornography Involvement

Not all child pornographers are created equal. There is a vast difference in engagement in the underworld of child pornography between a subject that searches for "naked young teen pictures" in Google and one that actively participates in forums, producing and sharing content. The level of involvement can be used as a general guide to the amount of time a person has been accessing, distributing, and/or producing child pornography. Questions that assess child pornography involvement include the following:

- **Question**: We find adult pornography on every computer we analyze, and we've found it on your machine. There's nothing wrong with looking for adult pornography, but we see people obtaining it in many different ways. How do you generally find your pornography when you are looking for it?
- **Discussion**: The purpose of this question is two-fold. First, it establishes that everybody views pornography, which normalizes the behavior in the mind of the subject. Second, it gets the subject to tell you where and how they search for pornography in general. The depths the subject goes to in finding pornography will provide a clue as to their general involvement. A subject that has purchased subscriptions to multiple websites is more likely to have a deep involvement with pornography than a person who casually browses free websites on a whim.

- **Question**: What search terms do you use when you look for adult pornography?
- **Discussion**: Answering what search terms they put in a browser is easier for the subject than answering "what sexual activities are you into". The terms they provide are clues as to what they are interested in, and if the forensic exam results are available, what they left out may be even more telling. The investigator should listen for qualifiers like "legal nudes", which indicate the subject is trying to distance themselves from child pornography searches - a behavior that innocent parties aren't as likely to exhibit. If the subject provides a few terms, follow up with "What other terms have you searched for in the past?" and keep asking "What other terms?" until you are comfortable you have a comprehensive list. If the subject lists multiple terms, even if most of them are not of investigative interest, the interviewer should follow-up on all of them with the additional questions:

    - Where do you search for the term <XYZ>?
    - What do you find when you search for <XYZ>?
    - Have you ever had anything you didn't want to see come up when you were searching for <XYZ>?

  The final question gives the subject a rationalization for later theming if they indicate they saw underage pictures. Also, if the individual uses a qualifier like "Legal" or "Over 18", the investigator can follow up with the question "We frequently see individuals use the qualifier “Legal” to avoid seeing pictures of children. They tend to do this because they’ve come across images in the past that they didn’t want to see. Tell me about what made you start to use the term ‘Legal’”.

- **Question:** How often do you search for pornography?
- **Discussion:** This question seeks to quantify the amount of time the subject searches for pornography. The initial question is likely to get a very non-specific answer like “occasionally”, but the interviewer can follow up with more direct questions if that occurs. The interviewer should provide ranges to assist in the refinement of the answer. Breakdowns such as “Is it multiple times a day on average? Once a day on average?” are likely to generate a more specific response. Once the number of times a day/week/year is identified, the interviewer should then determine how much time is spent each occurrence (“Multiple hours? An hour?”). Then, how many websites per minute the subject views can be asked. Finally, how many images or videos per website are viewed can be quantified. Once the subject provides estimates on how frequently they have been searching, a quick calculation can be made. This can provide an overall number of images/videos viewed, and can add up quickly. For example, viewing five images per page, at five pages per minute, one hour and a half per day, for a year provides:

  5 x 5 x 60 x 1.5 x 365 = 821,250 images over the course of a year.

  This can be coupled in the interrogation with the percentage of images the subject views that are child pornography. Even if they admit that 1% of their searches are child pornography, in the above example that still provides 8,213 images.

- **Question:** Our tool/analysis/investigation showed the term “PTHC” appearing frequently. Tell me about that.
- **Discussion:** PTHC, or PreTeen HardCore is an acronym that is not well known outside the child pornography community. A typical response from an innocent subject would be to ask what that term means. If an individual shows knowledge of the term, or denies vehemently that the term would appear on their computer without the investigator explaining what it means, that is an indication of fairly deep involvement in child pornography. Depending on the specifics of the forensics, other terms that are equally unusual and strongly tied to child pornographers can be used (e.g. “PTSC”, “R@ygold”, “Nabult”, etc.) The absence of knowledge does not prove innocence – while PTHC is the most common search term used by those seeking child pornography, specific subgroups of subjects may not have encountered it – specifically those producing or trading within a small, tight-knit community and those who are new to the acquisition of the material.

- **Question:** We see a lot of people in here who have inadvertently come across explicit images of kids, usually when they are looking for adult pornography. A lot of times they are shocked and delete the images right away. Has that ever happened to you?
- **Discussion:** Despite the statement, ordinary web browsing does not generally turn

up child pornography. The answer to this may provide a later theme – if the individual states that this has happened, the investigator should ask follow-up questions about what the individual was searching for and what they thought when they saw the image. Further questions about what they did next and if they reported it, and why not, can then be asked in a non-accusatory manner. There may be a temptation to enter into the interrogation after this question, but the investigator is better off completing the interview unless the subject begins making a full confession without further prompting.

Contact With Children

The amount of contact a subject has with children is one direct indicator of the immediate threat of their committing a contact offense. While any offender can seek out children, one that has regular, repeated contact must be assessed for the likelihood of a contact offense. To that end, the investigator should assess the regularity of contact as well as the ages, sexes, and type of contact. A subject that tutors children one-on-one that matches their age and sex preference is of higher immediate interest than a subject that has no children in their household and has no routine contact with kids. The interviewer should listen to the specifics of the verbal responses during the course of the interview as well – referring to children as "my friend" as opposed to "my friend's kid", is telling information on how they view children.

- **Question**: What type of contact do you have with children?
- **Discussion**: The basic question is important, and can be used with subjects that have kids and those that do not. If the subject refers to children as their friends, or if they engage in age-inappropriate behavior those are threat indicators. Additionally, any one-on-one contact with children is higher risk than group behavior. If the individual only mentions group behavior, a follow-up on any times they are alone with a child can be asked. The type of group should overlap with other life aspects as well. Coaching their own child's soccer team is more typical than coaching a soccer team in a different age range than their own kids. There are many non-offenders that volunteer time to help kids, and a reasonable follow-up question is "What made you get into <activity>?" As with other questions, any activity with children the subject engages in that they explicitly leave out in their response is of interest.

- **Question**: Where do you most frequently encounter children?
- **Discussion**: Unlike the previous question, this question requires an answer as to the circumstances surrounding the subject's most frequent contact with children. If the subject has children of their own or has a job where they have extensive contact with children, the interviewer can ask "Other than at home with your own children..." as a qualifier. The investigator should listen for situations that would involve the subject being in an unusual place or, alternatively, interpreting a routine activity as "contact" with children. For example, a subject that provides the answer "When I'm

at the food court and I see them playing at the local mall every weekend" would be an example of a normal situation made unusual by the answer.

- **Question**: One of the nice things about the Internet is that no one knows who you are. Have you ever pretended to be younger than you are on the Internet?
- **Discussion**: One of the grooming behaviors for online predators committing contact offenses is to pose as someone younger than they are. An individual may offer what they deem is a "reasonable" explanation for doing so, but anyone who answers yes to this question should be probed for additional details. Individuals can be asked about specific accounts if known, but this question is primarily to elicit behavioral responses. If an individual admits to pretending to be younger than they are, the follow-up question to determine direct contact with children is "Have you ever met any of the people you communicated with in person?" A variant on this question, if the subject is evasive, is "Have you ever pretended to be anyone other than yourself?" on the Internet.

- **Question**: What types of activities do you engage in with your own children?
- **Discussion**: The specific activities the subject engages in with their own children, if they have stated they have children, can be used later in the interrogation. A potentially guilty subject may provide unusual activities that can be followed up on, for example "We give each other massages" in relation to a five year old, or provide mundane activities that can be used as contrast later in the interview. Routine activities that are age specific such as changing diapers or bathing a child can be asked about at this point to elicit any unusual wording or hedging in the subject's responses. Additionally, the investigator can ask what activities the subject engages in with their children's friends.

- **Question**: Have you ever taken pictures of children?
- **Discussion**: Taking pictures of your own children is normal, and should be expected. Taking pictures of other children is generally a questionable behavior. The clarification of what types of pictures and what situations the children are in can provide further context. If the subject states that they have pictures of children on their digital camera that they have taken, the investigator can ask if any of the children are unclothed, and the circumstances surrounding that. As with the questions above, the question can be phrased as "Are there any images that our forensic examiners may encounter that they may not understand the circumstances of how they were taken..." Any children that the subject admits to taking pictures of should be identified by the subject through detailed questions about their identities and contact information. Asking who the subject has shown the pictures to can be the basis for distribution offenses as well.

Behavior Provoking Questions

Behavior provoking questions are used by the interviewer to elicit a response that will be evaluated against an expected response. They can provide themes for use in the interrogation phase, and the subject's responses can be compared to the baseline acquired during the rapport and informational questioning phases. If there are multiple potential suspects, behavior provoking questions can be used earlier in the interview to identify which suspects have a higher probability of having committed the offense.

Behavioral Cues

Behavioral cues are used to evaluate the truthfulness of a subject's response. While they cannot determine guilt or innocence, they can identify questions that provoke discomfort in a subject, though the reason for the discomfort can be knowledge of an act committed by another party or internal psychological issues with a question unrelated to the crime being investigated. Cues can be broken up into three separate areas - non-verbal behavior, verbal behavior, and paralinguistic behavior. Single cues are not particularly helpful, but groupings of cues and overall changes in behavior related to specific questions can be good indicators for areas of focus.

Non- Verbal Cues

Non-verbal cues are the physical behaviors that a subject's body reveals to the investigator, generally without the subject being aware they are exhibiting the behavior. The cues can range from nervousness (grooming, blading the body away, avoiding eye contact) to anger (balled fists, clenched muscles, forward leaning). The interviewer must be constantly evaluating the subject's physical state at a meta-level. While microexpression and eye movement analysis have their advocates, they are beyond the scope of this book. Only gross motor movements and patterns of behavior will be covered. Key things to evaluate are as follows:

- **Posture**. A somewhat relaxed, upright posture is normal when answering innocuous questions. A standard response for both an innocent and guilty subject is to start our rigid, and to slowly relax during the rapport and informational questioning. A sign that the subject is ready to move on to more probing questions is the aforementioned relaxation. A forced, rigid posture is indicative of a subject that is trying to control their behavior. A slumped-over posture during interrogation is a sign of resignation, and an indication that is may be time to ask the alternative question.
- **Body Position**. Akin to posture, when talking to a subject they will generally have a slightly forward body position showing interest, and be directly facing the interviewer. Nervous subjects will blade their body away from the interviewer, showing their side. Additionally, they may attempt to physically move as far away from the interviewer as possible, either within their chair or by moving their chair. Additional positions of interest can include crossing the arms (a "guarded" position) or an overly-forward leaning position, which can be indicative of a subject getting ready to attack the interviewer. Overall movement of the body is another indicator - some shifting of position is normal in an extended interview. Constant shifting to get comfortable, foot tapping, or leg movement can indicate the subject's nervousness has increased.
- **Hand Movements.** When not in a controlled environment, investigators are told to

always watch the hands for officer safety. An individual who is hiding their hands may have something in them. Likewise, balled fists are an indicator of a coming attack. Interviewers have the same concerns, but have additional things to look for. Wringing of the hands, grooming behavior (moving the hands through their hair, picking at lint, etc.), and excessive movement are indicators of nervousness. When subjects become aware of their nervousness, they may sit on their hands or clasp them together to prevent movement.

- **Eye Movements.** In most Western cultures, it is normal to look an individual in the eyes when you are speaking to them, with intermittent glances elsewhere. In some cultures, however, eye contact is considered rude – the baseline for a particular subject can be assessed during rapport building. A guilty subject may have trouble looking the interviewer in the eyes. Alternatively, they may try to "stare down" the interviewer through socially awkward, extended eye contact. As with hand movements, eyes can be an investigator safety issue also. A subject that is staring at the investigator's holster or at an object that can be a potential weapon (a fireplace poker during a home interview, for example), may indicate an imminent threat. A subject that stares at the ground during an interrogation is another indicator that it is time for the alternative question.
- **Facial Expressions.** Some subjects have problems keeping a poker face. They will exhibit fake surprise, or will smile inappropriately. The forehead muscles and eye muscles move in a real smile (unless the subject uses Botox), but not a faked one without lots of practice. Subject may feign anger that goes away too quickly, or bring on tears that end abruptly. Any unnatural expression is likely to be a controlled behavior, and should be treated as such. Covering the face, especially the mouth, with the hand during question answering is frequently cited as an indicator of guilt if done selectively. Finally, a subject may shake their head "Yes" to an answer they verbally stated "No" to, or vice versa.

Verbal Cues

The linguistic behavior exhibited by subjects is one of the easier traits for an experienced interviewer to pick up on. Because active listening is the core skill in interviewing, non-answers, deflections, and hedging should jump out at the interviewer. There are several turns of phrase that are common indicators of deception, though any change in the structuring of answers for specific questions can be an indicator that something about that particular question is provoking a nervous response. Specific verbal cues that are indicators of deception include:

- **Repeating the Question.** Guilty subjects will repeat the question asked by the interviewer as a stall tactic to gain time to come up with an answer. "Have you ever touched your son's penis?" might be followed with "Have I ever touched my son's penis?" or "Are you asking me if I molested my child?" to cause a delay. The interviewer should repeat the question exactly and note the behavior, and should avoid answering counter-questions.
- **Hedging the Answer.** Hedging is taking an absolute and adding a qualifier. It can be done through the addition of "I believe", "I think", or "To the best of my knowledge"

to the beginning of an answer, or with the addition of a memory qualifier such as "I don't recall". The investigator has to assess the likelihood of the subject having legitimate difficulty answering the question – asking where the subject was on a Tuesday night three months earlier may very well generate an "I think" response, which may indicate a subject trying to remember and be helpful. When asked if they have ever had any sex with a child, "Not that I recall" is an extremely suspicious response. Depending on the question, the interviewer can request a probabilistic response, such as "How confident are you that you've never touched a child? 20%, 40%, 80%?" Anything less than 100% is a problem.

- **Answering a Different Question.** One of the harder things to pick up on for new interviewers is a subject that confidently answers a question that wasn't asked. The interviewer might ask "Have you ever had sex with anyone under the age of 18", and receive a response of "I'd never hurt a child", which wasn't the question that was asked (but may provide material for a later theme).
- **Overly Specific Answers.** Questions that are specific and involve criminality generally don't receive an exact response. "Did you touch your niece under her panties last Tuesday?" is likely to elicit "I've never touched my niece" or "I've never touched a child" from an innocent party. A response of "I did not touch my niece under her panties last Tuesday" is a more questionable response. Did the subject touch someone else under their panties on Tuesday? Did they touch their niece on Wednesday? Was it over her panties on Tuesday? If an overly specific answer is provided, the question can be broadened and re-asked.
- **Change in Grammatical Construction.** Most individuals will use contractions in honest denials. A subject that starts out using contractions and then for specific denials switches from "I didn't" to "I did not" indicates the question is in an area of interest.

Paralinguistic Cues

What a person says may be less important in a behavioral assessment than how they say it. Paralinguistic cues are the subconscious changes in how a person answers a question. A subject that is concentrating on phrasing responses properly and on controlling their body movements may still let paralinguistic differences show in their responses. When evaluating the importance of paralinguistics, just look at the misunderstanding that is possible in email messages. A simple sentence like "I'd love to help you move this weekend – it's not like I have anything better to do" may be a genuine offer of help, a forced offer of help, or a sarcastic way of saying no. Paralinguistic indicators include the following:

- **Volume.** The volume of a person's response can say a lot about their state of mind. A conversational tone should be the baseline. An individual getting angry will raise their voice, and an individual who is scared may lower their voice. In general, lowering their voice and trailing off are indicators of deception, but can also be indicators of an individual getting close to a confession as denials become weaker and softer. Because some of the questions regarding child pornography will deal with sexual activities, some individuals may lower their voice not because they are being deceptive but because of embarrassment due to the question.

- **Cadence**. The rate at which someone answers a behavioral question should be relatively similar to that observed in the baseline questioning. Some individuals are slower by nature, or may have difficulty understanding complex questions due to intellectual difficulties or language comprehension difficulties. A subject that slows down from their baseline for a particular response may be attempting to come up with a story on-the-fly, or attempting to avoid inadvertently saying something.
- **Verbosity**. There is a great deal of variance in the amount of time different subjects will spend answering questions. Some subjects will provide a long story to even the simplest question -asking their name may result in a story about how their parents came up with it - and others will be guarded and provide short, concise, and direct answers. Individuals who are verbose in their answers should be allowed to continue to the greatest degree possible, as an individual that is talking is an individual that is still participating in the interview. Individuals that provide short answers should be asked more open-ended questions that prevent them from providing yes/no answers. An individual that is generally long winded and provides a very short answer to a question of interest is a sign of deception. Similarly, an individual that tries to "run out the clock" by dancing around an answer to a question of interest for an inordinate amount of time is also an indicator of deception.
- **Editing**. Seinfeld captured this concept perfectly – George's girlfriend explains how her ex-boyfriend visited the night before and "yada, yada, yada ... I'm really tired today." Guilty parties will frequently provide extensive detail on innocent circumstances surrounding a criminal act, then become deliberately vague or leave out key pieces once the actions of interest occur in the retelling. A child pornographer who has committed a contact offense may discuss in detail brushing his teeth, eating breakfast, reading the paper, and then skip right past the details of their engagement with a child, only to go back into detail on eating dinner and watching TV. Any areas that are answered with less detail than others bear closer scrutiny.
- **Delay**. Individuals that are attempting to "think up" a story are likely to delay during questions that require them to provide details about an event. The delay may be a verbal delay, such as asking the interviewer what they mean or rephrasing the question back to the interviewer, or it may just be an extra-long pause before answering. Subjects may also fill the gap with meaningless statements such as "That's a good question" or just random musings "Hmmm.... Where was I yesterday morning... Let's see now..."

While covered as part of behavior provoking questions, behavioral cues should be assessed during all interview questions. The rapport building stage and informational questioning provide the interviewer with the baseline behaviors of the subject. The assessment questions can provoke changes in the subject's behavior that can indicate areas for follow-up, or areas to avoid (initially). The behavior provoking questions differ in that they are specifically designed to provoke behavior, whether positive or negative, in a subject. With these questions, the behavior itself is as important as the answer. No one signal should be read in isolation – crossing the arms may indicate a subject is cold, excessive leg movement could be from a medical condition, and inability to make eye contact could be a sign of introversion. An aggregate change in behavior is more important than individual elements.

Behavioral Questions

While behavioral questions are part of any comprehensive subject interview, child pornography investigations have a few specific questions that can be used to assess the individual's touch points, find theme material, and assist in the assessment of their guilt. Several of the behavioral questions are very direct, and new interviewers may feel awkward asking them. The interviewer should make every attempt to ask the questions in the same tone and pacing as they asked the informational questions. If the interviewer does not appear to be placing any additional emphasis on the questions, the subject is more likely to provide a response that is useful for a behavioral assessment. Some relevant behavioral questions include:

- **Question**: Have you ever viewed an image of a child engaged in sexual activity?
- **Discussion**: The answer to this question by an innocent party should be definitive – a straight up "No" or "Never" is a strong and positive response. A hedged response such as "Not that I'm aware of" or a weak denial are indicators of deception. Part of the reason to ask this question directly, however, is to compare and contrast the answers with related answers to contact offenses. Additionally, the question sets up the next behavioral questions. If the offense is distribution, the interviewer can substitute "shared" for "viewed". If it is production offense, "taken" can be substituted.

- **Question**: Why wouldn't you view an image of a child engaged in sexual activity?
- **Discussion**: Good answers to this question include "Because it's wrong", or "Because they are just children". A guilty party is likely to provide some theme material in their response. "Because I don't look for that material" allows for a "stumbled across it" theme. "Because I wouldn't want people to look at my kid" may be indicative of offenses at home. "Because it's illegal" provides the possibility of interrogation themes related to society not understanding the subject's behavior and inappropriately criminalizing it.

- **Question**: Why do you think people view images of children engaged in sexual activity?
- **Discussion**: This question requires speculation on the part of the subject. A common response would be "because they need help", which lends itself to a "can't help yourself" theme. This should not be confused with a response of "because they are sick", which is more likely to indicate innocence if delivered with the requisite vehemence expected of an innocent party. Similarly, another common response would be "because they accidentally downloaded it", which is one step away from an admission to receipt.

- **Question**: What should happen to a person who views an image of a child engaged in sexual activity?

- **Discussion:** This is another place where the interviewer should look for a strong response from an innocent party. Something to the effect of "lock them up and throw away the key" is a good response. Bad responses will almost certainly generate theme material - anything that involves needing to get help will be ripe for a medical theme, whereas any response that begins with "it depends" is likely to be followed by a scenario that will generate your first admission.

- **Question:** What could that person say to you that would make you reconsider <insert punishment here>?
- **Discussion:** If a subject provides a punishment that was fairly major as something they believed should happen to an individual who viewed child pornography, this follow-up allows the investigator to further probe for theme material. If the subject says "if they apologized...", a remorse-based theme can work. If the subject states "If they promised to never do it again...", a similar theme that includes making mistakes and taking responsibility might be successful.

- **Question:** Have you ever had sexual relations with a child?
- **Discussion:** This question has the same follow-up questions as the child pornography questions above. The reason to ask this is not only to assess the likelihood of a contact offense having occurred, but to assess the difference in punishments and reactions to the two different offenses. Comparing and contrasting distribution and production with possession can be done in a similar fashion.

The questions provided above are not meant to be comprehensive, and all of the questions do not need to be used in every instance. Ultimately, the interview is about eliciting information - both about the offense itself and for use in the interrogation phase. Interviewers should approach every subject interview with an open mind, and be receptive to unexpected responses.

13 INTERROGATION

It is more dangerous that even a guilty person should be punished without the forms of law than that he should escape.
Thomas Jefferson

Interrogations are often misunderstood, misapplied, and misinterpreted. Unfortunately, many individuals in law enforcement believe that an interrogation consists of Jack Bauer threatening to shove a towel down a subject's throat or Andy Sipowicz telling a subject that they are facing the needle if they do not admit what they did. While this makes for good television drama, real interrogation is about building trust with a subject, convincing the subject that you know what they did, then providing the subject a rationalization for their actions that allows them to retain some shred of their dignity.

Unlike interviews, interrogation involves the interviewer doing most of the talking and the subject doing most of the listening. The basic process of interrogation involves the investigator presenting a theme, which is simply a rationalization of the subject's behavior. The investigator develops and presents the theme to the subject, and watches their body language for signs of agreement or resignation. These may include affirmative behavior like nodding or signs that the subject has given up fighting and may be willing to accept the scenario presented, such as a hunched over posture staring at the floor with hands clasped behind the head.

When presenting themes to the subject, the single biggest trait the investigator needs is the ability to portray confidence. The interrogation usually starts by way of a direct confrontation, with the investigator informing the subject that the results of the investigation clearly show the subject's guilt. The investigator can provide general categories of evidence, but should avoid showing the subject any specific evidence if possible. As such, a sample opening statement might be as follows:

- **Primary:** Our investigation clearly shows that you downloaded pictures of children having sex. <brief pause> There is no question about the evidence, but what I don't know right now is why. The most important thing to me in these situations is to be able to understand the circumstances. We know what happened, but we need to understand why it happened so that we don't misinterpret the evidence. Here's what I think may have happened...

The confrontation may generate a denial, but anything short of the person walking out means that the subject is willing to listen to the reasons the investigator provides. The reasons, or themes, should be based on the responses to the behavioral questions during previous stage. There is no single, universal theme, but generally themes seek to rationalize, project, or minimize.

General Themes

Rationalization themes provide a reasonable-sounding story about why a subject took a particular action. The story generally involves answering the "why" question with a more desirable reason to the subject than the real reason. Thieves never steal money to buy drugs (at least as far as the interrogator is concerned), they steal it to put food on the table. Similarly, child pornographers never seek to hurt children, they only view the images because of a compulsion, or do so out of compassion, or as part of a general curiosity in unusual pornography. Most of the themes that will appeal to child pornographers are rationalization themes, for example:

- **Primary:** When I look at the movies you downloaded, I see that you are a man who has a lot of time on his hands and lets his curiosity get the best of him. I talk to a lot of individuals that are looking for adult pornography and stumble across all kinds of things that may not get them excited, but that they download anyway out of curiosity. I believe that may be what happened here.

Minimization themes generally try to take a deviant behavior and compare and contrast it to a more extreme behavior. Sometimes this can be done through a comparison to another individual, sometimes it can be based on numbers, and sometimes it can incorporate both. A sample minimization theme in a child pornography setting might be as follows:

- **Primary:** I think you may be blowing things out of proportion here. We found a couple dozen images of kids having sexual relations on your computer, but I like to keep things in perspective. I had a person sitting in that same chair last week that had over five hundred thousand images. When I see that, I see a person who has a major issue. What I see here is different – I see someone who may have just been a bit curious and got himself into a bit of a bind due to a rash decision.

Projection is the blaming of a person's actions on someone else ("If your boss had paid you for all the overtime you work, you wouldn't have needed to take that money") or something else ("If it weren't for the alcohol, I know that you never would have touched her"). While more applicable to contact offenses against children, projection can also be used with child pornography offenders. Blame can be placed on a spouse that is not providing sexual satisfaction, individuals in chat rooms that send unsolicited pictures (admitting they were solicited is the second step), or even the victims themselves:

- **Primary**: I don't know how much you read about this sexting phenomenon, but what happens is kids take movies of themselves with their smartphones having sexual relations. They then send them around to their friends and someone ends up posting them on the Internet. Those movies we found on your computer look just like the sexting videos I'm seeing a lot of nowadays. If the kids hadn't filmed themselves, and if their friends hadn't posted them on the Internet, I don't think we'd be sitting here right now.

Unfortunately, blaming victims or providing what sound like ridiculous rationalizations is difficult for new investigators. If the investigator doesn't sound like they believe what they are saying, the subject won't believe it either. This is a cause for concern, because many of the rationalizations are difficult to read, and even more difficult to present with any conviction (e.g. blaming a young child for soliciting the favors of the subject). To be successful, the investigator needs to treat the interrogation as an act - they are not stating their own believes, but rather playing a role that provides the subject a sounding board for the subject's own rationalizations, however twisted. Playacting interrogation themes ahead of time and holding murder board reviews of interrogation strategies with more seasoned investigators can help. Additionally, seeing the themes used successfully by a senior investigator before they undertake an interrogation can instill the confidence necessary to be successful.

Maintaining control of an interrogation is another area that can be difficult for new investigators. The subject may try to take control of the situation, or to interject their own statements while the interrogator is talking. Reid teaches their interviewers to raise an open hand in the "stop" fashion, while providing an interjection like "Let me finish what I was saying" or "Hold on to that thought for one minute". Another technique interweaves questions with the interrogation. This comes across as more of a conversation, but the interviewer still needs to maintain control and to not allow interruptions during their monologue periods.

The interviewer generally ends the monologue of theming the subject when they have exhausted multiple themes and the subject is showing no signs of giving in, or when the subject begins to exhibit signs that they are ready to confess. These can include a hunched over posture, hanging their head low and staring at the floor, or giving a sigh of resignation. Once the subject is in that state, the interviewer will end their theme with an alternative question.

The alternative question is one that provides the subject a contrasting set of two alternative possibilities, either of which will result in an admission. One of the possibilities is generally more positive than the other, and this allows the subject to maintain a semblance of dignity by choosing the more positive response. The contrast can be based on severity, intent, or moral reasoning, but should result in an admission to an illegal act with either alternative. Example alternative questions include:

- **Primary**: I occasionally see people in here with millions of images, but I think what we are talking about here is only a couple of hundred movies. Is it millions of

movies or only a couple of hundred?
- **Primary:** Did you force your son to touch himself on camera, or did you just happen to be filming when he was already touching himself?
- **Primary:** Are you running a criminal enterprise here selling these images, or did you just share a few images with some close friends?

Sometimes the subject appears to be on the verge of answering, but may not say anything. In these cases, the question can be followed up with a prompt toward the expected answer.

- **Primary:** Are you the type of guy who is out there grabbing kids off the streets and molesting them, or were you just trying to show love and affection to your daughter by photographing yourself having relations with her. I think you are the type of guy who was just try show affection. You were just trying to show her affection by touching her, right?

Innocent parties will generally not choose when provided the alternative question – they will tend to provide answers of "neither" or refute the question completely, whereas guilty parties will tend to take the path of least resistance and chose the alternative that paints their actions in the best light.

As a word of caution to interviewers, the alternative question should never address consequences, only actions. Questions like "Do you want to be honest here so that you can go back to your kids, or do you want us to call child protective services?" should not be used under any circumstances and will likely result in suppression of the admission.

Child Pornography-Specific Themes

There are several themes that can be used in child pornography interrogations. The choice of theme will depend on the answers to the behavioral questions and the specifics of the acts committed. Multiple themes may need to be presented, and an individual theme may need to be presented in a slightly different way multiple times. Examples of specific themes to use for child pornography subjects are listed below.

The Collector

General Theory

- Collecting child pornography isn't any different than collecting baseball cards, stamps, or coins.

When to Use It

- If the subject has indicated they have collection-based hobbies, either through observation of their office or residence (look for items being displayed) or through the organization of their electronic data (categorizing non-offending images or documents in a structured way). If distribution is suspected, an initial admission to possession as a collector has a natural progression to distribution themes.

Interrogation Dialog

- Adam, I think I can see what happened here. You told me earlier how passionate you were about collecting coins. I saw your comic book collection in your house and was very impressed. It showed a great deal of organization, and it must have taken years to put together. I think you treated the images of the young people we found on your computer the same way. You went online and stumbled across a few images. Because you like to collect things, you saved them to your hard drive and began categorizing them without even thinking about it. Just like with comic books, once you started to organize them you began to fill in the gaps by looking for similar pictures. I don't think this was about the content, but the collection.

Furtherance of the Theme

- For distribution, stress the sharing of information on collecting child pornography and the images themselves with other collectors. Online forums for child pornography can be likened to forums for other types of collections. Stress group membership to avoid "singling out" their behavior.

The Photographer (Artist)

General Theory

- Taking photographs is a form of art. One of the most frequently photographed objects since the invention of the camera has been the human form. Photographs of naked children are just one expression of that art form.

When to Use It

- If the subject has shown any interest in digital photography as an art. Possessing a high end digital SLR with expensive lenses, framed landscape photographs, books of artwork or other indicia that the subject believes they are the next Ansel Adams. This is a strong theme for production offenses, though it can be used as an "appreciation" theme in possession cases.

Interrogation Dialog

- Barry, I was really stunned by the quality of the digital pictures on your computer. I don't know much about photography myself, but I can see you know your way around a camera. Those pictures from your family trip to Yellowstone made me want to visit the park myself. We found several pictures of your children unencumbered by clothing on your computer – I can see you appreciate the human form. A lot of photographers have been misunderstood initially, but society is coming around. Robert Mapplethorpe made an extensive study of the youthful nude, and is now a celebrated artist. I think you appreciate beauty in any form, and just took those pictures of your kids as one expression of beauty.

Furtherance of the Theme

- If the pictures themselves are inherently explicit in their sexual content, this theme is effective. If they border on child erotica, the interrogator will need to obtain an admission to sexual stimulation from the images as a follow-on to the initial theme. For distribution, the need to "share their art" with other aficionados makes an effective follow-on.

The Photographer (Family Photos)

General Theory

- Digital photography makes taking photographs of anything easy. Sometimes people get caught up in the camera and end up take photographs of candid moments without thinking.

When to Use It

- If the computer examination shows thousands of images of family gatherings, vacations, and friends at social events. Subjects sending large numbers of camera phone images or having printed books filled with family photos are good candidates for this theme. It is a variation on the artist theme and centers on production, but focuses on the obsession with the camera as opposed to the obsession with the victim.

Interrogation Dialog

- Chuck, I was amazed by the number of pictures on your phone. I saw a lot of pictures of you and your friends and family on there. It's amazing how much camera phones have changed the face of photography – we see pictures on the news every day from world events that were captured by someone with a camera phone. I can see you like to take pictures with your phone, and I think that's great. I did see a few pictures of your kids playing with each other without their clothes on, and need to know where they came from. What I think happened was that you had your phone out like you frequently do and may have gotten caught up in the moment and may have captured a candid act.

Furtherance of the Theme

- If the person has sent many MMS messages using their phone (or sent images through email or other means), sending the images of child pornography can be stressed as being "the same" as sharing other pictures to show distribution.

The Addict

General Theory

- People can't help what they get interested in. Many times they don't even understand themselves why they like something. Child pornography isn't any different than alcohol or drug addiction.

When to Use It

- The addict approach is merited in two circumstances. First, if the subject is caught with child pornography in a relatively high-risk environment such as their workplace. Second, if the subject, during the behavioral interview, tells the interviewer that he believes people who view child pornography "have a problem" and "should be given help", this is an effective theme.

Interrogation Dialog

- Daryl, I don't know if you are familiar with the Diagnostic and Statistical Manual. It's a book that the medical profession uses to look at illnesses and addictions. We've known for years that an interest in children can be an addictive behavior. There are millions of people like you who are good folks and don't want to be downloading images of children, but they can't help themselves. I think that you don't set out in the morning to download those pictures, but that sometimes, when you've had a really bad day at work, when the stresses of life start getting to you, you can't help yourself. I've seen many people like you struggling with this, and they just want to get help but they are afraid to ask.

Furtherance of the Theme

- The addiction theme can be turned into a contact offense theme ("sometimes the pictures aren't enough") or can be turned into a distribution theme - visiting online forums and talking with others with similar predilections is like attending an AA meeting.

The Free Thinker

General Theory

- There are many closed-minded people, who believe they know what is best for society. They try to impose their own rigid morals on others, even when they aren't backed up by strong evidence. Contact with children is healthy and shouldn't have arbitrary boundaries imposed on it.

When to Use It

- The subject that has an ACLU card in one wallet pocket and a NAMBLA membership card in the other is the target for the "free thinker". The approach is also effective with subjects that express disdain for society's judgment in the behavioral interview. Because it uses a logical approach this theme can be used with those that may have sociopathic tendencies. Interest in "nudist" websites is an indicator for this theme also.

Interrogation Dialog

- Enrique, I can see you are a well-educated man and have high ideals. That tells me that you are a free thinker, and that maybe some people don't always understand your point of view. I can tell you, there is a lot of evidence to show that kids enjoy sexual contact. I think that you are afraid to talk about the images on your computer out of fear of being misunderstood. I've read the research and can tell you the popular opinion isn't always correct. Back in the 60's a professor named Kinsey did a study that showed that children as early as 6 months old can experience sexual pleasure, and that people's interests aren't black and white but shades of gray. They originally questioned his work, and now he is celebrated as a pioneer in the field of sexual education. I think what we have here isn't a black-and-white issue, but a shade of gray.

Furtherance of the Theme

- The "shades of gray" approach works with other themes, and can be a lead in to walking the person down in terms of age of the victims or the extent of a contact offense. Additionally, the theme works well when paired with the "tender touch" theme below.

The Tender Touch

General Theory

- Many kids are introduced to sex in a less than perfect way. By introducing kids to sex in a caring environment you teach them love and tenderness.

When to Use It

- If the subject contrasts types of contact or makes remarks about sexual contact being wrong only if it is "against their will" this theme works. Even in cases where there is non-sexual physical abuse, the subject may not view themselves as being abusive. This can work for both contact and non-contact offenders by highlighting how the kids being depicted appear to be enjoying themselves.

Interrogation Dialog

- Fred, I can see that you are a caring person. You do volunteer work to help troubled kids, you have a loving family, and I don't think you are the type of person who would ever intentionally hurt anyone. A lot of times we see kids that have had really bad first sexual experiences – sometimes things happen in a way that makes the experience less than special. I've looked at the files on your computer, and there are a few videos of kids acting out sexually. What I noticed about all of the images, though, is that the kids appear to be enjoying themselves. I've seen folks come through here that seek out images of kids being hurt and crying, but with you I don't see that. I think that you don't want to see kids hurt, and that it makes you happy to see kids enjoying themselves. This is all about seeing the kids happy, isn't it?

Furtherance of the Theme

- The tender touch theme is one of the core crossover offender themes. It can be used with any of the general excuse themes, and can lead to production charges if they admit to sharing "tenderness" directly.

The International

General Theory

- The United States has very strict societal standards. Other world cultures are more open and expressive to the sexuality of children.

When to Use It

- The International theme is effective in cases of sex tourism, and in cases of the importation of child pornography. Individuals may find it easier to admit they downloaded and viewed child pornography overseas and not in the United States. This theme is a tremendous benefit in charging importation instead of possession.

Interrogation Dialog

- Greg, I can see that you are a worldly guy. I know you've travelled extensively, and I find that travel opens people up to different cultures and different ideals. In this country, we are a bit stodgy when it comes to sex – we don't even allow topless beaches. Other countries are much more open – it's not unusual for people to get married at 12 or 13 years of age in half the countries around the globe. I don't know what the laws are in Thailand, but my concern is United States laws. If you downloaded these pictures of naked boys here, that's one thing, but I don't think you did. I think that maybe, while you were in Thailand, you got caught up in the local culture and viewed a few images out of curiosity. I'm betting that you only did this over there and would never have done the same while you were in the United States.

Furtherance of the Theme

- The International theme relies on subjects not knowing that US law does extend to actions overseas. It can easily be turned into a sex tourism theme (travelling for the purposes of sexual relations overseas) and the patriotism aspect can be played up relative to US law. Contrasting other offenses such as the legality of marijuana can support the theme, depending on the facts of the case.

The Historian

General Theory

- The United States became ultra-conservative when it comes to sex back in Victorian times. We coddle our children now and don't treat them as "adults" capable of making their own decisions the way we would have in the past. Asking a behavioral question of "At what age do you think a person can consent to sex?" can provide clues as to the use of this theme.

When to Use It

- The Historian is a good general theme for just about any child pornography or child contact offense. It plays well with anyone looking to rationalize their behavior, and gives a non-specific out for them to latch onto. The theme also works well for production offenses and may be a starting point if something beyond possession/receipt is suspected.

Interrogation Dialog

- Hank, I think you may be a victim of the times. We have these ultra-conservative ideals pressed on us these days that have no basis in history. Back in the Roman culture, the one on which most modern societies are based, wealthy families would send young boys to a patron to be educated in the ways of society, including sex. It was considered an honor for a family to have their eight or nine year old son be taken under the wing of a prominent senator from a good family and to be shown the ropes both culturally and sexually. Julius Caesar, Cicero, Homer - all of these great figures were raised this way and it certainly didn't appear to affect their success and may even have contributed to it. I can see how gentle you were in the video, and it looks to me like you were focused on teaching the kids. I think that you were just trying to show the kids in this video the ropes in a safe, nurturing environment.

Furtherance of the Theme

- Moving into contact offenses is the obvious theme furtherance for the Historian. Quoting any past society and referencing early marriages, working at age 14 and starting a household, and how early monarchs were children themselves can further the theme. Using the term "young adult" in place of "children" can also further the theme, depending on where the subject draws the line themselves.

The Socialist

General Theory

- We coddle our kids these days for no good reason. Kids are more than capable of making "adult" decisions, including consenting to sex. Viewing images of kids that are consenting is a lot different than viewing images of kids being forced to do something.

When to Use It

- The Socialist is another good, general use theme. It can be played off any recent news story about over-parenting to make it current and topical. As with the Historian, it plays well to offenders that may have also committed a contact offense. The question about age of consent may give clues as to this being an effective theme to use.

Interrogation Dialog

- Irwin, I read stories in the newspapers about “helicopter parents” that accompany their grown children to job interviews at age 20. I think that’s just ridiculous – our society doesn’t give kids enough credit. Historically, a boy was considered to be a man at age 12 or 13 and expected to go out and get a job. In the Jewish faith, we have a Bar Mitzvah at this age, and in the Catholic faith a Confirmation at this age. We recognize kids as being able to make their own decisions at this age, yet there are groups in society that still insist on coddling kids. Kids can even get married as young as 12 in some states. I don’t know about you, but the young adults in that video certainly looked like they knew what they were doing and were consenting. If they can legally have intercourse, all you are doing is looking at a couple that made a decision to share a sexual experience. I don’t see you as the type that would ever view kids being forced into something.

Furtherance of the Theme

- The Socialist theme transitions well to a “consenting” theme for getting the subject to admit to a contact offense. Highlighting that kids have sex all of the time at whatever age the subject had contact with, and focusing on them being capable of adult decision making can further this theme.

The Wanderer

General Theory

- The Internet is a big place. It is very easy to stumble across material, then before you know it get caught up in that material without thinking.

When to Use It

- If the person spends a lot of time on the Internet, and appears to have large amounts of pornography on their system, both child and non-child. Subjects who spend much of their time socially isolated and online are good candidates for the Wanderer theme. When asking the question about what the subject does on the Internet if they rattle off a list of dozens of activities then this theme may be effective.

Interrogation Dialog

- Joe, I can see you’ve been to the ends of the Internet. It looks to me like you go just about everywhere – you told me that you do everything from playing World of Warcraft to writing a blog on stamp collecting. I don’t go online that much myself, but I know that you can occasionally stumble across things you weren’t looking for. What I think we have here is a few images that you stumbled across during your extensive travels on the 'Net. I don't think you went online and made a beeline for these pictures, I think you were just following links and maybe clicked on a few pictures of younger folks having intercourse. You maybe got to a site and spent a little time there, just like you would a site on table tennis, and then moved on to something else. If this was just one quick stopover in your travels on the Internet instead of your intended destination, I can certainly understand that.

Furtherance of the Theme

- The Wanderer is mostly a receipt-based theme. It can be an easy-to-rationalize first theme to try if contact offenses are not suspected, although it doesn't preclude moving to those offenses. It can be furthered by talking about "going back" to places previously travelled, just to see if there is anything new there, similar to going back to the daily news sites.

Curious Cat

General Theory

- Curiosity is a trait that gets a lot of very bright people into trouble. It's also human nature – we can't look away when we see a car crash, even though we know we shouldn't watch.

When to Use It

- Curious Cat works well for individuals that have higher IQs, or who believe they have higher IQs. It can be played off an individual who appears to have a myriad of interests, and ties in with the Wanderer theme for individuals that list multiple online or offline interests in the behavioral interview.

Interrogation Dialog

- Kyle, I think we have a case here of a person whose curiosity may have gotten the better of them. I found all sorts of adult pictures on your computer. There were pictures of fat people, thin people, and old people. I even saw a picture of a woman pleasuring a horse. We see that same horse picture on thousands of computers we look at every year. What I think happened with these images is that you were curious and just couldn't look away. I think you shared that picture of the woman and the horse with your friends just because it was different. I don't think you were sexually attracted to the horse, were you <nods no>? I didn't think so – I think the images you have of the kids having sex are the same thing. Sometimes, even things that disgust us we can't look away from. Did you view those images just because you stumbled across them and couldn't look away, or did you do it because you were sexually interested in children?

Furtherance of the Theme

- Curious Cat can lead to an "experimenting" theme for contact offenses, or to a sharing with friends theme for distribution ("I see you shared lots of images you found interesting...") by showing that they frequently share news items or other things with their network and equating that to sharing child pornography.

The Researcher

General Theory

- The subject read about child pornography or about a specific incident on a news site, and that got them curious. They went looking themselves to try and better understand the news story.

When to Use It

- Another general use theme, The Researcher can be played effectively off of just about any current news story. It is primarily a receipt/possession theme, and may play well for well-educated subjects.

Interrogation Dialog

- Larry, you look to be the type of guy who likes to keep up on the news. This Penn State trial of the coach who was abusing children in the showers is a great example. It's on the front page of every newspaper and you can't turn on the TV without hearing about it. If you are like me, you read a story on Yahoo! News about swordfish, and then to learn more about the topic you go to Google and type in "swordfish" and read everything you can about the subject. I think that may be what happened here – you read the stories about the Penn State coach and maybe put in terms from the story like "child pornography" into Google, not realizing where they would take you. Next thing you know, you are looking at images of children as part of trying to understand the coach's behavior. I don't know if you know this, but Pete Townshend of the Who, one of the greatest guitarists of all time, had the same thing happen to him. I caused a pretty big misunderstanding – is that what we have here?

Furtherance of the Theme

- "Researching" is not an affirmative defense in the United States. Likening "cutting clips" of news stories to saving the images can be an easy next step. After the admission to downloading the images, getting the person to admit they were aroused by some of them is the next step in the interrogation.

The Dabbler

General Theory

- We found a few dozen images of child pornography on your computer. It wasn't as though there were millions of images. This was likely just a passing fancy.

When to Use It

- If the subject expresses a general interest in pornography, or in lots of non-related topics. Alternatively, this can be vetted as a theme by doing a contrast question in the behavioral interview: "What do you think should happen to a person that has tens of thousands of sexually explicit images of children?" v. "What do you think should happen to a person that only has a few sexually explicit images of children?"

Interrogation Dialog

- Mike, we found a few sexually explicit images of children on your computer. To be frank with you, my forensic team told me that the analysis of your machine was really quick compared to some they do. We had a case last week where the person sitting in that same chair had over a hundred thousand sexually explicit images of children. That person clearly spent a lot of time thinking about and finding pictures of kids. I think we have something different here – I think that, while trading pictures, you got a couple dozen pictures of children. I think that you saved them without thinking, and they got lost in the tens of thousands of pictures on your drive. This was just something you dabbled in briefly and not an obsession, like the guy last week.

Furtherance of the Theme

- The Dabbler is a good starter theme if the subject doesn't provide additional behavioral clues during the interview. The transition theme becomes "you started out dabbling in this any may have gotten a bit carried away before you knew it" to grow the number of images and the number of views.

The Pop-up Victim

General Theory

- While casually browsing the Internet, a pop-up advertisement appeared showcasing pornography. The site turned out to have child pornography. If not for the pop-up ad (or email enticement), the subject never would have sought child pornography.

When to Use It

- During the behavioral interview, one of the most common answers to the question of "Is there any reason our forensic team would have found sexually explicit images of children on your device?" is to speculate that a "pop-up" appeared while they were surfing. While there is no evidence that "pop-ups" with child pornography have ever inadvertently appeared for Internet users casually browsing innocuous websites, when interrogating subjects that provide this justification the interviewer can use their excuse as a starting point and build upon it.

Interrogation Dialog

- Ned, you told me that you encountered a few pop-ups that had what you thought may have been pictures of children on them. That fits with what my forensic team is telling me – they are seeing that you came across a few images. My digital forensics team has some of the best trained examiners in the field, and they are also telling me there are more than just pop-up images on your machine. Here's what I think may have happened – you encountered a pop-up with a sexually explicit image on it. You had probably never seen anything like that before, and clicked on it just to see what was behind it. Before you knew it, you had clicked on several of the links from that site and a viewed a bunch more images out of curiosity. I don't think you originally set out to find child pornography, and I think that if you hadn't encountered that pop-up you never would have set out to find those images. I also think that, once you found the images, you got caught up in the moment and viewed a few more of the images than you would have if you had stopped to think.

Furtherance of the Theme

- The next step is to have the subject admit that they were aroused by some of the images. It can be furthered to increase the number of images by having the subject admit that they "went back" to the sites they stumbled upon a few times, The theme can also be used as a "gateway" excuse to explain other offenses related to child pornography.

The Poor Judge of Age

General Theory

- The subject is a poor judge of age and may not realize how young the individuals in the images really were. If they had realized how young they were, they may not have viewed the images.

When to Use It

- If the subject does not have children or admits to infrequent social interaction with children, this is an effective theme. It allows the subject plausible deniability in their own mind about the actual age, and focuses on development. Unusual answers to the question "How do you know the people in the pictures are over 18?" can be an indication for this theme. If the subject admits to viewing "developing" or "budding" images, this theme is also effective.

Interrogation Dialog

- Oscar, I think we may be talking past each other. You are telling me that you never looked at images of anyone under 16, but that isn't consistent with what my forensic team is telling me was found on your iPad. I believe we have a problem of nomenclature. You may not realize this, but puberty is the point at which most children developmentally become "adult". It's during puberty that we see individuals with "developing" breasts, and this generally occurs at around 13. I think what happened was that you didn't realize that "developing" breasts meant the person was that young. Given what I've told you about development, did you come across images that you now realize were in that age range but maybe didn't at the time?

Furtherance of the Theme

- This technique can be used iteratively to walk a person downward in terms of the ages of individuals depicted. It can start with pubescent, then lead to pre-pubescent ("there were a few pictures that hadn't started budding yet") or even younger children. A secondary theme is to blame the dress ("the way kids dress these days - it's sometimes hard to tell their age"). The next step is to ensure the person admits that they knew the individuals were really in their age range of interest. The theme works equally well with contact offenses.

The Worrier

General Theory

- There are a few images on the device – the subject may be making more of this than necessary.

When to Use It

- This is the general minimization theme that can be applied to just about any crime. With child pornography, it is applied based on the number of images (smaller than "usual"), the age of the victims ("not too young"), or even the makeup of the images ("nothing too explicit"). It is a general purpose theme that works for any of the charges, and for contact offenses as well.

Interrogation Dialog

- Pete, I think you may be making more of this than you need to. I see people coming in here every week with tens of thousands of images, with children as young as six months old. Just last week I had a case come in for which my forensic team has already identified over one hundred thousand images. I don't think we have that here. I think you downloaded a few images of younger adults having sex. I think you knew they were a little bit over the line, and made a mistake, but I think that all we are talking about is a few images of younger teenagers. Is it only a few images of younger teens we're talking about?

Furtherance of the Theme

- Like a few of the other themes, this can be used iteratively and the numbers are irrelevant as long as a sufficiently large alternative is used ("it's only a few thousand images, not millions"). If the numbers appear too high, break them down by a period of time. A "few images a day" doesn't sound as bad as "over a thousand images last year", but they are both charged the same.

The Giver

General Theory

- The subject only provided these images because someone asked for them. If they hadn't asked, the subject never would have shared them.

When to Use It

- Any individuals that are found to be sharing files on a distribution charge are good candidates. The Giver is a good starting theme for subjects that are identified through peer-to-peer connections as providing child porn. The only subjects to avoid this theme on are commercial producers, although a corollary theme of "you aren't in this for the money", and ironically the opposite theme "you are only in this for the money, not to hurt kids" will both potentially work for those distributing for profit.

Interrogation Dialog

- Quincy, we know that you were sharing sexually explicit pictures of kids. There is no question about that - our investigation clearly shows this. What I need to know is why you were sharing the pictures. We see people producing these types of images and selling them for a profit. I don't think we have that here. I think you just turned on sharing to give back to the community. I see that you were sharing other files as well - movies and games according to the report I have here from my forensic team. That tells me that you share everything, and that these were just a few of the many files you shared.

Furtherance of the Theme

- This works for sharing over forums and sending messages via email as well - they were only providing them to friends, and not doing this for profit. A variant on this theme where there is email or forum-based trading is to blame the recipient. The subject never would have sent the images on their own but the recipient asked for them.

The Out-of-Character Experience

General Theory

- The subject was acting outside of their normal behavior. In fact, the downloading of images goes against everything we know about the subject.

When to Use It

- The acting outside of character theme works well with individuals who are in positions of trust or who have a proud history of service, whether it is to a company, the government, or a civic organization. It doesn't matter if the person actually has a good history, only that they believe they have a good history. This can even be used on those with extensive criminal backgrounds "I can see from your record that you've snatched a purse or two, but this doesn't seem to fit with what I have read about your character".

Interrogation Dialog

- Rodney, I've been reviewing your record and I see that you served honorably in the Army for over a decade. I've asked around about you, and the answers I get are universally positive. That's why, when I see the images we found on your system, I think that it's a case of you acting out of character. I think that maybe you used bad judgment and went to a site or two that you knew you shouldn't visit. I know it's a stressful time with the current economic crisis, and I think that you may have acted here without thinking and downloaded some pictures that you ordinarily would not have sought.

Furtherance of the Theme

- In contact offenses, drug or alcohol use can be leveraged as "reasons" for acting out of character, though they are not particularly good for image-only offenses. Stress can always be used as a factor in any offense as a reason to act out of character while online.

The Innocent Bystander

General Theory

- It's not the subject's fault. It's the fault of their spouse for not paying enough attention, of the victim for enticing them, of the ISP for allowing access to the content, or of society in general.

When to Use It

- If, during the behavioral interview, the subject blames anyone else for their actions this is a good theme to use. It is a good crossover theme for contact offenses, and blame can be assigned to anyone, however illogical. It works well for married subjects (in blaming the spouse), for subjects with kids they've filmed (the kids asked them to film them) or for those participating in chat rooms (the bad guys sent the images).

Interrogation Dialog

- Steve, I think you are getting jammed up for something that isn't your fault. I know you recently got divorced, and I know how hard that can be. Your wife leaves you, and dating in this day in age isn't easy. Like all guys, you have needs and end up going online to look for movies to satisfy those needs. What you may not realize is that a lot of commercial sites that claim to offer adult pornography can sometimes have movies of kids that are a bit below 18 on them. They don't make it clear to the viewer all the time what they are watching, and before you know it you've downloaded a few videos where the girls aren't 18 yet. We found a few of those videos on your smartphone. What I think happened is you went to one of these sites and the site steered you to these videos. Being curious, like all guys are, you downloaded a few of them. I don't think you would be in this predicament if your wife hadn't left you and that site hadn't steered you to an area that had the younger images.

Furtherance of the Theme

- The blame theme can be applied to non-persons also. For contact offenders, the use of alcohol or drugs can be blamed (and used with the Out-of-Character theme). It can also be used with minimization themes by blaming the producers "I know that you aren't producing these movies - if there wasn't someone out there doing that you'd never be in this predicament".

The Reluctant Participant

General Theory

- The kids were the ones who wanted to be filmed and coerced the subject into filming them.

When to Use It

- This theme works well for production offenses and is another variant on blaming the victim. The theme builds on the fact that the subject has mentally sexualized the children, and believes they are willing participants. By blaming the children, the subject becomes a willing - but reluctant - participant.

Interrogation Dialog

- Tom, I saw the videos that you took on your iPhone. What I saw when I looked at them was a kid that looked to be acting in a very adult way. Kids nowadays are growing up much faster than they did even 10 years ago, and the Internet makes it so that they exhibit mature behaviors much earlier. I think that what happened here is that the girl in that video convinced you to do something you would not have ordinarily done. Kids love to film themselves - just look at YouTube and Facebook - and I think that she kept bugging you to film her until you gave in and did it. If this was her idea, that's an important fact for me to know.

Furtherance of the Theme

- A variant can be used for receipt cases by stating that the subject really didn't want the images, but they felt obligated to ask for them out of politeness. For distribution, they didn't really want to send the images to anyone but the other person was insistent so they sent a few across.

The Abuse Victim

General Theory

- The subject was a victim of abuse themselves, and that made them the way they are. They can't help acting out the same way.

When to Use It

- If, during the behavioral interview, the subject recalls stories of their own abuse as a child this is an obvious theme to lead with. Although sexual abuse rates for subjects of child pornography investigations are higher than the general public, many subjects will lie about being abused in order to obtain sympathy or to excuse their behavior. If you believe a subject is lying about being abused as a child, do not confront them on it but use it in the theme.

Interrogation Dialog

- Uri, it pains me to think of what happened to you as a child. Your stepfather never should have treated you that way, and I'm sorry you had to go through that. I see a lot of victims of abuse like you in these cases. They tell me all the time that they still have trouble processing what happened to them as children, even now that they are adults. What I see a lot of victims do is to go online and to look for images that help them remember when they were abused. They use the viewing of these images as a form of therapy. Have you used these images we found to help you cope with what happened to you?

Furtherance of the Theme

- Like other themes that don't involve intent, the next step is to have the subject admit they were aroused by the images. Blaming their abuser for sexualizing the images for the subject works here also.

The Dark Passenger

General Theory

- The subject has a "dark passenger" weighing down on them, causing them to act in a way that they generally don't want to act. They resist as much as possible, but sometimes they can't help themselves.

When to Use It

- If the subject is showing intermittent viewing of images, this theme works. It also works for recidivists who haven't run afoul of law enforcement for a period ("I can see that you were able to control your urges for six months"). This is not a primary theme for distribution offenses, but doesn't preclude the use of other themes in that area.

Interrogation Dialog

- Vince, I can see the pain you are going through, and I feel sorry for you. I meet with a lot of people who have a desire to look at images of kids, even though a large part of them doesn't want to. The good ones struggle almost constantly to fight their urges. I see from your downloads that you go for weeks at a time without downloading images. I think that, during those weeks, we are seeing the real you. That you are a strong person, and that you are in control of your urges. But, the pressure builds and builds and you have a really stressful time at work and then stumble across something you didn't intend and your dark passenger takes over. I don't think that's the real you, Vince, and I think that with a little help you can completely control your urges.

Furtherance of the Theme

- The dark passenger theme works for contact offenses following admissions to possession. The possession can be flipped to be the baseline, with the contact being the occasional behavior ("I see that you control your urges by just looking at pictures most of the time, but sometimes that's not enough.")

The Holy Man

General Theory

- Whatever religious figure the subject believes in can forgive them, but they need to accept responsibility to get there.

When to Use It

- If the subject repeatedly swears to God, Allah, Jehovah, Zoroaster, or the Flying Spaghetti Monster during the behavioral interview this is a good theme. The presence of religious paraphernalia on their person or in their house, or a response to the "Why wouldn't you ..." question that involves the subject citing their religious beliefs make this a go-to theme. If the interrogator isn't familiar with the subject's religion, they can relate a religion they are more familiar with to the subject's situation. Any of the child pornography offenses are good candidates for this theme.

Interrogation Dialog

- Wu, I can see you are a very religious person. Being a devout Christian means striving to do what's right. God knows that no one is perfect, and that everyone makes mistakes. And God is all-forgiving – there is no one that has strayed too far to ask for forgiveness. It's not for me or anyone else to offer forgiveness, we can only stand witness. The only thing God asks is that you accept responsibility for your actions and that you are sincere in your regret. We know that you made the movies on your computer, but I think that you are regretting it right now. Regret is the sign of a good person who made a mistake. Are you willing to accept responsibility for your actions? Are you looking for forgiveness?

Furtherance of the Theme

- Religious or not, just about all subjects will have regret at the time of the interview, even if it's only regretting that they got caught. Subjects that will swear on a holy book and then lie will still go for this theme if they believe that asking forgiveness will paint them in a better light.

The Guilty Soul

General Theory

- We need the subject's help to identify victims and get them assistance. A good person would want to provide that help.

When to Use It

- This is a good knock-and-talk theme if other information isn't available. The investigators can claim that they are trying to find a missing child, and that they believe the subject may have been sent pictures of that child. It works with possession cases the same way, only with the investigators showing an interest in tracking down the distributor.

Interrogation Dialog

- Xavier, to be frank with you we need your help. We found some of the videos you were sharing with those kids in them, and one of the kids matches the picture of a child that has gone missing. I need your help in finding that child. I don't think you produced the movie – it's clearly not you in the movie. But I do need to know where you got it from. We need to find that child quickly and you can help us find out where it came from – you are the critical link in helping us find them. Are you willing to help us?

Furtherance of the Theme

- This theme can also be used as a guilt-based theme for producers who claim they were abused as children – the investigators need the subject's help in finding the child to get them the help the subject never received.

The Vigilante

General Theory

- The subject was patrolling the Internet as a public service trying to find illicit material. They just never got around to reporting it to the authorities.

When to Use It

- If the subject feigns outrage during the behavioral interview or shows an active interest in law enforcement (or is law enforcement in some capacity), The Vigilante can be used. This is a starter theme for possession cases where the subject may have collected and cataloged images. It can be played with the "wanting to help" themes above as well.

Interrogation Dialog

- Yancey, we found the images on your hard drive, and saw that you have bookmarked a lot of the sites. Your hard drive looks a lot to me like how we'd catalog evidence down at the station. You told me in the interview that you were disgusted by people who produced child pornography. I think that you may have acted on that disgust and started to track down some of the people doing this online. Originally, we saw people joining the neighborhood watch, but in the cyber age we see a lot of folks going online and using their tech skills to track the bad guys. You've done half of our job for us in tracking these folks down – we just need a little more help understanding how you found them.

Furtherance of the Theme

- Admissions to possession with this theme need to be expanded by getting the subject to admit that they may have become aroused by some of the images after extensive exposure. This can be a crossover theme for those working with children (law enforcement, pediatricians, and social workers) as part of a general "going the extra mile" and "became a victim to the exposure" duo of themes.

The Hail Mary

General Theory

- The subject isn't going out and victimizing children, they are just looking at a series of bits and bytes online. They would never even think about acting out on a real child.

When to Use It

- Unfortunately, this is the go-to starting theme for many child pornography interrogations because it is an "easy" theme to use. It is called The Hail Mary because it should be a last-ditch theme, not a primary theme due to its preclusion of contact offenses at the onset. It can be used to get an initial admission if the subject has vastly different answers to the questions "What do you think should happen to a person that downloads sexually explicit images of children?" and "What do you think should happen to a person that touches a child sexually?"

Interrogation Dialog

- Zach, we found some pictures on your computer I want to talk to you about. People look at pictures for lots of reasons – sometimes it's idle curiosity, but sometimes it's something more sinister. Anyone can look at a few pictures out of curiosity – that's just human nature. It's one thing to look at a few pixels on the screen – I can understand curiosity. If you are acting on these impulses and are out there grabbing kids off the street, there's not much I can say. On the other hand, if all you did was download a few images, that's something we see all the time. You aren't going out and grabbing kids off the street, are you?

Furtherance of the Theme

- Though this theme appears to preclude moving to a contact-offense theme, it doesn't completely do so. The use of "grabbing kids off the street" is a much better alternative than "acting out with your own children" because it is much rarer that a subject grabs strangers off the street. Additionally, even if the subject is molesting strangers, the interrogator can recover by using any of the "loving" themes above or playing the "grabbing kids" as an out-of-character action. That said, even though a skilled interrogator can get out of the hole, it's always better not to get into the hole in the first place, making this a last-resort theme.

Interrogation Mistakes

There are several mistakes that novices make during the interrogation process, generally based on bad advice from "old school" interviewers who stress the need to show the subject "who the boss is" or from poorly written television dramas that aggrandize the aggressive confrontation. A few of the mistakes include engaging in self-indulgent behavior, arguing over evidence, bluffing the subject and giving up the monologue too soon.

Self-indulgent investigators are more concerned that they appear "tough" coming out of an interview than they are with getting the confession. They would rather strut and posture, and would never consider backing down when a subject tries to provoke them. When an investigator rises to the occasion based on the goading of the subject, they have lost control of the interview. Instead, the interviewer should deflect any provocations if possible, and any increase in volume of protests by the subject should be met by a decrease in volume and a focus on calmness by the interviewer.

A behavior frequently seen in self-indulgent investigators is making threats against the subject. Instead of coming off as strong statements, threats make the investigator seem desperate. Consider the following two statements:

- **Primary**: You are going to be going away for a long time if you keep playing games and holding out on me. I've only got one deal on the table, and either you or your partner gets it. You were both there with that little girl, and we have the pictures of her abuse. Right now, I'm thinking it'll be your partner that gets the deal with the attitude you've been giving me. You've got 30 seconds to decide before I offer the deal to him.

The statement above is an indirect threat, followed by what is perceived to be a carrot by the investigator but doesn't sound that great from the other side of the table. It is more likely to cause the subject to go on the defensive or to shut down. Consider the confidence shown in another approach:

- **Primary**: Our investigation clearly shows that you and your partner took pictures of the girl having sex. There isn't any room for doubt in what you did, but what the evidence doesn't tell me is why you did it. I look at your background and I see nothing but good things until this incident, so that tells me that maybe your partner talked you into something that you are now regretting.

Both statements could be made about the same production offense. The second statement comes across as much more confident, while at the same time keeping the rapport going with the subject. It also provides an escape valve or an "out" for the subject that makes their behavior seem more understandable. Without providing them an out, it is much harder for the subject to confess.

A third form of self-indulgence involves focusing on the consequences of the acts. The first statement above mentions not only jail, but going to jail for "a long time". While the investigator is never permitted to offer leniency for a confession (unless the prosecutor has provided that right to them in advance), they can downplay the consequences. Consider the following response to a direct question about consequences:

- **Subject**: Am I going to prison for accidentally downloading a few pictures?
- **Primary**: I'm just here to gather the facts, and what is most important to me is to capture them accurately. Our evidence clearly shows you downloaded the pictures, but things can be taken out of context. What I want to be able to do is to hear your side of what happened so that I can capture the circumstances accurately.

The investigator has sidestepped the entire question of jail, and re-opened the door for the subject to tell their side of the story. It is very difficult for a subject to refuse a request by the interviewer to make sure the record is accurate and that what they say is reflected in the write-up of the investigation.

Another mistake common in new investigators is giving in to the desire to show the subject all of the evidence the investigation has uncovered. It sounds logical – providing them details on the case may make them realize the futility of continuing to make denials. Unfortunately, this generally backfires on the investigator.

First, showing evidence to a subject is exactly what many guilty subjects are looking for when they participate in an interview. The initial inclination of guilty subjects that do not request an attorney is to either try and talk their way out of the situation, or to see what evidence the investigators actually have on them. If they are trying to find out what evidence exists, they may weigh their chances of going to jail as lower when confronted with the sum total of what the investigation has uncovered.

Second, providing evidence to a subject takes away one of the most powerful tools the investigator has at their disposal – the subject's own imagination. Because the subject knows every action they took, they may be imagining the evidence the investigator found to be much worse than what was actually uncovered. By keeping the totality of the evidence hidden from the subject, it ratchets up their tension during the interrogation.

Third, by showing evidence to the subject, the investigator opens the door to a discussion about the evidence. As an example, showing a subject copies of the forensic report on their computer allows them to argue against the report or the process, or to simply deny they were the ones responsible for the acts. The interviewer can easily lose control of the interview at this point and have it become a discussion about the validity or strength of a piece of evidence. Subjects may even respond irrationally when presented with direct evidence – many subjects have denied that they are the person pictured in a photo or movie, despite a clear resemblance. This sets the interrogation back a few paces, and provides the subject a platform from which to argue.

The most important reason to not show evidence to subjects is independent corroboration. If a subject confesses, the investigator should have forensic details that have been withheld that can be compared to the confession to gauge its veracity. This can help ensure that the confession is complete, and that a false confession was not obtained due to mental instability, attention seeking, or through inappropriate pressure from the investigator.

While showing all of the evidence is not recommended, showing a fragment of evidence and implying the strength of the remaining evidence can be a helpful technique to break through a sticking point with a subject. If the subject balks and won't admit to a basic fact (for example, being at the scene of the crime), the investigator can provide a single piece of evidence to the subject. It is still recommended that the subject not be shown the evidence, just provided the knowledge of its existence. As an example:

- **Primary:** I'm not sure I made it clear what house we were talking about – I apologize for that. We have your fingerprints all over Bobby's house [Investigator hold up the case folder], independently confirmed, in addition to a few other things that I am not at liberty to share at this point, and I think there was a misunderstanding based on my description of the home. We were talking about Bobby's house – the red one over on Maple Street. Since there isn't any question as to you being in the house, when did you first go over there?

In line with mistakes about showing evidence, another mistake made by overly bold investigators is bluffing and being caught. While bluffing can be a powerful technique, it can also bolster the confidence of the subject if the investigator is caught in a lie. In the above scenario, if the investigator is bluffing about having fingerprint evidence, the technique can backfire. The subject may have worn gloves and be confident that they never left fingerprints, destroying any rapport the investigator built and emboldening the subject with a single assertion.

Bluffing should be used sparingly, often as a last resort to break down a subject on a key point, and there are two things the investigator should do with any bluff. First, the investigator should make the bluff as general as possible, to allow the subject's own imagination to fill in the blanks. If investigator did not have fingerprint evidence in the above scenario, a better bluffing statement would be as follows:

- **Primary:** I'm not sure I made it clear what house we were talking about – I apologize for that. We have forensic evidence that you were there at Bobby's house [Investigator hold up the case folder], independently confirmed, in addition to a few other things that I am not at liberty to share at this point, and I think there was a misunderstanding based on my description of the home. We were talking about Bobby's house – the red one over on Maple Street. Since there isn't any question as to you being in the house, when did you first go over there?

In addition to keeping a bluff general, the investigator should always have a fallback position in the event the subject calls their bluff. The fallback, or "out", should allow the investigator to gracefully retract what they stated in a way that is non-alerting. As an example:

- **Primary:** Why would our forensic team find evidence that you were searching for pictures of minors on your computer?
- **Subject:** I bought that computer a week ago and haven't turned it on yet.
- **Primary:** I didn't expect there would be any evidence found, but I had to ask the question before I go and commit digital forensics resources to look at a piece of media. Is there any other media from your house that you have purchased recently and we can rule out?

The final note of caution on bluffing is to avoid creating false evidence. The investigator can imply the presence of evidence, but should not, *under any circumstances*, seek to create false evidence. Doing so is unethical and will likely result in any confessions obtained being suppressed later on.

The final mistake made by many investigators is on the timing of the interrogation. Less experienced investigators will have a tendency to make interrogations both too long and too short.

Interrogations that are too long involve multiple hours spent going over the same material with a subject. With younger subjects, individuals with lower IQs, and those with psychological disorders, excessive time can result in a false confession. In longer interrogations, the subject should be afforded the opportunity to get a drink or some food and to use the restroom. Taking frequent breaks provides the interviewers a chance to regroup and strategize about new approaches, and reduces the risk of the confession being suppressed. Even with breaks and with a subject who is not in one of the special categories above, spending too many hours interrogating the subject may result in them saying things like "I'll say anything you want me to" or "what do I have to say to get out of here". If the interviewer ever hears statements like that, it is time to wrap up the interview and continue on another day.

On the other side of going too long, newer interrogators may have difficulty providing a monologue related to a theme for an extended period of time. They may only talk for a couple of minutes before giving up on theming the subject, and not provide enough time, or enough themes, to obtain a confession. As with all tactics, practicing monologues with colleagues can be an effective way to prepare for difficult interviews.

Following an admission, the interviewer's job is not finished. Developing an admission into a confession requires just as much skill as obtaining the admission in the first place and is the final step in the interview process.

14 CONFESSION

We only confess our little faults to persuade people that we have no big ones.
François VI, Duc de La Rochefoucauld, Prince de Marcillac.

La Rochefoucauld might very well have been relating the experiences of a 17th century inquisitor, and it is as much true today as it was back then. Rarely when an individual makes an admission will it be to all of their relevant crimes – most subjects will continue to minimize their actions even after the first admission. The admission itself is likely going to be lacking in the detail necessary to obtain a conviction, and may consist of a barely uttered "yes" or "no".

Following the admission, the interviewer needs to get facts that are specific to the alleged criminality – the confession. Confessions provide detail and context to an admission, and seek to elicit facts that map to the elements of the crime. This chapter details how to obtain relevant details in a confession. Additionally, taking written statements properly and guarding against false confessions are covered.

Expanding the Admission

The initial admission is likely to be very narrow in scope. It may be a non-definitive answer ("I might have sent the picture out"), an admission to a technical but difficult to charge violation ("One of the boys in one of the videos was probably 17"), or an admission to a single instance ("I accidentally clicked on a pop-up this summer that had a picture of a kid on it but immediately closed it"). The investigator should consider this a starting point, not the end game, and should seek to expand the admission to identify all relevant behavior. A few techniques for doing so are detailed in the following sections.

Investigator Misunderstanding

The "misunderstanding redirection" is an advanced interview tactic. Using this tactic, the investigator is always responsible for either misinterpreting an answer or for not being clear with their question. Because a subject may lie initially, for example, about the number of images on their computer, they will have a tendency to try to stay with that initial statement so as not to appear to have lied. If the investigator misinterprets that lie, however, it provides the subject a reasonable out to tell the truth. The misinterpretation could be a clarification that allows for expansion, or just a changing of the parameters. Examples of obtaining admissions on the same question based on different misinterpretations could be as follows:

Example 1

- **Primary:** How many images of minors having sex do you have on your computer?
- **Subject:** No more than two or three.
- **Primary:** That's what I suspected – it was only a few. How many *movies* of minors having sex do you have?
- **Subject:** Only three or four of those.

Example 2

- **Primary:** How many images of minors having sex do you have on your computer?
- **Subject:** No more than two or three.
- **Primary:** I can see that you only view a few at a time, then – we see a lot of people who do that. How many old images do you have that you haven't deleted yet?
- **Subject:** Probably a few dozen, but I was going to wipe them out.

Example 3

- **Primary:** How many images of minors having sex do you have on your computer?
- **Subject:** No more than two or three.
- **Primary:** Only a couple of images of minors, then. I also see folks with a lot of borderline images, and I know you had a bunch of those as well. Borderline images are those of individuals who are close to 18, but not quite there – generally people who are 13 – 17 years old. How many borderline images did you download?
- **Subject:** Probably a couple dozen. It's sometimes hard to tell the age.

Walking Downward

Even if the subject has been viewing pictures of infants, they are likely to make their first admission to viewing a 16 or 17 year old. Part of this is for acceptance – they are looking to see if the investigator shows disgust or contempt when they make their first admission. Another part is the knowledge that it sounds more plausible to mistake a 16 or 17 year old for an 18 year old than to mistake an infant for an 18 year old. The investigator can capitalize on this fact, and can lead the subject down to the actual age in question. In general, walking downward involves giving the subject a plausible reason to drop the age and to provide understanding when they do. A sample walk-down might go as follows:

- **Subject**: I may have viewed an image of a 16 year old.
- **Primary**: That's very understandable. It's pretty hard to tell sometimes how old a girl is – there are high school girls with fake IDs that get into bars all the time and fool bouncers. I've seen girls as young as 14 pass for adults. Were some of the girls you looked at more likely to be 14 year olds who just looked older?
- **Subject**: One or two of them may have been 14, but most of them were closer to 18.
- **Primary**: When you looked at the pictures did any of the girls look like they were before puberty or were they more in the developing stage?
- **Subject**: They definitely weren't little kids if that's what you're asking. A few of them may have been developing.
- **Primary**: I talk to a lot of people who have trouble estimating ages. You told me that you had two boys, so you probably aren't as familiar with estimating the ages of girls – that's completely understandable. What you probably didn't know is that girls today are reaching puberty younger than when we were kids. Some girls start developing as early as eight, but most are in process by 10. How many of the girls were closer to eight and how many were closer to 10?
- **Subject**: I think most of them were closer to 10. There definitely weren't any eight year olds in there.
- **Primary**: What I've seen in these instances is that the person downloading the images is interested in a particular age range – say, for example, girls that are developing like we talked about. They go on a website and look for developing girls, expecting to find girls that are just becoming women in early puberty, but the links take them to girls that were younger than they were expecting. You are looking for a developing 10 year old and you end up with a few six or eight year olds that were mislabeled. What is the youngest you ever downloaded, even if you weren't looking for it?
- **Subject**: I did get a few that were younger than I was targeting, maybe around six or eight years old. It wasn't very many, though.
- **Primary**: It is hard to know what you'll get when you download images – so many of them are mislabeled and you unfortunately can't trust everyone on the Internet. When my forensic team looks at these computers, they frequently find images of three or four year olds that are labeled as pre-pubescent, which I personally think is deceptive. Have you ever encountered any three or four year olds in mislabeled images?
- **Subject**: Absolutely not. I don't know who would be interested in that kind of thing, but it's certainly not me.

The walk-down does not need to go down to the actual age that is present in most cases. If the subject has pictures of infants on their computer and they will only admit to five year olds, that is still sufficient for charging. The walk-down should be stopped once the themes stop working and the subject becomes adamant about not going beyond a certain age range. There are two exceptions to stopping the walk-down – in cases where there is differential charging and in cases where the offender has access to children of a younger age than they admit to looking at.

Many states, and in some proposed federal statutes and sentencing guidelines, the age of the victim matters. If you know the subject has images of eight year olds, but the maximum penalty doesn't increase below 12 years of age (which is the cutoff in federal sentencing), there is no need to get an admission to anything lower than 12. An admission to knowingly searching for, receiving, or viewing images of 11 year olds to show intent followed by victim identification and confirmation of their age is sufficient.

If the subject has images of eight year olds on their computer and they have an eight year old daughter that the investigator suspects may be at risk, it is to the benefit of the investigator to get them to admit to having pictures in that age range as preparation for obtaining admissions to contact offenses.

Walking Upward

Following the walk-down, there are several options. First, if the investigator has not already done so, they will need to walk-up the number of images/movies. Following that, they need to obtain a breakdown as to the number of images in each category.

In general, it is best to start walking up the number of images as a series of small steps. This will be more productive than getting the subject to guess at a "total number" of images they have viewed, possessed, distributed, or produced. It also provides for more context in terms of the number of sessions, the duration of each session, and the number of years the subject has been conducting these activities. The approach is the same as the walk-up for the number of adult pornographic images from the assessment questioning, and if this number is high enough this step can be skipped and the percentage that are child-related can be identified.

The walk-up starts with a simple question of how often the subject searches for child pornography when they are on the Internet. This should be couched in terms of the shortest time period possible – the number of times a day is a good starting point. If the subject states that they do not search for child pornography every day, the investigator should ascertain the number of times per week or per month, but the smallest timeframe that the subject will admit to should be used. Once the subject has given an initial number, the investigator now has a starting point to walk-up from, though most subjects will minimize their first response. The investigator should work on getting an accurate number of times that the subject views child pornography in a given timeframe first, before working on the longevity of their browsing or the number of images per session.

Following the subject admitting the frequency of their viewing (or distributing or producing – the same technique is used for all of the offenses), the investigator should seek to find out how long the subject has engaged in the offending behavior. The easiest way to start this conversation is to ask the subject when they first got access to the Internet – the subject is not likely to dissemble on this fact, and it is a low stress question. The investigator should also ask if they had access to the Internet continuously since that point to ensure they accurately represent their usage. If the subject was incarcerated or lived in a remote location, there may be long periods where they didn't have access. Once the subject provides a date, the investigator should ask how long after obtaining access it was before the subject first encountered child pornography. The investigator should provide a range of small time periods – was it the first day, or was it a few weeks before the subject first encountered child pornography? The date provided should correspond to the first date that the digital forensics showed child pornography present. If the date provided by the subject is later than the dates of the child pornography on their devices, the investigator can provide the subject with the earlier examples of dates identified to obtain an explanation in a non-confrontational way.

The final step in the walkup is to ascertain the number of images/movies that were viewed during each session. This can be further broken down into searches/sites/thumbnails/images to obtain the necessary granularity. By obtaining an accurate estimate at each individual level of granularity, the investigator can get to a realistic number of views and reduce minimizations by the subject. All three walk-up areas can be reordered as needed to maintain the flow of the interview – if the subject begins talking about a typical session, start there. Alternatively, if the subject talks about how many years they have been on the Internet, start with the duration.

As noted, the walk-ups for distribution and production are extremely similar. An example of a walkup (for distribution) may go as follows:

- **Primary:** We've talked about the child pornography that you provided to our investigator over IRC. He said that you seemed to be very familiar with IRC. How long have you been using it?
- **Subject:** I've been using since I was in college.
- **Primary:** When did you attend college?
- **Subject:** On and off from about 2000 to 2005.
- **Primary:** Did you start using IRC your first year?
- **Subject:** It was more like my second year.
- **Primary:** Okay, so would 2001 be an accurate estimate?
- **Subject:** That sounds about right.
- **Primary:** How many times a day to you generally logon to IRC?
- **Subject:** I dunno, maybe once or twice.
- **Primary:** I understand it varies – some days I'll check my Yahoo! mail ten times and sometimes I'll go for a couple of days without checking it. If you are going on once or twice a day, would about ten times a week be an accurate estimate for the number of times you logon to IRC?
- **Subject:** I think eight times a week is probably more accurate.
- **Primary:** Sounds fair. Your logs looked pretty consistent according to my forensics folks for the past few years. Have you dropped off IRC at any point during that time?
- **Subject:** Well, I had a little trouble with a DUI back in 2006 that ended up with me being put away for a bit, and they didn't let me have Internet access for like six months.
- **Primary:** It's tough to be away from the Internet – even paying your bills can become a problem, so that must have been rough. Other than that six month period, you've been on IRC consistently?
- **Subject:** Yeah.

- **Primary**: I see that you have multiple chat rooms in your logs. How many chat rooms are you typically in at once?
- **Subject**: Probably about two or three.
- **Primary**: I also see you have multiple screen names. How many different private sessions are you typically covering in each room at any one time?
- **Subject**: Probably about the same.
- **Primary**: Two or three per room?
- **Subject**: That's about right.
- **Primary**: You must be pretty quick with the keyboard. I can't even keep one conversation straight, but it sounds like you average about ... two or three per room, and two or three rooms ... how many conversations on average does that mean at any one time?
- **Subject**: Maybe like five or six. No more than seven or eight, though.
- **Primary**: So somewhere between five and eight. What would be the average?
- **Subject**: Let's say eight.
- **Primary**: I spoke to the investigator that you sent those pics to a few weeks ago and have been on IRC myself, so I'm somewhat familiar with how things go. Most folks won't share pics with you unless you share with them first, has that been your experience?
- **Subject**: Pretty much, unless they know you.
- **Primary**: I've found the same thing when I've gone undercover in the chat rooms. You have about eight conversations a session, about how many of those conversations do you need to share pics?
- **Subject**: Probably only about half. Some of the folks just don't seem right, or I've seen them before and they don't give you anything back.
- **Primary**: So only about four chats each session will you have to share something. How many pics would you say you share each time?
- **Subject**: It's not always different pics, but I usually only give 'em about three pics to see if they'll send something back. If not, I block them.
- **Primary**: Your chat rooms seem to be more female-focused. When you say pics, just so I'm clear, you'll send pics of early pubescent girls having oral sex like the ones you sent me?
- **Subject**: Yes, sir.
- **Primary**: So you do about three pics for four chats, so probably about 12 pics per session? And about two or three sessions each day, so would 25 pics a day be typical?
- **Subject**: That sounds right.
- **Primary**: That comes out to about maybe 750 times a month. You've been on for about a dozen years, so you've sent out about 750 explicit pictures a month similar to what you sent to my investigator for that whole period, except for the six months where you didn't have Internet access?
- **Subject**: That's right.

If the subject has used other mechanisms to transmit/produce/distribute images, the investigator can repeat the above exercise with each of the mechanisms. A simple "we've talked about IRC, what about peer-to-peer?" can be used as a transition.

As with the walk-down, the number of images is only important up to the maximum sentencing guidelines. The federal sentencing guidelines under U.S.S.G. § 2G2 provide enhancements at 10, 150, 300, and 600 images. Because a movie counts federally as 75 images, getting the defendant to admit to as few as eight movies will suffice to obtain the maximum penalty, and additional movies will not provide further enhancement. There are two caveats to this. First, if the number of movies/images reaches the "shock the conscience" level, it may be worthwhile to obtain the number in hopes of a post-Booker upward departure. Second, it helps to have a larger number of images than are needed for sentencing in the event that the defense contests the age on some of them.

The Breakdown

The breakdown is the stage in which the investigator gets an estimate of the number of images per age category, or the percentage of offending images, following a walk-up. If the subject is already saying that all of the images they traded are child pornography, the percentage that are offending isn't relevant, but the percentage that are in each age group may be relevant for sentencing purposes. A breakdown for a subject that has admitted to downloading 100 movies a night for several years on eMule, but has admitted to downloading other content also, in addition to admitting to possessing child pornography of boys as young as 10 might go as follows:

- **Primary:** The movies we saw on your system looked pretty typical of what we see all the time. You said that you download about 100 movies a night. Are they mostly movies of young boys having sex?
- **Subject:** Some are, but I download a lot of music videos also.
- **Primary:** That's understandable – some are and some aren't. Is it 50% young boys having sex? 75%?
- **Subject:** No way, it's probably more like 25%.
- **Primary:** So the majority of the movies are music videos, and only 25% are of young boys having sex?
- **Subject:** Yeah, that's right.
- **Primary:** Let's look at that 25% that are boys under 18. What percentage of them is over 15 and under 18?
- **Subject:** Probably like half.
- **Primary:** So half are between 15 and 17. What percentage is between 12 and 15?
- **Subject:** Maybe like 30%.
- **Primary:** So only 20% are younger than 12?
- **Subject:** Yeah.
- **Primary:** What's the youngest you've ever come across?

The final statement can be left off, but it gives the subject another chance to drop the age of the children depicted in the movies even lower and the walk-down can be resumed if their answers are still inconsistent with the forensics.

Details

Once the magnitude of the offense has been quantified above, the investigator should seek to obtain the details on the elements of the offense that are necessary for prosecution. The details should include intent, confirmation of image contents, and corroboration of the subject's statements. As many details as possible should be obtained to provide the most accurate picture of the subject's actions.

Intent

Many of the statutes dealing with child pornography require intent – that the subject knowingly viewed or trafficked in images of children engaged in sexual activities. There are several ways that intent can be covered:

- **Search Terms.** By asking the subject what terms they used to search, or by confirming the terms the analysts found during the forensic review, the investigator can show that they knowingly looked for illicit content. If the subject provides an obscure search term like PTHC, the investigator can ask about the meaning of the term and what the subject typically found when they used that term.
- **Repetition.** If the subject claims they went to a site or a chat room that contains child pornography "accidentally" during their initial admission, this can be disproven through repetition. By getting the subject to state that they went to a site or used particular terms repeatedly, intent to view the underlying content can be established.
- **Nomenclature.** Often the subject will download files or go to chat rooms with explicit names. By eliciting from the subject that they joined a forum called "NY Giants Fans" to talk about football, the interviewer can then elicit that they went to a "Child Sex Slave" forum to find bondage pictures of children. Similarly, by having the subject admit that they named directories where they stored their child pornography using phrases like "Good Stuff" or "Top Pics", intent can be established.
- **Hiding Behavior.** Having the subject admit that they took steps to hide their child pornography shows guilty knowledge and differentiates it from other, innocuous material. Mislabeling folders or using encryption for certain material shows intent. Having the subject admit they only attempted to obfuscate their child pornography activities as evidenced in the forensic review further establishes intent.

Image Contents

The confirmation of the contents of the images is done to establish the fact that they are child pornography and to identify sentencing enhancements based on the particular material present. Secondarily, having the subject provide details on the image contents not only shows intent by indicating that the subject knew what was in the images, but also provides corroboration to protect against false admissions, assuming the descriptions match files found on the subject's media.

For an image to meet the federal standard for child pornography, the following definitions from 18 USC § 2256 must be satisfied:

(8) "Child pornography" means any visual depiction, including any photograph, film, video, picture, or computer or computer-generated image or picture, whether made or produced by electronic, mechanical, or other means, of sexually explicit conduct, where—

(A) the production of such visual depiction involves the use of a minor engaging in sexually explicit conduct;

(B) such visual depiction is a digital image, computer image, or computer-generated image that is, or is indistinguishable from, that of a minor engaging in sexually explicit conduct; or

(C) such visual depiction has been created, adapted, or modified to appear that an identifiable minor is engaging in sexually explicit conduct.

Additionally, sexually explicit conduct is defined in the same section as:

(2)(A) Except as provided in subparagraph (B), "sexually explicit conduct" means actual or simulated—

(i) sexual intercourse, including genital-genital, oral-genital, anal-genital, or oral-anal, whether between persons of the same or opposite sex;

(ii) bestiality;

(iii) masturbation;

(iv) sadistic or masochistic abuse; or

(v) lascivious exhibition of the genitals or pubic area of any person;

Because the definition of a minor is anyone under the age of 18 years for this statute, the first confession point should be to establish the subject's knowledge of the age of the children depicted. This can be done by revisiting the initial confessions as to the age of the victims, or with more direct questioning, based on behavioral answers previously provided:

- **Primary:** We discussed that a portion of your movies that you downloaded were of girls between the ages of 10 and 12, and that you had put in terms related to age like "10yo" into your eDonkey client to find these. I know you probably got a lot of images that were not what you were expecting – how did you know for sure that the ones you kept were 10 years old?
- **Subject:** I didn't know for sure.
- **Primary:** Obviously you didn't have their birth certificates, but you seem to be a very observant person. You've seen sitcoms on TV where the girls are 10 years old – how did the images compare to those girls?
- **Subject:** They looked like they were mostly about that same age. They didn't have any hair "down there" yet.
- **Primary:** Were their breasts developed yet?
- **Subject:** Not really, no.
- **Primary:** What about the rooms depicted in the movies?
- **Subject:** They had lots of stuffed animals and things that little girls have.

The more details the subject can provide as to how they determined ages the better. If the subject provides information that indicates they may have underestimated ages, that information must be documented as well as potential exculpatory material.

With respect to the nature of the images, one of the sticking points in the federal definition is the difference between child pornography and child erotica. Because child pornography requires not just nudity but sexual activity, having the subject describe the contents of several images will solidify the charges. If the majority of the images are nude children where their genitals are displayed, the subject can later claim they were artistic images. To avoid this, the interviewer can establish they were lascivious through the subject's admissions. Lascivious is defined as "Wanton; lewd, driven by lust, lustful". The easiest way to establish that they were not obtained for their artistic value is to have the subject admit that they masturbated to the images or attempted to:

- **Primary**: All guys have viewed pornography at one point or another – there's a reason it's a multi-billion dollar industry. You've told me about your adult pornography and we've talked about the images of the young boys on your computer. How often do you masturbate to adult pornography as opposed to the images of the young boys?
- **Subject**: I only masturbate to the adult stuff. I was just curious with those other pictures.
- **Primary**: That's very understandable. What I find talking to folks is that they may get aroused by something outside their control. They don't mean to, and a lot of good people like yourself get aroused but fight the temptation. A lot of times they feel ashamed afterward. Were you initially aroused by the images, but never acted on it?
- **Subject**: Yeah – I was aroused. But I swear I never jerked off to any of the images of the boys.
- **Primary**: Most people I talk to will touch themselves instinctively when they get aroused, but many that feel ashamed will stop before they ejaculate when they realize what they are doing. Is that what happened with you and the images of the young boys, or did you ejaculate to them?
- **Subject**: I never ejaculated to them. When I realized I was touching myself I stopped right away.
- **Primary**: Did you ever ejaculate to them accidentally? Sometimes guys get aroused quickly and ejaculate, then regret it afterward because they never meant to ejaculate to them. Did that ever happen with those pictures?
- **Subject**: Maybe once or twice, but it wasn't a regular thing.

The federal sentencing guidelines also provide an upward departure for an image that "portrays sadistic or masochistic conduct or other depictions of violence". Having the subject admit that some of the images involved this conduct can be a sentencing differentiator. If the subject has material that fits this definition but is reluctant to provide details in the confession, the interviewer can go back to a contrast statement. Stating the interviewer's belief that the subject "preferred" the "loving" images, and just downloaded a few bondage images out of "curiosity" may elicit an additional confession to this point.

Corroboration

No matter what the contents of the images, the investigator should seek to corroborate any of the information that the subject provides. Corroboration can be done by obtaining detailed descriptions of specific images, what is depicted in them, and how they were obtained. The interviewer can ask for details about the first time they viewed child pornography or about the most recent time to get information to match up with the forensics. It is generally not a good idea to show subjects copies of the images they have trafficked in, but the investigator can provide details on the directory structure and have the subject describe how they cataloged their images, if relevant.

Further Expansion

Expansion looks at taking the initial admission, generally to possession, and covering the bases with respect to other chargeable offenses. The first area federally to expand to is generally receipt, followed by distribution and potentially production. Finally, expansion into potential contact offenses should be done.

Receipt, or receiving child pornography, is confirmed by the subject stating how the possession occurred. Unless the subject produced the images, the child pornography on their computer was received. Because receipt offenses in the federal system carry a five year mandatory minimum sentence and possession has no mandatory minimum, it is always advantageous to identify how the subject obtained the material, and then confirm the subject's statements via forensics.

If the subject uses the word received, this should be explicitly noted by the interviewers and included in any written statements. If the subject claims no knowledge of how the child pornography got on their system, the interviewer can utilize a production vs. acquisition theme by contrasting an individual that simply downloads images as opposed to an individual that directly touches a child and films it. Before using this contrast, the investigator must be reasonably certain the offending material was not produced by the subject.

Once the subject has confirmed that they received the information, the investigator should solidify the details of how they received it. For peer-to-peer or web downloads, the investigator should obtain details on the software used, the timeframe, the search terms, the sites and/or servers they connected to and the filenames of the identified images. For IRC, email, or IM based receipt, the investigator should confirm the software used, the chat room names, the handles of both the sender and recipient, and any solicitous wording used prior to the transfer. With either method, the investigator should confirm the location that the content was stored at, any subsequent accesses of the content, and any actions taken on the content (moving it, changing it, deleting it). If any of the material was purchased, the investigator should obtain details about where the subject purchased it, how much was paid, and what payment mechanism was used.

If the subject has traveled outside the country recently, charging importation may be a possibility. Because subjects may believe it is okay to download child pornography in another country, they are more likely to admit to importation than general receipt. An expanded theme to get the subject to admit to importation may be something similar to the following:

- **Primary:** I saw you just came back from Thailand. I think that maybe you

> downloaded the child pornography while you were over there. I don't know what the laws are in Thailand, but I know a lot of people sometimes act outside themselves when they go over there, and do something they wouldn't do stateside. Did you download the movies while you were over there, or were all of them downloaded back here?

The second tier of expansion is to identify any distribution. Distribution is the sending of child pornography to other individuals, and it can occur as an unsolicited one-way transaction, as barter for similar material or other goods/services, or for financial gain. Any distribution carries an enhanced penalty in the federal system, with further enhancements for barter or commercial gain. Because of this, the investigator will want to evaluate the potential for the subject having provided the images to another party.

With peer-to-peer software, distribution can be proven by showing that the subject knowingly had file sharing enabled. Asking the subject what their share folder for uploading is called can confirm this, and the investigator can discuss the subject not wanting to be a "freeloader" as a potential theme. Additionally, the investigator can ask about the limitations of the sharing, contrasting the act of sharing temporarily while downloading with the long-term sharing of content. Either way, the investigator should obtain specifics about the software used, the amount of time and number of files shared, and the specific content that was shared.

For distribution offenses using other software, the subject should be asked about any content the subject provided to others. Unless a commercial enterprise is suspected, the investigator can bring up the fact that the subject never received money for their sharing as a positive. Reasons for sharing could include:

- Confirming the person they were communicating with had content available.
- Being a "nice guy" and wanting to give back to the child pornography community.
- Uploading content as a requirement to join a particular forum ("You only uploaded the bare minimum needed")
- Being pressured into it by a demanding chat partner.

Once distribution has been established, any content received in-kind should be ascertained. The investigator can compare and contrast the amounts distributed against the amounts received as another theme at this point ("You weren't a major distributor of this material, you only shared with a few people to get them to trust you and send you images"). As above, the investigator should detail the software used, the people/forums that the content was distributed to, the amount of content, and how the content was labeled.

In general, stumbling across commercial distribution is not likely in a typical knock-and-talk scenario. The investigator will, most often, have a priori evidence of commercial transactions. However, if material is present in the forensics that is suggestive of distribution for profit, or if the subject has bad behavioral responses to questions regarding commercial distribution, the investigator should proceed to explore the possibility of commercial distribution.

The general approach to a commercial distribution expansion of admissions is to blame the purchasers. It is always the purchasers that offered the subject money, and sometimes even forced it upon him for the purposes of theming. If the subject is also a producer, a theme about sharing funds with the victims or the victims requesting the material be made commercially available are a backup theme ("You used the money you received from the pictures of your daughter to pay for that private school she goes to"). If commercial distribution is admitted, the investigator should obtain details about distribution channels, volumes, and payment methods. The ultimate destination of the payments - where the money went to - and any items purchased with the funds should be identified if possible for later seizure as part of asset forfeiture.

For any of the distribution charges, the investigator should obtain details on the individuals the subject distributed the material to. Any identifiers that the subject can provide should be noted, and specifics about transactions covered. If the subject was distributing over chat-based systems, the investigator should attempt to ascertain if any of the recipients were minors, providing another sentencing enhancement in the federal system. This can be done using a minimizing theme – the subject only provided like-aged images to minors, at ages it would be natural for them to have an interest in.

The final enhancement in child pornography deals with contact offenses – production of sexually explicit material involving minors. Once admissions to possession are solidified, the investigator should be on the lookout for unusual behavior by the subject when they are questioned about how the material got on their system. If material is found on a camera or a cell phone with a camera, extra attention should be paid to the likelihood of production. Production themes ranging from "kids like to be photographed" to "personal use but not distribution" can be brought up again to obtain to a production admission. Of primary importance in production cases are the identification of each location of production, the identification of any other parties present (co-abusers, camera persons, relatives, etc.), and most importantly the identification of any victims.

Because global distribution cases can start with a simple possession charge, the investigator should never forget that the ultimate goal of prosecuting child pornography offenses is to prevent the victimization of children. For distribution admissions, all of the individuals that received child pornography should be further investigated or sent out as leads - the Internet Crimes Against Children taskforces or the Child Exploitation and Obscenity Section of the United States Department of Justice are great starting points. If the subject purchased child pornography from a commercial service or received it from an identifiable source, that source should be pursued. In the worst case scenario, if the subject produced child pornography, the investigator should work aggressively to identify all of the victims to ensure their physical and emotional safety.

Contact Offenses

No case on child pornography investigations is complete without transitioning to contact offenses. While this book is about the child pornography itself and dealing with contact offenses warrants its own book, the two are at least partially intertwined. The transition from an admission to child pornography offenses to contact offenses is difficult, except in the case of production, where the transition occurs naturally as part of victim identification following the admission. The possibility of a contact offense can result in an entirely new interrogation. Fortunately, the building blocks are there already:

- The interviewer has already established rapport with the subject.
- The subject has already made admissions to criminal acts, and has observed the fact that the interviewer has not judged them.
- The subject has expressed an interest in children through their admissions.

The final building block before starting an interrogation related to contact offenses is the threat level identified in the questioning phase and an assessment of the behavior associated with contact offense questions. If the subject has no ready access to children and has good behavior related to child contact offense questions, it is at the interviewer's discretion whether or not to enter an interrogation about child contact offenses. If there are questions regarding potential contact offenses, the investigator needs to, at a minimum, explore those issues.

Unlike the transition to the primary interrogation, the subject should be rewarded for their admissions before this transition. Providing the subject something to eat or drink, and thanking them for their hard work discussing tough issues can be valuable. This leads into a nice transition statement – "We just have one more thing that we need to cover before we can say the file has been fully documented".

Following the transition statement, the investigator should seek to build on the admissions that the subject made to the possession of child pornography. The same minimizations can be used to obtain child contact offense details. This includes blaming the victim, blaming the circumstances, and society not understanding the subject. Minimizing the offenses themselves follows a similar pattern – the number of offenses was small, the child was not that young, or the contact was loving and not hurtful. A sample transition dialog follows:

- **Primary**: Thank you for providing the context for those images we found – without that context things may have been misconstrued. We just have one more thing to cover before we are finished up here. Like we discussed earlier, all of the pictures appear to have been loving in nature. We spoke earlier about your daughter. Have you had any loving contact with your daughter like we saw in those images.
- **Subject**: Not really. I don't do that.
- **Primary**: I've found that a lot of kids do things without thinking. One of the people I spoke with last week had his daughter constantly walking in on him in the shower and grabbing at him. Has anything like that ever happened to you?
- **Subject**: Maybe once, but I told her she shouldn't do that.
- **Primary**: Tell me about what happened.
- **Subject**: I was getting ready for work in the morning and my daughter came in and kissed me on my privates. I told her that she shouldn't do that.
- **Primary**: Kids do some strange things. How long did she kiss you for?
- **Subject**: It couldn't have been more than a few seconds.
- **Primary**: Then what happened.
- **Subject**: I told her she shouldn't do that and I got dressed.
- **Primary**: When she kissed you, were her hands on your privates or were they around your waist?
- **Subject**: They were around my waist.

- **Primary**: I know kids sometimes do what they see on TV or have heard about at school. Did she put her mouth around your privates while she was kissing it, even if it was just the tip?
- **Subject**: Yeah, but it was only the tip and only for a few seconds.

In addition to any domestic contact, if the subject has traveled recently to a high risk area the investigator should determine if the subject had contact with children while traveling. Similar to downloading child pornography while overseas and importing it, the subject may be more likely to admit to committing a contact offense, or filming a contact offense, if production is suspected, when the conduct occurred overseas. A sample theme would be:

- **Primary**: I saw you just came back from Thailand. I don't know what the laws are in Thailand, but I know a lot of people sometimes act outside themselves when they go over there, and do things they wouldn't do stateside. They seek out some comfort from a boy or a girl from one of the brothels there, and the proprietor convinces them that the younger escorts need money to eat and suggests the traveler help them out. I think that may be what happened – were you just doing something you would never do here and before you know it you were having relations or did you set out to travel there just to have sex with a minor?

Because there is no requirement in the statute that the subject intended to travel just for the sake of sexual relations with a minor (the law used to require it), any reason the subject provides is still an admission to a felony contact offense.

As with the child pornography offenses, the investigator should obtain as many details as possible about the contact offenses. The same concepts apply of expanding upon the initial admissions, finding the names of victims, identifying additional contacts, and documenting the results.

The Wrap-Up

Ultimately, the gold standard for proving intent is to show the subject knew that what they were doing was illegal. While the investigation can collectively show the subject's knowledge through the sum of the parts, from the content itself to the attempts to conceal the activity, there is no substitute for the subject clearly stating their knowledge of the act being illegal. As a capstone action, once the other offenses have been covered, the investigator can attempt to elicit a final admission. One effective approach is to present a statement like the following:

- **Primary**: Based on everything we've talked about here, I think you know that what you did was wrong, and I can see that you are regretting your actions. That tells me that you are a decent person. Is my assessment of you accurate? You did something you knew to be illegal, but you regret that decision now, you will never do it again and are willing to make amends. Is that the case?

The capstone statement, in addition to obtaining an admission that the subject knew their actions were illegal, opens the door to requesting a written statement. Not all subjects will provide a statement, but if they will, and if the prosecutor agrees, the subject's own words written freely and containing statements against self-interest can be compelling evidence.

Asking the subject directly to write down all of their criminal behavior is not likely to be successful. Many subjects will write minimalist statements and not address the relevant actions. To avoid this, the investigator should explain the need for accuracy and for the subject to provide an accounting in their own words to avoid misinterpretation:

- **Primary:** Thank you again for being honest with us. What I'd like to do now is to give you an opportunity to put down what you just told me in your own words. I've found that is the best way to ensure nothing is misinterpreted and that we get all of the facts straight. Would you like to write it yourself or would you like me to type up what you told me and let you see it and make any changes you want?

The final question provides an alternative to the subject in which both options involve providing a statement. There are four primary ways to take a written statement, each with their own advantages and disadvantages.

Unsupervised by the Subject

In this scenario, the investigator provides the subject with an ample supply of paper and a pen, or a computer to type on, and leaves them alone for an extended period to write whatever they want. The investigator should provide the subject the chance to use the restroom and offer a drink or food as appropriate at this stage.

In general, a subject will not provide the necessary detail in their initial statement. The investigator may get anything from a life story to a simple "I'm sorry for anything I may have done" statement. If the initial statement does not contain the details the subject provided in the interview, the investigator can walk the subject through their statement and then ask the subject to recall what they had told the investigator and fill in that information. It may take several tries to get the subject to provide the detail in writing that they provided verbally. The subject may also regress on some of their statements and further minimize numbers or ages. If this occurs, the investigator should gently remind the subject of what they said in the interview, state that the investigator believed what they said was true, and ask if they want to correct or amend their statement.

The advantage of the unsupervised subject statement is that it is in the subject's own words and will be the most natural response, reducing any concerns that the investigator misinterpreted the subject's actions. The disadvantage is that many subjects will try to further minimize their actions or provide no details at all.

Supervised by the Subject

In the supervised statement, the investigator should review their interview notes and re-ask the subject the same direct questions regarding their actions. The subject should then be requested to write or type the answers to the questions as they re-state them. The investigator can remind the subject of what they stated in the interview if the subject deviates from their original statements.

While time consuming, the primary advantage of the supervised subject statement is that it ensures that all points addressed in the interview are covered. The subject is prevented from "wandering" in their statement, and the statement itself will be in their own words. The disadvantages are that it takes time to obtain a thorough statement, and the subject may try to change earlier statements they made.

Unsupervised by the Investigator

In the unsupervised statement, the investigator types or writes the information provided by the subject in the interview into a statement. The investigator should first summarize all of the key statements provided by the subject verbally to confirm their accuracy prior to writing the statement.

When writing the statement, the investigator should write in the first person and use the exact words, where possible, that the subject used. The investigator should not include any additional information, even if known to the investigator, that was not provided by the subject, and should include all exculpatory statements or explanations provided by the subject. Once the statement is complete, the investigator should provide it to the subject to read in its entirety, and to make corrections as needed.

The unsupervised statement will be the most concise and contain the most accurate recollection of the statements presented to the investigator. The investigator can ensure that nothing is left out, that the details that are necessary to meet the elements of the crime are included, and that the subject does not have a second opportunity to minimize their actions. On the downside, the subject can later argue that the investigator was putting words in their mouth.

Supervised by the Investigator

As a compromise between the investigator writing everything and the subject being provided a blank piece of paper, the supervised statement is written by the investigator in response to contemporaneous verbal answers by the subject. In taking a statement this way, the investigator asks the subject a question and writes down exactly what they respond, in their own words.

The primary advantage of the supervised statement written by the investigator is that it ensures that all of the questions that need to be addressed are covered. The disadvantage is that the subject may rescind or minimize earlier statements. The investigator can reduce the impact of this by reading to the subject what they stated during the interview prior to asking the question.

Both of the options that involve the investigator writing the statement may be necessary for a subject that is illiterate or would otherwise have difficulty writing a statement. If the subject is illiterate, the investigator must, with a witness present, read the statement aloud in its entirety to the subject and make any changes the subject requests verbally.

If the subject does not agree to provide a statement, the investigator can request they write a letter to the victims (or to their employer/friends/family/etc.) apologizing for their actions. If the subject does provide a formal written statement, especially a supervised statement, the subject should be afforded the opportunity to make a statement expressing remorse at the end.

Any changes/corrections to the statement should be crossed out with a single line and initialed by the subject. If the investigator is authorized to take oaths, the investigator and the witness should stand and the subject should be asked to stand and raise their right hand. The investigator should then ask the subject "Is the information provided in this statement true and accurate to the best of your knowledge?" and include their response in the interview notes.

Following the swearing of the oath, each page of the statement should also be dated and initialed, and any whitespace crossed out and initialed. The final page of the statement should be signed and dated by the subject, the investigator, and a witness.

Once the statement has been provided, the investigator will either release the subject or arrest them, depending on their admissions, prior evidence, and local protocols. In either case, the investigator should follow the guidance in the rapport section at the end of the interview, in the event that a future interview is necessary to obtain additional details. One final question that can be asked of the subject is "Do you feel that you've been treated fairly?" If the subject states that they have, it reduces the potential for complaints of coercion. If the subject states that they have not, the investigator should pay attention to what the subject says as it will be a direct reflection of the subject's perception of their technique.

15 FINAL THOUGHTS

If you give me six lines written by the hand of the most honest of men, I will find something in them which will hang him.

Armand Jean du Plessis, Cardinal-Duc de Richelieu et de Fronsac

The quote frequently attributed to Cardinal Richelieu can be taken as a cautionary warning to those investigating child pornography offenses. Although the sexual victimization of children is among the most heinous of acts, those investigating child pornography should not form fixed opinions on the guilt of subjects identified as part of an investigation. In the United States legal system, all subjects are presumed innocent until proven guilty by a jury of their peers, or a judge if the right to a jury trial is waived. Assuming the guilt of a particular subject can lead an investigator to misinterpret statements and evidence in a way that supports that conclusion, a form of confirmation bias.

During the interview, the investigator should be prepared to hear any explanations the subject provides and to re-evaluate their working theory of the crime at any point. While pop-up ads with child pornography have not been seen in the wild, there is always a first time. The SODDI defense is generally assumed to be the last resort claim of guilty parties, but may also represent the genuine lack of knowledge by an innocent subject. Although it is very difficult to accidentally receive child pornography, there may be a situation where a subject is sent unsolicited images that they never opened. A good investigator will constantly challenge their assumptions and be willing to accept any new evidence, especially if it is contrary to their initial theory.

Confirmation bias is not limited to interview statements. Forensic examinations can be inadvertently slanted by analyst bias. The analyst's job is not to theorize how an action occurred and then find evidence to support that theory. The job of the analyst is to identify factual evidence present on a particular device or group of devices. All evidence, especially exculpatory evidence, needs to be fully explored and recorded in a forensic report. One trick from the scientific method that can come in handy is to take the allegations provided by the investigative team and to try and *disprove* them. This ensures that the analyst takes an unbiased look at the facts, and starts from the right viewpoint – a presumption of innocence.

Even alleging an individual is a child pornographer can have devastating consequences on a person's life, and care must be taken not to overstep the investigative boundaries. This should be considered when talking to potential witnesses, employers, relatives, and others associated with the subject.

If all investigators assigned to these cases can remember one thing from this book it is that they are investigating the criminal *acts* associated with child pornography, and not the *person* alleged to have committed those acts.

Thank you for your efforts to make this world a safer place for the children.

ABOUT THE AUTHOR

Chad Steel has performed hundreds of digital forensics examinations. He has been involved with every aspect of child exploitation investigations from interviewing and interrogating subjects to performing digital forensics analyses of devices ranging from cell phones to servers. As an adjunct faculty member, he developed and taught the Computer Forensics graduate course in Penn State's engineering program and has instructed federal and local law enforcement, commercial clients, and graduate students in conducting child pornography investigations. His experience includes serving as head of IT investigations for a Global 100 corporation and as managing director of the Systems Integration and Security practice at Qwest Communications. He is currently an adjunct professor at George Mason University in Virginia.

Made in the USA
Lexington, KY
16 September 2015